MW01102649

CONGREGATIONS AT THE CROSSROADS

FAITH'S HORIZONS

RONALD E. VALLET
general editor

Stepping Stones of the Steward, second edition
Ronald E. Vallet

The Mainline Church's Funding Crisis
Ronald E. Vallet and Charles E. Zech

Christian Voluntarism
William H. Brackney

Living in the Maybe
Christopher Levan

*Congregations at the Crossroads:
Remembering to Be Households of God*
Ronald E. Vallet

Other volumes forthcoming

CONGREGATIONS AT THE CROSSROADS

*Remembering to Be
Households of God*

RONALD E. VALLET

William B. Eerdmans Publishing Company
Grand Rapids, Michigan/Cambridge, U.K.

REV/Rose Publishing
Manlius, New York

© 1998 by REV/Rose Ministries, Inc.

Published by Wm. B. Eerdmans Publishing Co.
255 Jefferson Ave. S.E., Grand Rapids, Michigan 49503 /
P.O. Box 163, Cambridge CB3 9PU U.K.
All rights reserved

Printed in the United States of America

03 02 01 00 99 98   7 6 5 4 3 2 1

Library of Congress Cataloging-in-Publication Data

Vallet, Ronald E., 1929-
Congregations at the crossroads: remembering to be households of God /
Ronald E. Vallet
p.   cm.   — (Faith's Horizons)
Includes bibliographical references and index.
ISBN 0-8028-4367-0 (pbk.)
1. Stewardship, Christian. 2. Church.
I. Title. II. Series.
BV772.V25 1998
250 — dc21   98-17305
                                        CIP

The Scripture quotations in this publication are from the New Revised Standard Version Bible, copyright © 1989 by the Division of Christian Education of the National Council of Churches of Christ in the U.S.A., and used by permission. All rights reserved.

*To Christian congregations in North America
struggling to become households of God
and
to Matthew, Nikita, and Nicholas*

Contents

Contents

An Overview of the Faith's Horizons Series

A human observer, facing in a single direction, can see only one part of the physical horizon. By using mirrors, photographs, or technological devices, a person may see all 360 degrees of the horizon at one time. Even then, however, it is seen as "in a mirror, dimly."

And so it is when we look at the horizons of faith. The horizons of faith in God's world are breathtaking! Yet no one view, no one perspective, can capture a full understanding of the reality of God and God's interactions with the people who inhabit our world. A mosaic of views, though it will not provide a complete view of faith's horizons, does offer a view that is wider and fuller than a solitary perspective can be.

The Faith's Horizons series, which began in 1994, is an attempt to provide such a mosaic about God's work in the world God created. Different titles in the series, which involves several writers, explore God's mission from a variety of vantage points: individuals, congregations, denominations, theological education, and our relationship to the world God created.

As I have carried out my responsibilities as general editor of the series, I have found the work to be challenging and fulfilling. My hope and prayer is that the Faith's Horizons series will be an instrument that, when used by God's people, will help to accomplish God's mission in the world. A look at existing and future titles will illustrate these hopes and prayers:

THE FAITH'S HORIZONS SERIES

The *first* title in the Faith's Horizons series was *Stepping Stones of the Steward: A Faith Journey Through Jesus' Parables* (Ronald E. Vallet, 1994). Using 14 parables, *Stepping Stones* explores dimensions of the faith journey of the Christian. The emphasis of the book is on the *individual* as a steward of the gospel and of God's creation. Indeed, it is argued that the image of steward embodies the identity of the Christian. The theme of the book centers on the faith journey of the individual Christian, set within a community of faith.

In the *second* volume of the series, the *Mainline Church's Funding Crisis* (Ronald E. Vallet and Charles E. Zech, 1995), the emphasis shifted to *denominations,* of which individual Christians and their congregations are a part. This work deals primarily with the mission funding crisis of mainline denominations in the United States, Canada, and Australia. Its main conclusions are: 1) the funding crisis among mainline denominations is real and actually began before the generally accepted date of the 1960s; 2) the main factor behind the funding crisis is the church's surrender to and entrapment in the reigning assumptions of modernity; and 3) the Christian congregation holds the key to a revitalized church in the emerging post-modern world — a world that will play to the strengths of congregational life.

Christian Voluntarism: Theology and Praxis (William H. Brackney, 1997), the *third* book in the series, provides biblical, theological, historical, and sociological bases for asserting that the spirit and practice of *voluntarism* are essential parts of the life of the church and its members. The individual Christian lives and functions in the context of the institutional church and a particular society. This book first looks at the biblical backgrounds and the theological bases of Christian voluntarism. This is followed by an in-depth historical perspective on Christian voluntarism over the centuries, focusing on the experience of Christian voluntarism in Britain and North America.

The *fourth* title — *Living in the Maybe: A Steward Confronts the Spirit of Fundamentalism* (Chris Levan, 1998) — is a strong reminder that to love God and to follow God involves a willingness *to live in the maybe*. To know God and to do God's will is not as simple as opening and following a road map. There are many twists and unexpected turns in the faith journey of the steward — the Christian disciple. In *Living in the Maybe,* Chris Levan provides readers with a breathtaking view of the horizons of faith. The perspective that the life of faith is lived in the "maybe" is refreshing, especially when contrasted with the dogmatic certainties that have deviled the Christian faith over the centuries. And, as Levan points out, the context and content of that dogmatic certainty has shifted back and forth across the centuries.

This book, *Congregations at the Crossroads: Remembering to Be Households of God* — the *fifth* volume in the Faith's Horizons series — focuses on *congregations.* It explores and expands on ideas about the congregation that were only touched on in *The Mainline Church's Funding Crisis. Congregations at the Crossroads* represents my efforts to describe a congregation that remembers who it is and whose it is — a household of God — and forsakes being a household of amnesia.

The next volume, number six in the Faith's Horizons series, will be a parallel to *Stepping Stones.* Based on Old Testament stories and the connecting thread of *covenant, The Steward Living in Covenant* (Ronald E. Vallet, 1999), will look at the promise and command aspects of God's covenant with God's people as a vital dimension of what it means to be a steward.

The seventh book in the series (Ronald E. Vallet, 2000) will look at biblical and theological dimensions of our relationship to the *environment* that God created and for which God calls us to stewardship.

The eighth title, currently being planned and projected for publication in 2001, will look at the possibility of *theological education* being rooted in the concept of the Christian as steward, with the role of the pastor being "theologian in residence" for the congregation he or she serves. An important question to be explored is whether theological education prepares men and women to be theologians in residence, or merely therapists or chief executive officers. Several theological educators in both the United States and Canada will contribute to the book.

Ronald E. Vallet,
general editor of the Faith's Horizons series

Foreword

It has long been recognized that Ronald Vallet possesses peculiar gifts and acute sensitivity in the vexed arena of Christian stewardship. This volume, however, moves well beyond his previous contributions in terms of fresh expression and serious rethinking, and presents a coherent, comprehensive statement of a theology of stewardship that is geared to the real life and practice of the church. Vallet has thought long and well about the cultural setting and crisis of the "oldline" churches in North America, and has come to see that the consumer culture around us is slowly eroding our passion for giving and undermining the convictions that make giving a sustainable mode of life.

Without setting out to do so and being compelled by no radical agenda of his own (beyond the agenda of the gospel), Vallet arrives at the inescapable conclusion that the church as a giving community marked by passion and generosity is indeed *an alternative community*, alternative to the "bread and circuses" ambience of dominant culture. There is in his argument deep theological and christological roots and profound ecclesial implications. But none of this is in the least way obscure, technical, or esoteric.

Vallet is a churchman whose life is in the real church, on the ground. His vision is of the church as a caring community of people who intend to live their lives in obedient response to the goodness of God. Such obedience cannot be a haphazard, hit-and-miss operation but must be a sustained enterprise formed by a larger narrative account of who we are and who we are called to be. Vallet provides that larger narrative account by considering the church as a "household" of memory, hope, and obedience that determinedly refuses the despair and amnesia of dominant culture. While Vallet is deeply informed by the work of M. Douglas Meeks (an excellent guide in such matters), it is his own work in a fresh and suggestive way. He is practical for the life of the church. He turns a phrase and offers an image that opens up interpretive possibility and permits new recognition of self and community in faith.

Congregations, stewardship committees, and pastors will find here grist for the endless "burden of finance." Beyond that, there is expressed here a most accessible *reframing of life* in the joys and fidelities of our faith. This serious rethink bodes well for the "recovery of nerve" so urgent now in a church context that can no longer go on with business as usual. This is "alternative business" out of and toward an alternative possibility for our common life.

Walter Brueggemann
McPheeder Professor of Old Testament
Columbia Theological Seminary
Decatur, Georgia
February 5, 1997

Preface

The second volume in the Faith's Horizons series dealt primarily with the mission funding crisis of mainline denominations in the United States, Canada, and Australia.[1] Its main conclusions included these points: (1) the funding crisis among mainline denominations is real and actually began before the generally accepted date of the 1960s; (2) the main factor behind the funding crisis is the church's surrender to and its entrapment in the reigning assumptions of modernity; and (3) the Christian congregation holds the key to a revitalized church in the emerging postmodern world — a world that will play to the strengths of congregational life. Significantly, the book viewed the Christian congregation as called to be a household of God (also described as a household of Jesus Christ) and listed some of the characteristics and rules of such a household.

As the manuscript for *The Mainline Church's Funding Crisis* was completed at the end of 1994, it became clear to me that a companion book focusing on the congregation was needed. I envisioned it as exploring and expanding on ideas about the congregation that had only been touched upon in the earlier work.

But other events were to take place. On May 9, 1995, without prior warning and quite suddenly, I experienced pain and a feeling of pressure in the center of my chest. Within a minute or two, the

---

1. Ronald E. Vallet and Charles E. Zech, *The Mainline Church's Funding Crisis: Issues and Possibilities* (Grand Rapids, Mich.: Wm. B. Eerdmans Publishing Co.; Manlius, N.Y.: REV/Rose Publishing, 1995).

pain increased. It was obvious that something of a serious nature was happening. I told my wife, Rose Marie, what was happening and asked her to call 911. Within five minutes, two medical emergency technicians were with me in the living room. After asking a few questions and checking my vital signs, they placed me in the ambulance and transported me to a hospital emergency room.

Using an echo cardiogram, the cardiologist determined that a heart attack had taken place, with some damage to the heart. He then observed that a second heart attack was beginning to take place. Even as he was sharing this information, he interrupted himself to say, "Look, it's reversing." *Before his eyes, the second heart attack was reversed.* A few minutes later, I saw the reversal on videotape. With some new insight, I thanked God for divine reversals.

In my own life and in a most dramatic manner, a divine reversal had taken place. I had believed in divine reversals before. The reversal in the emergency room gave me an existential perception of reversal.

The Bible is a story of divine reversals: Moses led a people from bondage in slavery to release from captivity; Israel in the death of exile was restored; God triumphed over the power of death in the resurrection of Jesus Christ.

In *The Mainline Church's Funding Crisis,* I had described the divine reversal in Ezekiel's vision of the valley of dry bones. My personal experience deepened my conviction that God can and will bring reversal to the life of the church that *remembers* who and whose it is.

This book, the fifth title in the Faith's Horizons series, represents my efforts to describe such a congregation. Like its predecessors, it explores factors affecting the church in order to find places of hope where a new perspective — faith's horizons — can identify potential points of faithful change. The *horizon* is the line where the sky seems to meet the earth. As such, it is the boundary between the visible and the invisible — the seen and the unseen. It is also a reminder that a change of position or perspective can bring a view not seen before. With new views can come insights. Even more, beyond the horizon a new vision beckons people of faith. It is my hope that this book will help the church find points of change and will also suggest ways that faithful change can be brought about.

This book is based on the premise that the church, as a household of God — *a household of faith* — provides a setting for nurture and sustenance. The church, however, too easily forgets that it *is* a community of faith. In North American culture, metaphors of management and psychological therapy control and sometimes overwhelm the call to the church to be a faithful, hopeful, loving community.

It is my judgment, based on my work and experience in Christian ministry on the local, regional, national, and international scenes — both denominational and ecumenical — that the church has largely forgotten who it is, what it is called to do, and whose it is. It has become a household of amnesia. A divine reversal is needed if the church is to become the household of God that God intends. Much of the work on this book occurred in the year and a half following my heart attack. My hope — indeed, my expectation — is that God will bring about a divine reversal in the life of the church in North America as it enters the twenty-first century.

My thanks go to Rose Marie Vallet, my wife and valued colleague, for her great help in editing and proofreading. Other colleagues in both Canada and the United States read the manuscript and provided feedback that did much to make this a better book than it would have been without their input. My gratitude goes to Leslee Alfano, Vincent Alfano, Walter Brueggemann, William R. Herzog II, Robert Wood Lynn, M. Douglas Meeks, Kenneth R. Morgan, Donald M. Scott, L. E. "Ted" Siverns, William W. Vallet, and Laura E. Wright. I appreciate each one.

A special word of gratitude goes to M. Douglas Meeks. His presentations at a number of ecumenical and denominational meetings provided several seminal ideas, especially in relationship to the characteristics and rules of the household of God and the instruments of Christian stewardship.

Working on this book has been a labor of love and of hope. If it helps Christians to understand more fully why God desires reversal from a household of amnesia to a household of God, and how it may come to pass, those hopes will have been met. My prayer is that it will be so.

Ronald E. Vallet
Manlius, New York
Epiphany 1997

INTRODUCTION

Forgetting or Remembering?

Memory is critical for a congregation striving to become a
household of God. Without a memory, a state of amnesia
will continue to shroud the life of the congregation.

Vital Questions

The most vital question confronting the church in North America as
it approaches the twenty-first century relates to whether the church
knows who it is, what it is called to do, and, especially, whose it is.
The question *Is the church a household of God?* can be phrased another
way: Can the church remember its origins and its stories and live
them out? The danger is that the church is so caught up in the allures
and mentality of a consumer society that it is not the household of
God that God called it to be.

Is the church a household of amnesia instead of being a household of God? The answer for the North American church in the
waning period of modernity, as it enters a postmodern age, seems
to be that the church is a household of amnesia. If this answer is
correct, the logical next questions are: Can the church be freed from
the spell of amnesia and remember that it is called to be a household
of God? What does a faithful household of God look like? How can
a congregation remember the biblical stories that will inform it as it
seeks to become a household of God? How does stewardship as
"household" management relate to becoming a household of God?

1

How can meaningful change take place? This book will consider these questions, particularly from the point of view of the Christian congregation.[1] How can a Christian *congregation* become *a household of God* — a household of Jesus Christ?[2]

A Parable About Forgetting

A modern parable illustrates the danger of forgetting: "On a dangerous seacoast where shipwrecks often occur there was once a crude little lifesaving station." So begins a parable written by T. O. Wedel[3] many years ago. The parable speaks as powerfully now as it did then. Originally the lifesaving station was a hut, with only one boat and a few devoted members who kept watch over the sea. With no thought for themselves, they went out day and night to search for those who were lost. Many lives were saved and this wonderful little station became famous. Some of the persons who were saved and others who lived in the area wanted to be associated with the station and gave of their time and money to support its work. New boats were bought and new crews trained. The lifesaving station grew.

Some of the members grew unhappy that the building — the hut — was rude and poorly equipped. "Should not a more comfortable place be provided as a refuge for those saved from the sea?" they asked. They enlarged the building, put in better furniture, and

---

1. In Ronald E. Vallet and Charles E. Zech, *The Mainline Church's Funding Crisis: Issues and Possibilities* (Grand Rapids, Mich.: Wm. B. Eerdmans Publishing Co.; Manlius, N.Y.: REV/Rose Publishing, 1995), we concentrated on the plight of mainline denominations in the United States, Canada, and Australia. One of our findings in that book was that the primary locus of hope for denominations lies in the *renewal of congregations,* specifically, that congregations become households of Jesus Christ.

2. Since this book deals with *Christian* congregations, the term "household of Jesus Christ" and the term "household of God" are used interchangeably when referring to Christian congregations.

3. T. O. Wedel, "Evangelism — The Mission of the Church to Those Outside Her Life," *The Ecumenical Review,* Oct. 1953.

replaced the cots with beds. Soon the lifesaving station became a popular gathering place for the members. As it began to be used as a sort of club, it was decorated beautifully and furnished exquisitely. Fewer members were willing to go to sea on lifesaving missions so they hired lifesaving crews to do this work.

> About this time a large ship was wrecked off the coast, and the hired crews brought in boat loads of cold, wet, and half-drowned people. They were dirty and sick and some of them had black skin and some had yellow skin. The beautiful new club was in chaos. So the property committee immediately had a shower house built outside the club where victims of shipwreck could be cleaned up before coming inside.[4]

A split in the club membership developed at the next meeting. A large number of the members argued in favor of stopping the club's lifesaving activities because they were unpleasant and hindered the normal social life of the club. A smaller number of members insisted that lifesaving was their primary purpose and that they were still a lifesaving station.

> But they were finally voted down and told that if they wanted to save the lives of all the various kinds of people who were shipwrecked in those waters, they could begin their own lifesaving station down the coast. They did.
>
> As the years went by, the new station experienced the same changes that had occurred in the old. It evolved into a club, and so yet another lifesaving station was founded. This story continued to repeat itself, and if you visit that sea coast today, you will find a number of exclusive clubs along that shore. Shipwrecks are frequent in those waters, but most of the people drown.[5]

This parable makes clear how important it is that a congregation remember *who* it is and *what* God has called it to do. A congregation needs to have a clear sense of its purpose — its mission — and set priorities and determine goals and objectives that are consistent with

4. Wedel, "Evangelism."
5. Wedel, "Evangelism."

that overarching purpose. Above all, a congregation must know *whose* it is.

Assumptions of This Book

As Christian congregations in North America enter a new century, many have settled into a survival mode in which the prevailing question is: "How can we pay the bills and make it through another year?" Even a congregation that has moved beyond a survival mode to formulate a mission statement that speaks of more than managing to pay its bills may forget what God has called it to be: a community of faith, that is, a household of God.

The basic assumptions of this book are threefold:

1. God calls each Christian congregation to be a household of God — a household of Jesus Christ.
2. The major barrier to becoming a household of God is amnesia — a loss of memory.
3. God can bring reversal to a congregation so that it becomes a household of God.

The Urgency of Memory

The most urgent matter requiring attention in the life of the church is the regaining of memory. Without a memory, there is no story. Without a story, there is no identity. The greatest danger of our churches today is that we are losing our memory. We live in a world affected by the twins of amnesia, in which we forget who we are, and anesthesia, which numbs us into insensitivity about what is happening to the church. We can't remember the stories of our community, of our family, even our own story. In a consumer, market society, one doesn't need to have a memory. In fact, those who don't have a memory may be more "successful" than those who do. But because the promises of the church's future are given in its past and nowhere else, it is a disaster for the church to lose its memory. Today,

4

it seems, the North American church has lost its memory and doesn't know who it is or whose it is.

The story of a young lion illustrates the importance of knowing who and whose we are:

A young lion got lost one day and his family couldn't find him. After a while he wandered into a community of lambs and was being brought up by them. They taught the little lion how to baa. It sounded silly to him, but that's what everybody was doing. They taught him how to munch on grass. It tasted lousy, but that's what everybody else was eating. Once in a while he would look down and wonder why he didn't look like everyone else. But, he figured, that's just the way it is.

While he was out munching on grass and baaing one day, there was a huge roar up on the hill. All the little lambs scattered as fast as they could. But somehow it sounded familiar to the little lion, so he went padding off to find out what it was.

When he got there, the big lion looked down and said, "What do you think you're doing?"

The little lion said, "I'm munching on grass."

"But what are the funny noises you're making?"

"I'm baaing."

"Come here," said the big lion. He took the little lion over to a pond of water and said, "Look in the water."

The little lion looked in the water and the big lion gave a roar. The little lion's eyes lighted up and he said, "I'm like you."

"Right," said the big lion. "Now you know who you are and whose you are."[6]

Most Christian congregations in North America live in a world of amnesia, not remembering their stories and what it means to be God's household. Biblical illiteracy is rampant. The Letter of James reminds Christians that they are to be doers of the word, and not merely hearers, lest they forget: "For if any are hearers of the word and not doers, they are like those who look at themselves in a mirror;

6. Based on a presentation by John H. Westerhoff III at Syracuse, New York, in May 1982, at a conference sponsored by American Baptist Churches of New York State.

for they look at themselves and, on going away, immediately forget what they were like" (James 1:23-24).

The church needs the *miracle of memory*. To "re-member" is to bring something *from* the past *into* the present. It is not simply to go back into the past, but to bring the promises — the fermenting grace of God — from the past into the present. The congregation must seek and live by texts that provide the miracle of memory and thus serve as "a powerful alternative to the kind of self-deceiving amnesia reflected in Deut. 8:17."[7] ("Do not say to yourself, 'My power and the might of my own hand have gotten me this wealth.'")

A congregation afflicted by amnesia forgets that members of the household cannot do the work alone and on their own. The work of the household of God is the work of *God*. These words need to be remembered and blazoned on our banners and in our literature:

"Unless the LORD builds the house, those who build it labor in vain." (Ps. 127:1a)

Faithful Change Cannot Be Divorced from Faithful Decision Making

If a congregation is to become a faithful household of God, change is needed! The congregation must first come to the realization that it is a household that has forgotten to whom it belongs. This will be an act of confession. Yet, even then, faithful change cannot and will not take place unless and until appropriate and faithful decisions are made by the members of God's household.

At any given moment, the life of a congregation is in change — either minor or major. The change may be intended or not intended. The change may be sought or it may be feared. No congregation can stay as it is — nor should it. Change is inevitable. The wise congregation anticipates change and makes faithful decisions ahead of time, before the options are less desirable. Faithful decisions

---

7. Walter Brueggemann, "The Book of Exodus," in *The New Interpreter's Bible*, vol. 1 (Nashville: Abingdon Press, 1994), p. 963.

require that the congregation remember that it is called to be a household of God and seek, with God's leading and help, to become such a household.

One of the major barriers to remembering is the relationship of the congregation and its members to money. A popular conception about the relation of money to the church is that money is tainted and therefore the only reason the church must deal with money is because money is a necessary evil to pay the bills and to carry out ministry. "The ideal situation," it is thought, "is one in which all the financial needs of the congregation would be met without ever having to ask anyone to contribute money." Many pastors and lay leaders are embarrassed and reluctant to ask for money or to make economic decisions. Asking, they feel, seems too much like begging. Of course, "pocketbook protection" is also a major part of the equation. As a consequence, economic decisions are assigned a low level of priority — driven by necessity, more than by being related to Bible study, theological reflection, and prayer.

The truth is that the life of a congregation — especially when change is contemplated or is taking place — is vitally connected to its economic decision-making processes. And economic decision making is directly connected to faithfulness as a household of God. Indeed, the word *economy* comes from the Greek *oikonomia,* which means "stewardship" or "household management." Money is more than a way to pay the bills. *Attitudes about money have a vital relationship to faith.* Economic decisions made by the congregation shape more than budgets and programs; they have a strong effect on the discipleship and life-styles of the members.

A reading of how the relationship between faith and money is viewed within a congregation may come when some congregational leaders think that an opportunity for renewal exists within their congregation. Some would like to see their congregation truly become a household of God. Other leaders may fear change and sense dangers — both real and perceived. At such times, financial factors may become a reason — or an excuse — to avoid meaningful change. The question then becomes: will the opportunity to become a household of God, as perceived by some members, be overwhelmed by the dangers perceived by other members? Or, putting it another way, will the work of the household be perceived as the work of God? The important subject of money will be explored further in chapter two.

Disjointed Decision Making

When change is occurring, or is about to occur, both opportunity and danger appear. Members of a congregation contemplating change will usually discover that *perceptions* about objectives and methods do not change as quickly as the need for change calls for. History shows that attempts are often made to use once successful methods in pursuit of goals and objectives that are no longer appropriate or relevant. Seeking to maintain the status quo so as to perpetuate objectives and methods of yesterday will not result in a favorable outcome. Decisions must be made with the desired outcome as the overall goal. Otherwise frustration and apathy will follow.

For example, agendas of congregational meetings often do not reflect priority goals but rather represent a traditional ordering of items. As a result, today's agendas many times may look nearly identical to those of ten or even twenty years ago. Even when new goals are established, the expectation that they are to be implemented is often accompanied by an equally strong expectation that past programs are *also* to be carried out. Such a failure to establish priorities grows out of confused, disjointed, and fragmented decision making.

The ancient parable of several blind men who met an elephant on the road may well serve as a metaphor for the disjointed decision-making processes of some congregations. Different members of a congregation see the same "elephant" — their congregation — from a different angle or perspective.[8]

8. This application of the parable to the life of a congregation is an adaptation of John Godfrey Saxe's "The Parable of the Blind Men and the Elephant," in *Concern: Communication*, ed. Jeffrey Schrank (Morristown, N.J.: Silver Burdett Co., 1970), pp. 16-17. The reference was provided by L. E. Siverns.

Those members whose interests and concerns focus on the financial needs and administration of the congregation may be like the blind man who felt the elephant's leg and decided a tree was blocking the way, sensing only the immediate problem of money and budget.

Those who are concerned with pastoral ministry and interpersonal relationships may be like the blind man who felt the writhing, twisting trunk of the elephant and decided that a snake was threatening, feeling barred from accomplishing what they want to accomplish.

Others who are concerned with matters of church education, reaching young people and young adults, intergenerational education, higher education, and related resources and materials may be represented by the blind man who touched the elephant's ear and thought it was a fan, as they perceive a blowing and scattering of the diverse elements of their concern.

Those who have concern for the reaching of persons through programs of evangelism and outreach may be like the blind man who felt the elephant's belly and thought himself up against a wall, so massive seem the problems.

Individuals who are concerned with ministry to and with the community, the oppressiveness and dehumanizing of institutions, and evils such as racism and sexism may be like the blind man holding on to the elephant's swinging tail, feeling it as a rope pulling to go to another place.

In the parable, each of the blind men disputed loud and long as to what the elephant was. Though each one was partly right, they all were in the wrong! If the blind men had exchanged places in order to experience the portions of the elephant that they had not felt previously and then shared their experiences, they would have been better able to agree on what the elephant was really like.

What is needed, of course, is that the leaders and members of a congregation do all possible to experience the congregation in its wholeness, realizing that the whole is more than any single part, or perhaps even greater than the sum of the parts. Such a holistic approach will enable planning processes and decision making that reflect the call to become a household of God amid the allure of modernity and in the context of an emerging postmodern world.

Conflict Between the Short Term and the Long Term

A fundamental conflict nearly always exists between the short-term and long-term consequences of policy changes. Decisions exist only in the present, but their consequences reach into the future. Jay W. Forrester wrote that decisions leading to a series of actions aimed at short-run improvements can eventually burden a system with long-run depressants so severe that even heroic short-run measures will not suffice. Conversely, a series of actions aimed at long-term improvement will be likely to have their cost during the short term.[9]

As congregational leaders plan and make decisions, they need to consider both the present and the future — both the short run and the long run. Difficult though this may be, it is an essential part of decision making.

Wise leaders recognize the dangers of focusing on a part rather than the whole and of focusing on the near term to the neglect of the long term. They are then in a better position to make recommendations regarding purpose, needs, objectives, programs, financial resources, organizational structure, and staffing patterns that will help the congregation remember that it is called to be a household of God.

Sorting Out Principles

In a delightful book that describes the life of a mythical Presbyterian church in North Haven, Minnesota, Michael L. Lindvall narrated the life of the Second Presbyterian Church through the cycle of a typical year.[10] In his telling, the origins of Second Presbyterian Church go back to more than a century before, when the newly founded First — and only — Presbyterian Church had a church fight. One Sunday

9. Jay W. Forrester, "Counterintuitive Behavior of Social Systems," in *Toward Global Equilibrium: Collected Papers*, ed. Dennis L. Meadows and Donnella H. Meadows (Cambridge, Mass.: Wright-Allen Press, 1973), pp. 13-14.

10. Michael L. Lindvall, *The Good News from North Haven* (New York: Doubleday, 1991).

in June, half the congregation walked out during the sermon and founded Second Presbyterian Church. Lindvall described the results:

> All memories agree as to what the fight was about: whether young women ought to lead discussions at Christian Endeavor meetings or keep a low profile and ask questions when they go home, as St. Paul seems to have counseled. What memories do not agree on is who was on what side. Some people now say that the Second Presbyterian group that left was in favor of women speaking at meetings, some say they were against it. Whatever the truth, everyone agrees that Second Presbyterian Church was squarely established on the firm foundation of an important principle, even if no one is now quite sure what that principle was.[11]

Lindvall concluded this story by writing that a few years after the split, the building of First Presbyterian Church burned. They had no fire insurance, by conviction, and did not rebuild. Most of the members joined Second Church after the fire. A handful refused to do so as a matter of principle and became Methodists.

A principle that seems important at one point in a congregation's history may seem less important, or even be forgotten, as years go by and new chapters in the life of the congregation unfold. Does this mean that principles are unimportant? No. It does indicate that points of discussion and disagreement on which no compromise can be made may be seen as much less crucial a few years later. Congregational leaders must assess the situation and distinguish carefully between principles that must be held as an intrinsic part of the Christian faith and those that can be yielded and compromise sought. The distinction is not always easily made. A faithfully executed planning process, which is bathed in Bible study, theological reflection, and prayer, can help a congregation *sort out long-lasting principles from passing fads*. To know and heed God's call to a particular congregation is a process of embarking on a faith journey.

God's people, as Lindvall noted, can be "often stiff-necked, a little vain, a little jealous, and a little afraid." But you can also witness

11. Lindvall, *Good News,* p. 2.

11

"grace at work, so gently and surprisingly in these same people."[12] A faithful congregation will do its planning so that God's grace will work through the people involved in the process as the congregation moves to become a faithful household of God.

Guidelines for Becoming a Faithful Household of God

What guidelines will enable congregations to move toward becoming and living as faithful households of God — households of Jesus Christ? How can congregations chart a course and navigate their way faithfully and effectively through changing times? These twelve guidelines are recommended for use in beginning the planning process that is described in chapter eight:

1. Engage in Bible study, theological reflection, and prayer to reach agreement about what it means to be a faithful household of Jesus Christ.
2. Agree and be clear about the purpose — the *raison d'être* — of your congregation.
3. Adopt and implement goals, objectives, and strategies that are consistent with that purpose.
4. Acknowledge that economic decision making by the congregation affects individual discipleship and life-styles.
5. Plan for the long term, recognizing that long-term plans have short-term consequences. (Aiming only for the short term can burden congregations with severe depressants and undesired results.)
6. Provide opportunity for all members to be involved in decision making.
7. If disagreements emerge, seek agreement and consensus, again through Bible study, theological reflection, and prayer.
8. Recognize and acknowledge when a congregation is leaving an old chapter to move toward a new chapter in its life.

12. Lindvall, *Good News,* p. 7.

9. Be sure that plans adopted and implemented are holistic and comprehensive.
10. Provide ways in which all members may share the risks and costs of leadership.
11. Appreciate and encourage leaders.
12. Value and care for each member.

The Household's Beginning Point

Where does the household of Jesus Christ begin? M. Douglas Meeks has said, "The household of Jesus Christ begins with the dancing and laughter of Easter, or it does not begin at all. The household of Jesus Christ lives between two realities: the destruction of death in Jesus Christ and the destruction of death in all things. The in-between-time history in which we live is the time we call mission."[13] Yet, if one takes an honest, objective look at the life of most congregations, it is usually only around Easter that real celebration is made of the resurrection of Jesus Christ. It is rarely mentioned during other times of the year, and it is forgotten that the reason most Christians gather for worship on Sunday is because that was the day Jesus rose from death.[14] The church is a miracle that really does depend upon the resurrection work of God.

In Germany a growing number of people are choosing to be buried anonymously, without ritual or even a farewell from relatives.

13. M. Douglas Meeks in July 1993 at an educational event for stewardship leaders held in Bolton, Ontario.
14. Several New Testament texts (Matt. 28:1; Mark 16:2, 9; Luke 24:1; and John 20:1, 19, among others) place the resurrection of Jesus on the first day of the week. The Lord's Supper was celebrated on Sunday (Acts 20:7). Interestingly, one reminder that the gathering was to be on the first day of the week came as a statement about saving for the collections: "On the first day of every week, each of you is to put aside and save whatever extra you earn, so that collections need not be taken when I come" (1 Cor. 16:2). Thus, it may reasonably be concluded, the first day of the week, Sunday, was adopted by the early Christians as the day of worship based on the fact this was the day of the resurrection.

There has been a large increase in anonymous burials, where the ashes of the deceased are buried in a nameless urn. Most German cemeteries now have these kinds of burial grounds. It is reported that "Visitors who cannot cope with their grief wander around aimlessly, searching for the place where the ashes of their relative or friend might be buried. In the end the bereaved randomly lay down some flowers on the ground and walk away."[15] In a pastoral statement, the Roman Catholic bishops of Germany decried this changing attitude toward dying and death. Such anonymity contrasts sharply with accounts of the impact of Jesus' resurrection on his disciples.

The role of memory is crucial. Peter Marty recounted the role of memory as written by Craig Dykstra:

> Without a narrative that sustains us, the world — and we ourselves — are virtually phantom. But the issue is not just whether one has a narrative or not. The issue is whether we have one that is true and genuine, one that can sustain us in reality, one that, having been given and committed to memory, frees us from desperately having to make one up.[16]

In writing about the two who traveled with Jesus to Emmaus, Marty concluded:

> Until Jesus reminded the travelers to Emmaus who the Messiah was and what his resurrection meant, they were as desperate as most of us are to make sense of life. Their existence was as phantom as their faith. Their identity was as elusive as people believed the risen Christ to be. Their hope was as uncertain as the future of their nation. Then they remembered. They remembered that they wouldn't have to make up life anymore. Jesus had set them free.[17]

---

15. This information about anonymous graves was reported in "Europeans Seek the Grave's Anonymity," *The Christian Century,* 15 May 1996, p. 541.

16. Peter W. Marty, "Living by the Word: Burning Hearts," *The Christian Century,* 10 April 1996, p. 397, quoting Craig Dykstra. The source is not given.

17. Marty, "Living by the Word."

Memory is critical for a congregation striving to become a household of God. Without a memory, a state of amnesia will continue to shroud the life of the congregation.

Recovery of Memory

If we indeed suffer from amnesia, how do we recover our memory? The household of Jesus Christ is built around the table. Table and bread are absolutely central. In the Jewish tradition at the Seder meal, a young child asks: "Why are we doing this?" That is, why are we doing this strange thing? The questions this raises for the Christian church are: "Are our liturgies odd enough that our children ask the same question? Are our practices enough out of step with the world to cause our children to ask, 'Why are we living this way?' Do our children never hear the story because it is the odd way of living that is the occasion for the question, 'why?'" If the church were living that way today, our children would ask, "Why are we living this way?" That becomes the occasion for the story.

When God gave a new kind of bread in the wilderness (Exodus 16), God was building a new household. The new kind of bread — manna — was not Pharaoh's bread. The exchange of bread as a *commodity* had led to slavery and starvation in Egypt. Manna was a *gift* of God — not a commodity to be exchanged. This new bread, if stored, would spoil. That is what distinguishes the household economy of God from the public household economy in which the church in North America lives and ministers. The people in the wilderness were told to keep an omer of the manna "throughout your generations, in order that they may see the food with which I fed you in the wilderness, when I brought you out of the land of Egypt" (Exod. 16:32). The people were told to *remember God's gift* of a new kind of bread and to keep some in a jar as a visible reminder.

In a household of amnesia, there is the bread of slavery, the bread of tears, and the bread of misery — Pharaoh's bread. This is the daily experience of most persons — rich or poor — in North America.

At Mount Sinai, God gave the rules of the household of God

15

— God's economy. Christians sometimes forget or minimize the reality that the Torah was at the heart of the ministry of Jesus. Christians are sometimes inclined to discount the importance of the Old Testament. The church must remember that these were the sacred Scriptures to which Jesus turned.

Likewise, the church must seek parallels between the household rules of Torah and what happened in Jesus' economy movement. The heart of the Torah is in Deuteronomy 5:15: "Remember that you were a slave in the land of Egypt, and the LORD your God brought you out from there with a mighty hand and an outstretched arm; therefore the LORD your God commanded you to keep the sabbath day." This statement of rationale occurs in the midst of the Ten Commandments given by God to Moses.

Only our memory lets us know about the bread of joy, the bread of freedom — manna in the wilderness. It is the same bread of which Jesus spoke when he said "I am the bread of life." In his ministry, Jesus had the same understanding of bread. When he fed the multitudes, there was no exchange of commodities. The offering of food brought by a young boy was multiplied so that there was enough for everyone, with food to spare.

In communion, the church lifts the bread and says, "This is my body." The bread is distributed by the principle of charis, which means grace or gift.

To become a household of God, a congregation needs to remember the biblical texts that inform it, or should inform it. Accordingly, we turn next to look at a biblical base for stewardship, particularly at biblical stories that relate to what it means to be a household of God. Then, because economic decisions are deeply involved in the life of a congregation, we will look in chapter two at fantasies and fears about finances in the congregation. Subsequent chapters will explore the history and present context of giving to the church in North America; the church as a household of amnesia caught in a culture known as modernity; the congregation as a household of Jesus Christ — including its characteristics, life, and work; worship in the household of God; and the roles of the pastor and laity. The book will close with a chapter on the congregation as a living household of God and two appendices that are sermons on some key biblical texts.

16

CHAPTER ONE

A Biblical Base for Stewardship

> In the biblical tradition, steward is the primary metaphor
> for ministry. The very heart of what it takes to become a
> steward is precisely the whole life of the congregation.
>
> M. Douglas Meeks

Stewardship in a Straitjacket

By and large, the church in North America does not remember its
stories; biblical illiteracy is rampant. When the church is without
a memory, there is no real knowledge of God's promises and
consequently no hope. The church needs the miracle of memory!
The church's amnesia is particularly evident in the arena of
stewardship.

Though many church leaders deny it and argue otherwise,
stewardship is a critical dimension of congregational life. Denials
of and arguments against this statement reflect a radical misunder-
standing of the nature of stewardship. Church leaders are mistaken
when they assume that stewardship is only a program to fund
ministry and mission in the church. Leaders who forget that
stewardship is rooted in the biblical story start out on the wrong
pathway. Leaders who assume that stewardship is something that
exists outside the basic worship and proclamation and sacramental
life of the church, and outside the *diakonia* and *koinonia* and mis-

17

sion, forget that *all of these things are necessary in order for a person to become a steward.* Churches often develop stewardship programs, but do not grow stewards. *Growing a steward requires the whole life of the congregation.* The church needs to release stewardship from its straitjacket so that stewards may develop and grow in the household of God.

A Look at the Word *Stewardship*

Oikonomia, the Greek word for stewardship, means household law or rules. In short, the word refers to household management. But whose household is it? For Christian stewards, it refers first and foremost to God's household.[1]

John H. Elliott noted that *oikos* is used over sixteen hundred times in the Septuagint, often conveying the communal identity and socioreligious solidarity of Israel.[2] Douglas Meeks wrote:

> The Old Testament traditions . . . appropriated *oikos* (or *bayith*) from their environments and used it with decisive theological intensity. Israel's life in relation to God and its historical environment is often described in terms of having a home or being at home in opposition to being homeless or being uprooted from home. The household is at the heart of most Israelite definitions of community. *Oikos* is a principal way of speaking of God's covenantal bond with Israel (Exod. 19:4-5). God has created Israel

---

1. Though not always recognized, the concept of "household" pervades Christian thought. The words *economy, ecology,* and *ecumenics* are related. *Economy* is taken from the Greek word *oikonomia* ("stewardship" or "household management"). *Ecology* also is rooted in the Greek noun *oikos,* "house." Thus, literally, ecology means a study of the household, referring to the creation or the environment. *Ecumenics,* as well, is rooted in the Greek noun *oikos.* Literally, it means "one household." It has, of course, been given a more specialized meaning in and by the ecumenical movement. Thus, the three words usually associated with financial management, environmental concerns, and the ecumenical movement are all rooted in the concept of "household."

2. John H. Elliott, *A Home for the Homeless: A Sociological Exegesis of 1 Peter, Its Situation and Strategy* (Philadelphia: Fortress Press, 1981), pp. 182-86.

as a household out of many tribes and is accordingly viewed as a constructor and ruler of the household.[3]

Meeks continued:

> The transformation of the church in our time depends on its rediscovery of its own *oikos* nature. A church that does not take seriously its character as the "household of God" will form its members only partially, which means that it will actually aid them in adapting to the predominantly defined *oikos* of the society. Thus theology in our time should think concretely, praxiologically, in the midst of the church's economy. Theology will not be able to overlook the fact that the economy of the church in North America has increasingly been conformed to market modes of living. Calls for the renewal and transformation of the church that do not deal concretely with this fact will be partial and ideological in character.[4]

From this understanding, I would argue that *the chief understanding of what the church is called to be is the household of God — the household of Jesus Christ.* Paul used the phrase "household of God" twice in his New Testament writings:

> So then you are no longer strangers and aliens, but you are citizens with the saints and also members of *the household of God.* (Eph. 2:19)

> I am writing these instruction to you so that, if I am delayed, you may know how one ought to behave in *the household of God,* which is the church of the living God, the pillar and bulwark of the truth. (1 Tim. 3:14-15)

A study of the English word related to stewardship is also revealing. The English word "steward" comes from "sty-ward": literally, the keeper of the pigpen. In a broader understanding, the term

3. M. Douglas Meeks in *God the Economist: The Doctrine of God and Political Economy* (Minneapolis: Fortress Press, 1989), pp. 33-34.
4. Meeks, *God the Economist,* pp. 36-37.

refers to the person who is appointed by the owner to be the manager or caretaker of the estate: the household. The ongoing, underlying question for the steward is: "Will everyone get what it takes to live, to survive or to live through the day?" For example, the steward manages things in the summer so there will be food in the winter. Joseph, in Egypt, managed things in the good years so that there would be food in the poor years. In contemporary North America, this question has been eclipsed by the economics of the marketplace, models of mass production, and consumption.

In the biblical tradition, however, *steward is the primary metaphor for ministry.*

God's Passion for the World

God's love for the world is clearly expressed in Scripture — perhaps most clearly and succinctly in John 3:16: "For God so loved the world that he gave his only Son, so that everyone who believes in him may not perish but may have eternal life." Unfortunately, however, we often misconstrue the words to mean, "For God so loved the *church*." This interpretation is grossly misleading. The message is clear: "God so loved the *world*." The Bible is the story of God's love for and redemption of the world. The human role in God's love of the world is to be a steward of God's household in carrying out God's mission.

God called the church into being to help carry out God's mission. Thus, it is fair to say, the church exists *for the sake* of God's passion for the world. God's mission is the plot. The church is a subplot. The work of the church as the household of God — the economic work of God, as it were — is to redeem the world. Understood in this way, stewardship is a function of God's redemption of the world. Stewardship, then, is managing and taking care of the household of God. "Housekeeping" does not appeal to most persons trapped in the assumptions of modernity and the Enlightenment. Stewardship as "housekeeping" is considered by many to be neither macho nor appealing.

Before turning directly to the biblical story, we will look briefly at the characteristics and conditions of a household.

20

Characteristics and Conditions of Home (Household)

Home provides the setting for life. Only home protects against death. In Robert Frost's poem "The Death of the Hired Man," Warren and Mary engage in a dialogue about the hired man who has come back to their home — to die:

> "Warren," she said, "he has come home to die: You needn't be afraid he'll leave you this time."
>
> "Home," he mocked gently.
>
> "Yes, what else but home? It all depends on what you mean by home. Of course, he's nothing to us, any more than was the hound that came a stranger to us out of the woods, worn out upon the trail."
>
> *"Home is the place where, when you have to go there, they have to take you in."*
>
> "I should have called it something you somehow haven't to deserve."[5]

Warren said that home is the place where they have to take you in. Mary countered that home is something that you don't have to deserve. Both responses indicate that home is a special place, with special characteristics.

Meeks noted these four important *characteristics* of home:[6]

1. Home is the place where everybody "knows your name." That is to say, everyone knows your story. Home is where most people gain a sense of identity so that they know "who they are." For most North Americans, gathering at the table at home for dinner is the occasion when persons catch up with the happenings in one another's lives — where each person's story is updated and touched again. Aspirations and hopes are

5. Robert Frost, "The Death of the Hired Man," in *The Complete Poems of Robert Frost* (New York: Holt, Rinehart and Winston, 1962), p. 53. The emphasis is added.

6. Meeks, *God the Economist*, p. 36. While the main points are Meeks's, the wording and added details are mine.

shared. To be without a name is to be homeless. To be homeless is to be subjected to death. All human beings — indeed all of God's creatures — need to have a home.

2. Home is also the place where each person can expect to be confronted, forgiven, hoped for, and loved. A person who is not being confronted and forgiven is probably not in a relationship that will lead to love and care. Home is where truth can and should be spoken in love.

3. Home is where there is always a place at the table. No member of the household is shut out or excluded. Each member of the household is accepted and loved for who he or she is. No one is a second-class member of the household.

4. Home is where what is on the table will always be shared with each member of the household. To be at home is to know that what is available will be used for the welfare of each person and for the good of the whole household. At home, individual wants and desires are set aside for the welfare of other members of the household — and for the whole household.

These characteristics describe home at its best and most desirable. The best does not always happen, however. Nonetheless, these characteristics reflect a deep longing within each human heart and speak to our innermost yearnings.

Home, at its best, gives access to life — to what it takes to live against the power of sin, of death, and of evil. God's redemption of the world involves the creation of the kinds of conditions that give people life against the power of death, of sin, and of evil. To create home is hard, but it is the work of God's steward.

Imagine for a moment that you and your family are in an isolated area, without a home, and that you have the job of finding a site for and creating a home. What things would be absolutely essential to have a home? Meeks suggested four conditions that would apply in every situation:

1. The household would have to have access to *water*. Indeed, it can reasonably be argued that water is the most essential element if a place is to become a home. Throughout human

history, the first question asked in deciding if a place could become a home has been: "Where is water?"

2. Every household must have a *table*. It is unimaginable to have a household without a table. Not all households in the world have the same kind of table, of course, but every household must have a place where household members come to share bread. The table becomes the social center for the household.[7]

3. *Bread,* that is to say, food, is a requirement for the household. The table cannot be a bare table. Members of the household have a need to share with one another and to receive nourishment and sustenance — both in terms of food and personal interaction.

4. The household must have a *towel*. Used for many purposes and called by many names, the towel becomes a symbol of service within the household. Meeks described the towel as the supreme symbol of stewardship in a household that lives against death.[8]

If we accept the premise that God wants to create the *characteristics and conditions* of home, we must explore what that would mean in the life of Christian congregations. That exploration will be done later in this book, especially in chapters five and six. We turn now to look specifically at the biblical story related to stewardship.

7. In a letter to the author, L. E. Siverns wrote about a fight at a Sikh temple near his home. Some wanted to sit at tables; some insisted on eating while sitting on the floor. The argument was that sitting on the floor showed that no one was better than any other person. Siverns added that the same could be said of sitting at a table. A "table" can take many forms.

8. Meeks reminded us that often when a person is ordained, a stole is given on that special occasion. Actually, Meeks said, the stole is nothing but a towel hung around the neck to signify that one is authorized to serve at table. He told about a synod executive who, when a pastor, put a stole around the neck of every person who came into the membership of the church. Before becoming members, people were prepared for the specific ministry for which they were commissioned upon their entrance into the church. The ministries were called Abrahamic groups, each with a particular focus in ministry.

The Biblical Story

The biblical story can be summarized: "Once we were slaves. God has set us free and made us part of God's household." That's the radical beginning — and the radical ending. The story of the deliverance of Israel from the bondage of Egypt is comparable to the resurrection of Jesus. The Old Testament story climaxes: "Remember that you were a slave in the land of Egypt, and the LORD [YHWH] your God brought you out from there with a mighty hand and an outstretched arm" (Deut. 5:15a). Israel was taken out of the household of slavery and made part of the household of God. The deliverance from Egypt and the resurrection of Jesus, along with other biblical texts that speak to stewardship understood as being part of the household of God, will be explored in the remaining part of this chapter. And, as we shall see, God's promises and God's commands are part of many biblical stories.[9]

Creation

Genesis 2:7-9 describes the creation of humankind and the pleasant environment that was provided:

> [T]hen the LORD God formed man from the dust of the ground, and breathed into his nostrils the breath of life; and the man became a living being. And the LORD God planted a garden in Eden, in the east; and there he put the man whom he had formed. Out of the ground the LORD God made to grow every tree that is pleasant to the sight and good for food, the tree of life also in the midst of the garden, and the tree of the knowledge of good and evil.

The Hebrew word translated "man" is 'adam. It does not refer to the male, but rather to a human being (an individual or the

---

9. A forthcoming volume in the Faith's Horizons series by Ronald E. Vallet will explore in depth a variety of biblical stories that deal with the concept of the steward living in covenant.

species). Only later does God create male (*'iysh*) and female (*'ishshah*) out of the undifferentiated *'adam*. The Hebrew words used in Genesis 2:23 for male (*'iysh*) and female (*'ishshah*) form a pun in Hebrew, even as they do in English (male/female and man/woman).

The environment, or home, for *'adam* was a luxuriant setting that included edible plants and herbs of the field planted by God. However, they did not grow apart from rain and human toil. The beauty of the trees and the provision of food are especially noted. This was a land that spoke eloquently of the *promise* of God to care for creation.

But there was also a *command:*

> The LORD God took the man and put him in the garden of Eden to till it and keep it. And the LORD God commanded the man, "You may freely eat of every tree of the garden; but of the tree of the knowledge of good and evil you shall not eat, for in the day that you eat of it you shall die." (Gen. 2:15-17)

Though the command to till and keep the ground involved some limits, it was not an oppressive command. Instead, it involved trust in what God said. Humans make decisions that concern not only themselves, but have profound implications for their relationship with God. *'Adam* is called to relate to God in trustful obedience.

The role given to *'adam* in Genesis 2 resonates with the dominion/servant role in Genesis 1:28. The Hebrew word *rada,* which is translated "have dominion," should be understood in terms of caregiving and nurturing, not exploitation. It is to rule with benevolence. The command focuses on the earth, particularly cultivation. It is *not* a command to subdue an enemy; no enemy is in view at that time. Unfortunately, misinterpretation of this command of God over the centuries has led to exploitation of the environment, abuse of animals, and a bad reputation for Christianity because of the distorted domineering interpretation that it gave to the command to "have dominion."

Abraham

Nearly fifteen hundred years after the time of Abraham, when Israel was in exile and struggling to remember who she was, words from Isaiah urged the people in exile to

> Look to the rock from which you were hewn,
>   and to the quarry from which you were dug.
> Look to Abraham your father
>   and to Sarah who bore you;
> for he was but one when I called him,
>   but I blessed him and made him many. (Isa. 51:1b-2)

The exiles were urged to carry their memories all the way back to Abraham and Sarah. Walter Brueggemann wrote: "Specifically, the memory championed here is the memory of Abraham and Sarah. It is telling indeed that in this particular place, the poetry does not urge a return to Moses and torah, but a recovery of Genesis and promise. Exactly in a season of dismay and despair, it is to these primal parents that reference is made."[10]

The call of Abram in Genesis 12 is considered by many interpreters to be the key to the rest of Genesis and the Pentateuch. The command/promise structure of the verses in Genesis 12 that describe the call of Abram follows a pattern that we shall see again in the covenant agreements God makes with other persons. The promise to Abraham is not one that will be fulfilled instantly. Rather, it begins with Abram and continues in the lives of his descendants. God's promises have a continuing, ongoing nature. As such, they can be appropriated in every generation by the community of faith.

In Ur of the Chaldeans, a city in southern Babylonia (present-day Iraq), God spoke to Abram in words that are among the most important in the Bible:

> Now the Lord said to Abram, "Go from your country and your kindred and your father's house to the land that I will show you.

---

10. Walter Brueggemann, *Biblical Perspectives on Evangelism: Living in a Three-Storied Universe* (Nashville: Abingdon Press, 1993), p. 84.

I will make of you a great nation, and I will bless you, and make your name great, so that you will be a blessing. I will bless those who bless you, and the one who curses you I will curse; and in you all the families of the earth shall be blessed." (Gen. 12:1-3)

The divine promise and command seen here are central to covenant. The *promise* is that God will make of Abram a great nation. The *command* is to "go from your country and your kindred and your father's house to the land that I will show you." Abram was called to leave his ancestral household and embark on a journey as part of the household of God. Abram responded positively to God's command.

Joseph

The story of Joseph is one of the more familiar stories of the Old Testament. Joseph was a young man who was greatly loved by his father, Jacob, and who aroused the jealousy of his older brothers who sold him into slavery to a passing caravan. His father was told that he had been killed by wild animals. Taken as a slave to Egypt, Joseph, over a period of years, rose to become second-in-command in all of Egypt: Pharaoh's chief steward. Joseph practiced good stewardship, as it is generally understood. He led the nation to save food during seven years of plenty so that there would be food during the seven lean years that followed.

But there is another part of the Joseph story, recorded in Genesis 47:13-21, that tells the story from the underside of history. Let's take a closer look at what happened during the seven lean years. Note especially the *exchanges* offered and accepted in this paraphrase of the dialogue:

People: "We are hungry."
Joseph: "Give me your money; here is food."

People: "We are starving."
Joseph: "I will exchange bread for your money."

People: "We have no money."
Joseph: "No problem, I'll exchange bread for your livestock [means of livelihood]."

People: "Shall we die before your eyes. We have no money; we have no livestock. We have nothing left but our bodies and our land. Buy our land in exchange for food."
Joseph: "No problem, I'll exchange bread for your land."

People: "We and our children are starving. We have no money; we have no livestock; we have no land."
Joseph: "Then I will exchange bread for the only thing you have left: yourselves."

In the series of exchanges, the people turned over their money, their means of livelihood, their land, and, finally, themselves.

The climax comes in verses 20-21, where we read that from one end of Egypt to the other, "the land became Pharaoh's" and the people became Pharaoh's slaves. A fundamental household question was raised: whose household was it? The answer, of course, is that the household was *the household of Pharaoh*.

This is a household question, even up to the present day. To whom does the land really belong? To whom do the people belong? In Romans 8, Paul wrote that the whole creation is groaning. For what? For a restoration of the household of God; for the freedom of the people of God. The people of God are never free unless and until they are members of the household of God. To be a member of the household of Pharaoh is to be part of a household of slavery and death.

Joseph, one of Israel's own children, became the instrument of Israel going into slavery: a household of a living death. That's what slavery is. Joseph, touted as a good steward, was a faithful steward of the household of Pharaoh — not of the household of God.

Moses

The story of Moses' early years is well known. After the remarkable circumstances of his birth into a Hebrew family and his growing up in the household of Pharaoh, Moses killed an Egyptian taskmaster who was beating a Hebrew. When Pharaoh learned what had happened, he tried to have Moses killed. But Moses fled from Pharaoh into the wilderness — into the land of Midian. After that, the oppression of the Hebrews by the Egyptians grew worse:

> The Israelites groaned under their slavery, and cried out. Out of the slavery their cry for help rose up to God. God heard their groaning, and God remembered his covenant with Abraham, Isaac, and Jacob. God looked upon the Israelites, and God took notice of them. (Exod. 2:23-25)

In the wilderness Moses married, had a son, and led an ordinary life, herding ordinary sheep. Then something extraordinary happened. The Bible describes it as a blazing bush that was not consumed and a voice that called to him out of the bush. The God who spoke to Moses at this pivotal moment in his life was not a generic, bland God. It was the God who was described in the book of Genesis. It was the God who described himself by saying:

> I am the God of your father, the God of Abraham, the God of Isaac, and the God of Jacob. (Exod. 3:6)

This was the God who had led Abraham to a distant land and promised him in a covenant agreement that he would be the ancestor of a multitude of nations. This was the God who had been with Isaac in his difficult struggles and blessed him. This was the God who had wrestled Jacob and given him the new name of Israel. This was the God who was to come among a people in slavery and promise them land and a future beyond their imagining.

When Moses turned aside to look at this strange sight, God spoke to him. The text from Exodus 3 and 4 continues:

Then the LORD said, "I have observed the misery of my people who are in Egypt; I have heard their cry on account of their taskmasters. Indeed, I know their sufferings, and I have come down to deliver them from the Egyptians, and to bring them up out of that land to a good and broad land, a land flowing with milk and honey, to the country of the Canaanites, the Hittites, the Amorites, the Perizzites, the Hivites, and the Jebusites. The cry of the Israelites has now come to me; I have also seen how the Egyptians oppress them. So come, I will send you to Pharaoh to bring my people, the Israelites, out of Egypt." But Moses said to God, "Who am I that I should go to Pharaoh, and bring the Israelites out of Egypt?" He said, "I will be with you; and this shall be the sign for you that it is I who sent you: when you have brought the people out of Egypt, you shall worship God on this mountain."

But Moses said to God, "If I come to the Israelites and say to them, 'The God of your ancestors has sent me to you,' and they ask me, 'What is his name?' what shall I say to them?" God said to Moses, "I AM WHO I AM." He said further, "Thus you shall say to the Israelites, 'I AM has sent me to you.'" God also said to Moses, "Thus you shall say to the Israelites, 'The LORD, the God of your ancestors, the God of Abraham, the God of Isaac, and the God of Jacob, has sent me to you':

This is my name forever,
and this my title for all generations." (3:7-15)

Moses, however, was still reluctant:

But Moses said to the LORD, "O my Lord, I have never been eloquent, neither in the past nor even now that you have spoken to your servant; but I am slow of speech and slow of tongue." Then the LORD said to him, "Who gives speech to mortals? Who makes them mute or deaf, seeing or blind? Is it not I, the LORD? Now go, and I will be with your mouth and teach you what you are to speak." But he said, "O my Lord, please send someone else." (4:10-13)

Notice that when God spoke to Moses, the word "I" was used by God numerous times: "*I* am the God of your father"; "*I* have observed the misery of my people"; "*I* have heard their cry"; "*I* know their sufferings"; "I have come down to deliver them." God cares about the crisis and is deeply involved.

But then a strange twist appeared: "So come, I will send you to Pharaoh to bring my people, the Israelites, out of Egypt." Suddenly, the word "you" appears. All of the things that God had resolved to do were suddenly assigned to Moses. A human being was an essential ingredient in the equation. And the work was dangerous. That is the way it often is in the Bible. And that is the way it is today.

*Out of the bush came the most important thing for stewardship —
a promise and a command. The household of Jesus Christ lives from
promise and from command. Moses' task was to lead Israel out of the
household of Pharaoh toward a promised land: the household of God. We
often fail by leaving out promise or command, or by leaving both out.
There can be no stewardship without promise — the promise of resurrection, life conquering the power of death.*

We often leave out command. We think of the church as a volunteer association. The church is not a volunteer association. The church is a covenanted community. That is the meaning of baptism. Baptism is the receiving of promises from God and the giving of promises to God and to each other.

More than three thousand years later, the story of Moses speaks to us with great force because it describes a *reversal of life* by the power of God. Some people have had an extraordinary reversal of life by the power of the living God. Others, possibly the larger number, have not had such an experience. But they long for such a moment that will bring an extraordinary reversal. The ordinariness of life does not satisfy. The power of God breaking into a life *does* satisfy. But be warned: when God breaks in and reverses a life, the status quo is unsettled.

*Moses' experience has everything to do with stewardship — whether
stewardship is possible in our churches. Can we remember what it was
like to be a slave? A commentary on the Torah could be summarized:
Every man and woman of the household of Israel (and the household of
Jesus Christ) should remember that he or she has come out of Egypt. We*
came out of Egypt. There are many kinds of slavery: addictions, obsessions, and so on. The Christian church — as the household of Jesus Christ — is called to be a household of freedom against slavery.

31

Meeks said that the Bible is an antislavery book. Its stories will make sense only if we can remember what it was like to be a slave. This is the same as remembering the crucified Christ. Only then can we understand and participate in the resurrection. Paul wrote: "While we were yet sinners [slaves, enemies of God], Christ died for us."

The whole business of the household of Jesus Christ is about what God has done and is doing to bring us out of slavery, out of sin, out of enmity with God. It doesn't mean we are no longer sinners — enemies of God. We are *forgiven* sinners and *reconciled* enemies. That makes all the difference. If we miss this difference and miss this story, we have missed everything and we simply conform to the way the world is.

Exile

God's promise was kept and the children of Israel were led into the promised land. There God established a covenant with the house of David. Yet, over the centuries that followed, the covenant was not kept by the house of David. As a consequence, the kingdom was divided into two parts. The Northern Kingdom (Israel) was defeated by the Assyrians, *ca.* 732 B.C., and most of the Hebrew population was sent to Assyria (2 Kings 15:29).

The story had a different ending when Nebuchadnezzar of the Neo-Babylonian Empire laid siege to Jerusalem in the southern kingdom (Judah), *ca.* 598 B.C. When the city was captured, King Jehoiachin of Judah, his family, the nobles, a large number of soldiers, and craftsmen were exiled to Babylon. Nebuchadnezzar also seized the temple treasures. A second deportation took place in 587 after Jerusalem was again besieged, leveled, and the remaining Jewish rebels (except for the poorest) taken into exile. A third deportation took place *ca.* 581. But unlike those who had been exiled from the Northern Kingdom, *the exiles from Judah were able to maintain their identity in a foreign land.*

The prophet Ezekiel ministered to his fellow captives for at least twenty-three years by bringing a message of hope and restoration. The promised restoration of both the land and the people and the bringing of life out of death by the spirit of God are recounted in Ezekiel 36 and 37.

A New Heart and a New Spirit

The text of Ezekiel 36:26-27 speaks eloquently of the new heart and the new spirit that come as gifts from God:

> A new heart I will give you, and a new spirit I will put within you; and I will remove from your body the heart of stone and give you a heart of flesh. I will put my spirit within you, and make you follow my statutes and be careful to observe my ordinances.

Bruce C. Birch wrote that the words "heart" and "spirit" used in Ezekiel 36:26-27 are not always understood in their ancient Hebrew context.[11] In modernity, we use the word "heart" to mean the seat of human emotions. For the Hebrews, the heart was the center of thinking and understanding. This does not mean simply a dry and barren rational process, however. "Out of understanding comes commitment and action, and a heart oriented to God (or as in our text renewed by God) [that] issues forth in compassion, justice, righteousness, and faithfulness."[12]

Birch also noted that the word "spirit," in the Hebrew context, is not a part of the human makeup, as it is in the Greek concept of persons as body/mind/spirit. For the Hebrew, spirit comes from God and enters or fills the person. "The spirit of God is often pictured rushing upon men and women as a mighty wind empowering them to faithful action."[13] Examples include Samson, David, and the birth of the church on the day of Pentecost. The spirit of God, in the Hebrew view, is a gift of God that enables a faithful, human response to the call of God.

One of the tragedies in the life of the church in modernity is that the role of Christians as stewards is often reduced to programmatic and

---

11. Bruce C. Birch, "A New Heart and a New Spirit," in *Stewardship Worship Resource* (Indianapolis: Ecumenical Center for Stewardship Studies, 1992), p. 16.
12. Birch, "A New Heart and a New Spirit," p. 16.
13. Birch, "A New Heart and a New Spirit," p. 16.

budgetary concerns and mission support of the institutional church. Such concerns and support are important work, but they cannot succeed if persons who make up the community that we know as the church do not have a new heart and a new spirit.

The words of Ezekiel were *God's promise and command* addressed to the community of exiles in Babylon. Jerusalem and the temple had been destroyed. All the normalcy of the culture they had known was destroyed. Exile was not easy. Birch wrote:

> Exile was a moment when all of those things that normally give life meaning were overturned. The mood of exile is despair. It is captured poignantly in Ps. 137 with its plaintive cry *"How can we sing the Lord's song in a strange land?"* The implication is that they cannot. There are no songs; the voices do not come forth. Exile is not a matter of geography. Exile is representative of those moments in human experience when even God's song no longer seems possible.[14]

Ezekiel's words are for this generation and every generation. We get entangled in the patterns of the culture around us, just as did the Israelites of Ezekiel's time. "Left to our own resources, we risk the hopelessness of exile in those places in our own lives where there seems no room for God's song."[15] Our hearts turn to stone. Idols attract our devotion and our loyalty. We exploit our neighbor and relegate God to less than first place in our affections. In every generation, the ultimate source of our stewardship stems from God's graceful gifts that enable us to fulfill God's call to live as God's people in the world.

God's promise of the gifts carries no preconditions, but the receiving of gifts calls for an obedient response. Promise and command are the twin elements of God's covenants with humankind. The spirit of God makes an obedient response possible. With, and only with, the empowerment of God's spirit and God's renewal of our heart, we can *"follow my statutes and be careful to observe my ordinances"* (Ezek. 36:27). This is a powerful reminder that we are not individuals, but community.

14. Birch, "A New Heart and a New Spirit," pp. 16-17.
15. Birch, "A New Heart and a New Spirit," pp. 16-17.

The Valley of Dry Bones

In captivity, the hope of Israel had been sapped. Widespread despair had taken hold. But a vision came to the prophet Ezekiel (37:1-14), a vision of a valley of dry bones:

> The hand of the LORD came upon me, and he brought me out by the spirit of the LORD and set me down in the middle of a valley; it was full of bones. He led me all around them; there were very many lying in the valley, and they were very dry. He said to me, "Mortal, can these bones live?" I answered, "O Lord GOD, you know." Then he said to me, "Prophesy to these bones, and say to them: O dry bones, hear the word of the LORD. Thus says the Lord GOD to these bones: I will cause breath to enter you, and you shall live. I will lay sinews on you, and will cause flesh to come upon you, and cover you with skin, and put breath in you, and you shall live; and you shall know that I am the LORD."
>
> So I prophesied as I had been commanded; and as I prophesied, suddenly there was a noise, a rattling, and the bones came together, bone to its bone. I looked, and there were sinews on them, and flesh had come upon them, and skin had covered them; but there was no breath in them. Then he said to me, "Prophesy to the breath, prophesy, mortal, and say to the breath: Thus says the Lord GOD: Come from the four winds, O breath, and breathe upon these slain, that they may live." I prophesied as he commanded me, and the breath came into them, and they lived, and stood on their feet, a vast multitude.
>
> Then he said to me, "Mortal, these bones are the whole house of Israel. They say, 'Our bones are dried up, and our hope is lost; we are cut off completely.' Therefore prophesy, and say to them, Thus says the Lord GOD: I am going to open your graves, and bring you up from your graves, O my people; and I will bring you back to the land of Israel. And you shall know that I am the LORD, when I open your graves, and bring you up from your graves, O my people. I will put my spirit within you, and you shall live, and I will place you on your own soil; then you shall know that I, the LORD, have spoken and will act," says the LORD.

In this, one of the most dramatic descriptions in Scripture, the prophet recounts his vision. From complete death the bones are brought together, joined by sinews, and covered with flesh and skin. But that is not the fullness of the miracle. The breath (or spirit) of God blows over the dry bones and life is restored. What a contrast! Death is swallowed up in the victory of life — a divine reversal. Then it is made clear that these are the bones of exiled Israel.

God said: "I will bring you back to the land of Israel. . . . I will put my spirit within you, and you shall live" (37:12, 14). After God spoke through Ezekiel, hope returned to the people. What had seemed to be an unattainable vision and shattered hopes were transformed to expectation and anticipation. Israel did go home. God brought the people back to their land.

The bones came alive and recognized God as Lord. A new community came into being through the action of God's spirit.

Today, when numbers decline in the congregations of North America and the vitality that once was known seeps away, people grow discouraged; a kind of numbness takes over. People forget the reality of the living God and what it means to be the people of God. The spirit of God can bring life today to a church that is regarded by many as dead or dying.

Jesus

It is generally accepted that Jesus talked more about money and possessions and their relationship to the human condition than he did about any other subject. Thus Jesus' teachings are an obviously important source for teachings about stewardship. The connection to stewardship, however, goes deeper than his teachings that deal with money and possessions. His birth, life, death, and resurrection teach and demonstrate what it means to be a steward of the household of God. Because of limitations of space in this book, we will focus on certain specific events related to Jesus' life.

Birth

Much has been written about the commercialization of Christmas in North American society. Because of that commercialization — and

36

perhaps because of the sentimentalism connected to remembering "a baby in a manger" — much of the deepest significance of the incarnation is lost amid all the observances of Christmas. The depth of meaning of the incarnation is set forth in Philippians 2:5-11:

> Let the same mind be in you that was in Christ Jesus, who, though he was in the form of God, did not regard equality with God as something to be exploited, but emptied himself, taking the form of a slave, being born in human likeness. And being found in human form, he humbled himself and became obedient to the point of death — even death on a cross. Therefore God also highly exalted him and gave him the name that is above every name, so that at the name of Jesus every knee should bend, in heaven and on earth and under the earth, and every tongue should confess that Jesus Christ is Lord, to the glory of God the Father.

The birth of the infant Jesus resulted from God's choice to take the form of a slave/servant/steward, being born in human form. This emptying by God was done voluntarily and deliberately. God became part of the *human household* so that humans could become part of the *household of God.*

The first chapter of the Gospel According to John uses household language: verse 11 describes Jesus as coming to his own people; verse 14 uses the Greek word *skenoo,* which means to tent or encamp as God did in the tabernacle of old, to indicate that Jesus lived among us. It could be understood as saying that Jesus "pitched his tent in our camp."

The very beginning of Jesus' story reveals episodes of giving. The message of John 3:16 is: "God loved the world . . . God gave. . . ." At the birth of Jesus, shepherds from the field went to the birthplace to give praise to God and to worship the "God come in human form." Later, magi came from the east and brought gifts to the young child who would be Emmanuel.

Baptism and Temptations of Jesus

Sometimes, without meaning to, Christians trivialize Jesus' temptation experience, concluding that it was recorded primarily to remind his disciples that Jesus was without sin and that, therefore, his lack

of sin is the "good example" for Christians. Such a limited understanding barely scratches the surface of the implications of Jesus'
temptation experience. Actually, the temptation experience defines
what the ministry of Jesus means. Immediately following his baptism
— which was in effect his ordination — his ministry began with a
wilderness struggle.

The heart of the matter — the key question — in the temptation experience is this: will human beings choose to be part of *the
household of the tempter* or members of *the household of God?* Appendix
One, a sermon titled "Jesus: An Alternative to Bread, Circuses, and
Political Power," puts the question this way: is there any other way
in the human situation to impose order other than by bread, circus,
or political power? Is the reign of God accomplished only through
the elements of bread, circus, and political power? The answer is no.
Jesus is an *alternative* to bread, circus, and political power, and this
will have meaning in our lives only if we remember who we are and
in whose household we are members. When we forget — or fail to
remember — that to be part of the reign of God is to be part of the
household of God, confusion and uncertainty inevitably follow.

Jesus' Teachings: Parables and the Lord's Prayer

Jesus talked extensively about stewardship, especially as related to
money and possessions. More will be said about Jesus' teachings
about money in the next chapter. All of Jesus' parables, in actuality,
are stewardship parables with implications for every dimension of
stewardship. In *Stepping Stones of the Steward,*[16] this author lifted up
fourteen of Jesus' parables as important in the faith journey of the
steward. Other parables could have been discussed as well. The
parables point out that the faith journey of a disciple of Jesus Christ
is an ongoing stewardship journey.

When the model prayer provided by Jesus is spiritualized and
placed largely in an other-worldly context, it is stripped of its real power.

16. Ronald E. Vallet, *Stepping Stones of the Steward: A Faith Journey Through
Jesus' Parables,* 2d ed. (Grand Rapids, Mich.: Wm B. Eerdmans Publishing Co.;
Manlius, N.Y.: REV/Rose Publishing, 1989, 1994).

Jesus rooted the prayer in the hard economic reality of the grinding, hand-to-mouth poverty experienced by the Palestinians of his time. Appendix Two describes some of those harsh economic realities in a sermon titled "Economic Dimensions of the Lord's Prayer."

Miracles

The miracles of Jesus, as well as his teachings, have implications for stewardship. It is beyond the scope of this book to list or examine the miracles in detail. Many of the miracles have to do with healing and thus deal with stewardship issues of health and illness — life and death. Behind the issue of healing in many cases are interpersonal issues and ways in which societal structures and forces affect the well-being of humans.

Other miracles speak directly to Jesus' call to share resources. A good example of sharing resources is the feeding of the multitudes, the only story recorded in all four canonical Gospels. This story was very important for the early church. One recounting of the story appears in John 6:4-14 and is presented here in paraphrased narrative and dialogue:

> When Jesus heard about the death of John the Baptizer, he withdrew in a boat to a deserted place by himself. But the crowd followed him on foot. When he went ashore, he saw a large crowd and had compassion on them and cured their sick. But when evening came, a problem arose. There were a lot of hungry people and there were no restaurants or supermarkets nearby.
>
> Jesus (to test Philip, indicating that this was a major problem): Where are we to buy bread for these people to eat?
>
> Philip: Six months' wages would not buy enough food. . . .
>
> Disciples: This is a deserted place. . . . Send the crowds away . . . to buy food for themselves.
>
> Jesus: They need not go away; you give them something to eat.
>
> Andrew, Simon Peter's brother: There is a boy here who has five barley loaves and two fish. But what are they among so many people?

Disciples: We have nothing here but five loaves and two fish.

Jesus: Bring them to me. Make the people sit down.

Taking the five loaves and the two fish, Jesus looked up to heaven, and blessed and broke the loaves and gave them to the disciples, and the disciples gave them to the crowd.
And all ate and were filled. (A divine reversal.)

Jesus: Gather up the fragments left over, so that nothing may be lost.

And they took up what was left over of the broken pieces, twelve baskets full.

The setting is reminiscent of the wilderness setting for the people of God, en route from slavery in Egypt to the promised land (Exod. 13:18) and God's giving manna to them (Exodus 16; Numbers 11; John 6:1-58).

They were on the east shore of the sea — Gentile territory — but the crowds were from the western, Jewish side. The disciples doubted that food could be provided in the wilderness (cf. Exod. 16:2-3; Mark 6:35-38).

The abundance of the leftovers documents the greatness of the miracle. It is a *counter*picture of the Mosaic manna, which could not be preserved (Exod. 16:4-5, 13-21), and portrays the messianic times, when *hunger will be replaced by extravagance.*

Death and Resurrection

The death of Jesus by crucifixion has been written and preached about by hundreds of thousands of writers and preachers over the past two thousand years. It is not my purpose in this book to delineate or to comment on the various theological and philosophical theories that have sought to interpret the significance of his death.

By way of contrast, however, the subject of Jesus' resurrection generally has received far less attention. Yet it is clear that if the early disciples of Jesus had not believed intensely in his resurrection, the Jesus movement would not have continued and the church would never have come into existence. Jesus, at most, would be a minor

40

footnote in the history of Palestine during the time of occupation by the Roman Empire.

The reality, of course, is startlingly different. Christianity became a major religion in the world's history. The early church grew steadily, if not spectacularly. One study maintains that the rate of growth was 40 percent per decade from A.D. 40 to A.D. 350.[17] While this may not seem spectacular, the cumulative result of such exponential growth over a period of 310 years led from 1,000 Christians in A.D. 40 to 33,882,008 Christians by the year 350, according to the study.

Viewed another way, the resurrection of Jesus is the pivotal event that provides access to the household of life and escape from the household of death. The resurrection is the New Testament equivalent to the Exodus event in the Old Testament. It is the supreme stewardship event. As we have seen, in both the Mosaic tradition and in the Jesus tradition, the way God works to redeem the creation against the power of death, of sin, and of evil is by creating for it the conditions of home. There is no other way to redeem the creation. Redemption will not come by military might or power; it will come as God's faithful stewards create the conditions that make home.

The apostle Paul described the significance of the resurrection in these words: "if Christ has not been raised, then our proclamation has been in vain and your faith has been in vain" (1 Cor. 15:14). Whether considered historically in terms of the growth of the early church or theologically in terms of the teaching of the early church, the resurrection of Jesus was pivotal for the early church. As we shall discuss in chapter five, the household of God is built on the resurrection of Jesus Christ.

The Great Commission

The text of Matthew 28:19-20 is often referred to as the Great Commission, though ironically neither the word "great" nor "commission" occurs in the passage. The text is well known:

17. Rodney Stark, *The Rise of Christianity: A Sociologist Reconsiders History* (Princeton, N.J.: Princeton University Press, 1996), pp. 4-13.

Go therefore and make disciples of all nations, baptizing them in the name of the Father and of the Son and of the Holy Spirit, and teaching them to obey everything that I have commanded you. And remember, I am with you always, to the end of the age.

Note the key elements of promise and command that we have come to associate with both covenant and stewardship. The promise is "remember that I [Jesus] am with you always, to the end of the age." The command is "Go therefore and make disciples of all nations." The Christian as steward is called to be a steward of the gospel of Jesus Christ — the promise and the command.

Paul

The Great Collection

The project often known as the "Great Collection" was the major focus of the apostle Paul's ministry for seven or eight years, probably from A.D. 48 to 56. William R. Nelson provided a succinct description of Paul's efforts in an article titled "Reflecting on Paul's 'Great Collection.'"[18] The Great Collection was an offering taken from Gentile churches for the benefit of the poor in Jerusalem. The idea for the Great Collection had come from the Jerusalem Council, described in the firsthand report of Galatians 2:1-10 and the secondary report found in Acts 15:1-29. Most of the written portion about the project itself was directed to the Christians in Corinth.

As described by Nelson, Paul's admonitions regarding the collection included two processes: (1) a consistent pattern of giving (1 Cor. 16:1-4) and (2) a management principle of delegation (2 Cor. 8:16–9:5).

Regarding the first process, Nelson wrote:

The first question is addressed in considerable detail: "On the first day of every week, each one of you should set aside a sum of

18. William R. Nelson, "Reflecting on Paul's 'Great Collection,'" *Journal of Stewardship* 41 (1989): 8-19.

money in keeping with his income [i.e., proportionately], saving it up [i.e., systematically] so that when I come, no collections will have to be made [i.e., not under duress]" (1 Cor. 16:2 NIV).

The emphasis was on systematic and proportionate giving on a regular basis. Furthermore, the mention of the first day of the week is an early reference to the gathering of the church for worship on the Lord's Day, that is, the day of the resurrection.

The principle of delegation by Paul is discussed in 2 Corinthians 8 and 9. "Paul made a conscious decision not to work at this task by himself. Instead, he commended a delegation of representatives who had the responsibility for completing the collection among the Corinthians and Achaians," wrote Nelson.[19]

The Corinthians were challenged to give sacrificially, based on the model of the giving by the churches in Macedonia (2 Cor. 8:3). More than money was involved: "they gave themselves first to the Lord and to us in keeping with God's will" (2 Cor. 8:5 NIV).

In verse 9, Paul wrote: "For you know the grace of our Lord Jesus Christ, that though he was rich, yet for your sakes he became poor, so that you through his poverty might become rich." The primary giving by Jesus was a primary motivation.

The privilege of sharing (Greek, *koinonia*) would be their rich reward (2 Cor. 8:4). *Koinonia* is not a word that North American Christians have usually associated with stewardship. It is most often understood as meaning "communion" or "fellowship." But it also can mean partnership, participation, social intercourse, benefaction, or *distribution.* As we shall see in chapter seven, it is a word rich in implications about what it means to be a steward and a member of God's household.

In 2 Corinthians 9:1-14, it is clear that to give is to be generous. Giving is to be both with thanksgiving and with singleness of heart or sincerity.

19. Nelson, "Reflecting," p. 14.

Reversal Does Not Always Come Easily or Quickly

A congregation cannot "reverse course" in order to change from being a household of amnesia to becoming a household of God without a willingness to risk and to experience pain. An example of the difficulty of reversal in the non-church world can be found in the long and painful struggle of women in North America to secure the right to vote.

In Canada, Nellie McClung, with women and men who shared in the cause, set out to change an Election Act that read, "No woman, idiot, lunatic or criminal shall vote." She was heckled, yelled at, and at times had run-ins with the law. She was advised to leave politics to the men, the ones who knew about and understood it. She had to put up with those who quoted Scripture for their purposes. Nellie McClung and her colleagues persisted and by 1918 women were voting in national and provincial elections.[20]

In the United States, a number of women, including Susan B. Anthony, were tried and convicted of voting. They died, convicted criminals, simply because they were women. In 1995, in Seneca Falls, New York, hundreds of people gathered to participate in the seventy-fifth anniversary of the ratification of the nineteenth amendment to the U.S. Constitution in 1920 that gave women the right to vote. The long struggle had begun in Seneca Falls in 1848 when a group of women and men made the first public demand that women receive the right to vote. The journey to obtain the vote for women carries with it many stories of courageous people.

The climactic vote to ratify the nineteenth amendment came on a hot August morning in 1920 in Tennessee. A 24-year-old, first-term legislator named Harry Thomas Burn was to cast a single ballot that would give millions of women the right to vote. Congress had passed the nineteenth amendment a year earlier. By June, thirty-five of the thirty-six states needed for ratification had approved it. The issue was dead in nine states and four were undecided: Ten-

20. This information about the struggle to secure the vote for women in Canada was provided by Vincent Alfano, executive director of the Toronto United Church Council.

44

nessee, Delaware, Vermont, and Connecticut. Of those four states, Vermont and Connecticut refused to call special legislative sessions; Delaware chose not to take any action. That left Tennessee. President Woodrow Wilson urged the governor to call a special session. Governor Albert Roberts agreed. The Associated Press described the scene in these words: "As the speaker rapped for order, hundreds of women with big floppy hats and floor-length skirts nervously fanned themselves in the nearly 100-degree heat. Some anxiously waited in the corridors, others crowded the chambers."

The battle line was drawn in Tennessee. It had become known as the War of Roses: Suffrage supporters wore yellow ribbons; their opponents red. Ultimately, it was a letter from Febb King Ensminger Burn, mother of the state's youngest legislator, that made the difference. As Harry Burn left for the legislative session on that hot morning of August 18, he slipped the letter into his pocket; in his lapel he wore a red rose.

The day before a motion had been made to table the resolution until the next session in January. The vote was 48 to 48. A second vote was taken after both sides claimed a miscount. It also was 48-48.

Thus, on August 18, Tennessee had no choice but to vote on the amendment itself. A tie vote would defeat the amendment. A change of one vote could defeat the amendment or give women the right to vote. Burn believed women should have the right to vote. But his constituents in the East Tennessee community of Mouse Creek, now Niota, were divided on the issue. And he had a race to run.

The clerk began the roll call vote. When the clerk called his name, Burn said, "Aye." A dead silence was followed by cheers and jeers, applause and hisses. The resolution had passed. Eight days later, on August 26, 1920, the nineteenth amendment to the Constitution became law. Incidentally, Burn was reelected by the voters in Mouse Creek.

And what was in that letter from his mother? It read: "Dear Son, Hurrah and vote for suffrage! Don't keep them in doubt. I notice some of the speeches against. They were bitter. I have been watching you to see how you stood, but have not noticed anything yet. Don't forget to be a good boy and help Mrs. Catt put rat in ratification." God used the words of a mother to reverse the course of history.

God causes reversals: a second heart attack that turns around shortly after it has begun; a people in exile who are restored to their homeland and rediscover community; the resurrection of Jesus the Messiah from death; a legislator willing to risk political defeat for what he knows is right; a church that has lost its way and becomes again a household of God and a true steward of the gospel.

In the next chapter we will look at how the church's fantasies and fears about money reflect a household of amnesia more than they reflect a church informed by a biblical base for stewardship.

CHAPTER TWO

Fantasies and Fears About Money in the Congregation

Money has power and an ability to allure that has us lusting after it. Money has the power to create and the power to destroy. Its power is ambiguous. Money can enable and help us to do ministry and carry out missions in the name of Jesus Christ. Money can also be an entrapment and a snare. We ignore something so powerful at our spiritual peril!

A Fantasy About the Stewardship Sermon

Those who stand in the pulpit to preach to a congregation Sunday after Sunday know both the hopes and the fears of preaching about money. Almost always, however, the fears outweigh the hopes. For many, the "annual stewardship sermon" is the most dreaded of the year. "Not again so soon," is the lament felt and sometimes voiced by the pastor. The end result of such preaching usually bears faint resemblance to biblical teaching about money.

Now and again, imaginations soar and a pastor may dream about what could be, or at least what he or she hopes could be. Patricia Wilson-Kastner gave voice to such hopes and dreams as she described a fantasy sermon in the reminiscing of a pastor. (In her book, the pastor is a "happy old rector.") In the moments just before the sermon, the pastor thought about how his people spend their money. He knew how much they spend on rent, mortgage payments, food, liquor, clothes, and trips. He also thought of the needs around the world and how little is given to the outreach budget for needs in the community and beyond the community. Then, in his fantasy, he stood to preach:

> So it all came at once to me, and I preached as I've never preached before or since. I preached my heart out, and even the ushers listened without yawning. I preached about how much God had given them, how badly they used it, and what good they could do in the church with their time and talents and money. Before I could even finish, people were throwing cash, checks, and pledge cards at me. They were weeping and cheering and signing up to pay the church budget for the next forty years. I've never needed to preach a stewardship sermon again.[1]

The fantasy is a *reversal* from business as usual. It is entertaining and for a moment leads us to drop our guard against the fears and perceived dangers of preaching a stewardship sermon — especially one about money. But the reversal is short-term; it is not real. The fears are real and soon return.

The Power of Money

A book written in 1914 by Harvey Reeves Calkins, a former missionary who at the time was stewardship secretary in the Methodist Episcopal Church, described the relationship between a man and his money. Writing long before the widespread usage of inclusive language, Calkins noted:

> in very truth, money is the most significant and potent force given into the hands of men, the most sought after and the most feared. The mere covetous love of it is the root of all evil, and the wise,

---

1. Patricia Wilson-Kastner, *Preaching Stewardship: An Every-Sunday Theme* (New York: The Office of Stewardship, The Episcopal Church, n.d.), p. 3.

unselfish use of it is the fruitage of all goodness. But the hidden power of this mysterious instrument, money, can be called forth and set in motion only by a man.[2]

However, after having argued that money has power and that the love of money is the root of all evil, Calkins then took a different tack by arguing that "righteous men" ought to covet it. His actual words were:

> Money is power. When power is committed to the hands of evil men there can follow none other than the works of evil. But power in the hands of righteous men multiplies the work of righteousness. If evil men seek after power, by *how much more ought righteous men to covet it!* And herein lies the miracle of money. Value came from God, and money, the measure of it and the receptacle for it, fashions it in the hands of righteous men until it fits God's purpose in the world; for life itself has value but in this, that it may fit God's wider circling plans.[3]

He continued: "It must be the preacher, and not the promoter, who calls men to be rich."[4] The preacher, Calkins argued, is to be the one who calls human beings to seek riches, if the person is righteous and the call has a noble purpose. In my view, Calkins himself succumbed to the allure and power of money. Adding a proviso that it be used to accomplish God's purpose still leaves great leeway for self-deception, mischief making, and corruption of institutions, including the church.

In the contemporary North American church, many voices are preaching a "prosperity gospel" that speaks of the convergence of wealth and religion. *Dare to Prosper* is the title of a book by Catherine Ponder, a minister with the Unity Church Worldwide in Palm Desert, California. It is reported that her seminars are "standing room only." An article by Joy Thompson concluded: "I'm wary of this preaching

---

2. Harvey Reeves Calkins, *A Man and His Money* (New York, Cincinnati: The Methodist Book Concern, 1914), pp. 174-75.

3. Calkins, *A Man and His Money,* p. 347 (emphasis added).

4. Calkins, *A Man and His Money,* p. 350.

of prosperity. God wants his followers to have hearts of gold, not have their hearts where their gold is."[5]

One may fairly conclude that attitudes about money are decidedly not simple. It seems that the church is taught on the one hand to embrace money, and on the other to fear it and shun the subject.

Money and Sex

In 1993 a survey was conducted by Worth and Roper/Starch to probe the financial psyche of Americans. The editors wanted to know, they said, "how Americans . . . spend, squabble over, and think about money." The results of the survey appeared in *Worth* magazine. The opening paragraph of the report stated:

> Your money or your life? Not a simple question, since most people can't seem to differentiate the two. Just read the dollar signs. Forty percent of Americans think about money more often than sex. Fights over money are the number-one source of marital discord (just slightly ahead of arguments about which television show to watch). Fifty-six percent of us say there comes a point in every marriage when money becomes more important than sex.[6]

Robert Wood Lynn, in a presentation to the North American Conference on Christian Philanthropy in 1994, commented on the article, noting that the phrase "more important than sex" could serve as a summary of the whole essay. He said: "The article confirms a long standing observation about North Americans: we are just as confused about the idea of money as about the idea of sex. Perhaps even more confused."

5. Joy Thompson of Knight-Ridder Newspapers, "'Prosperity Gospel' Doesn't Jibe with Scriptures," *Syracuse (N.Y.) Post-Standard,* 21 Dec. 1996, B2.

6. Robert Sullivan, "Americans and Their Money," *Worth Magazine,* June 1994. The article was accessed on the Internet at "www.worth.com/articles/Z9406CO1.html."

Lynn continued by noting that while mainstream Protestants in North America have at least tried to deal with the subject of sexuality over the past half century, they have paid little attention to the idea of money. He referred to theological education as a case in point:

> Consider, for instance, trends in seminary curriculum since the early 1940s. The offerings of theological schools constitute something of a barometer of public interest. Despite the conventional complaints about seminaries as "ivory towers" far removed from the concerns of church and world, these institutions have generally kept pace with the worries of their constituencies — sometimes a little behind, occasionally slightly ahead.
>
> And so it is revealing to examine the respective fortunes of the ideas of sex and money in our seminaries. While the numbers of courses on sexuality have slowly but steadily grown during the past fifty years and now occupy a prominent place in some schools, relatively few seminaries have ventured even close to the theme of money. Money remains the "forgotten" subject.[7]

According to Robert Wuthnow in *God and Mammon in America,* "Observers who live in other societies note that Americans are much more reluctant to talk about money than people elsewhere."[8] This taboo on discussing money is strongest among persons who attend religious services, according to Wuthnow's research:

> Among those who seldom or never attend religious services, about a quarter claim that all or most of their friends have told them how much money they make, but among persons who attend religious services weekly, the proportion drops to about one person in eight. On specific financial issues, church members differ most from nonmembers in being reluctant to talk about their incomes and what their major purchases cost. Regular church attenders differ most from infrequent attenders in their reticence on discussions about income and money worries.

7. Robert Wood Lynn in a presentation made to the 1994 North American Conference on Christian Philanthropy in Indianapolis, Indiana.
8. Robert Wuthnow, *God and Mammon in America* (New York: The Free Press, 1994), p. 138.

One would think that religiously involved people might be less isolated from their friends and neighbors and for this reason actually more inclined to discuss money with them. Especially within the same church or synagogue, where there are presumably shared beliefs and values, money might well be an appropriate topic of discussion. When those who attended religious services every week were asked how often they had discussed their personal finances with various *kinds* of people, however, a surprising pattern emerged. The *least* likely group with whom conversations about personal finances had taken place were fellow church or synagogue members: 95 percent said they had never or hardly ever discussed personal finances with them. Nearly as unlikely were members of the clergy, with whom 93 percent had not had conversations. In comparison, such conversations were somewhat more common among fellow workers (88 percent had not had them), and among friends (82 percent had not had them).[9]

Wuthnow concluded that "if religious leaders want to help people apply their faith to their finances, therefore, it seems clear from this evidence that breaking through the barrier against talking about money must be a first step."[10]

It is ironic that persons who are active church members are considerably more reluctant to talk about money and its relationship to faith than persons who are not active church members. The setting of "community" within a congregation, which we would expect to foster an atmosphere of more open discussion, is actually a place of greater reluctance. Even as North Americans aggressively pursue the acquisition of money, they do not want the relationship between faith and attitudes about money to be talked about in the context of the church. Perhaps the disparity between what one does and what one says leads to a conspiracy of silence.

Discussion about sex is in; talk about money is not.

9. Wuthnow, *God and Mammon*, pp. 139-40.
10. Wuthnow, *God and Mammon*, p. 141.

Two Levels of Fears About Money

Why is there such great fear of talking about money in church? Why is the "annual stewardship sermon," which invariably deals with money, the one that is most dreaded by pastors and by the people who sit in the pews? Why are pastors so afraid to preach and teach about money? Why are people so reluctant to hear about the subject of money in the context of church, especially in a worship setting? Why is *reversal* so hard to come by? The answers are not as simple as we may at first assume. The answers lie at two levels:

The first level is typified by responses such as these given by pastors and lay members of congregations in a 1994 study[11]:

1. The pastor will be viewed as self-serving, seeking to raise money to pay his or her own salary.
2. There is already too much preaching and talk about money.
3. The pastor wants to avoid unpopular topics so as to be liked.
4. If the pastor preaches about money, there is a danger that people may become angry, offended, or leave the church.
5. The pastor may feel a lack of sufficient knowledge to preach on the subject.
6. Money and possessions, it is perceived, are unspiritual. Money is the responsibility of boards or committees such as the trustees. The pastor is called to preach on spiritual matters, which do not include money. The connection between faith and attitudes about money is ignored or missed entirely.
7. Preaching about money is too personal; people resist changes in their personal lifestyles.
8. The pastor wants to avoid placing a financial burden on his or her people.

11. Adapted from a 1994 study done by Ronald E. Vallet for the American Baptist Churches of New York State. This study was also reported in Ronald E. Vallet and Charles E. Zech, *The Mainline Church's Funding Crisis: Issues and Possibilities* (Grand Rapids, Mich.: Wm. B. Eerdmans Publishing Co., 1995; Manlius, N.Y.: REV/Rose Publishing, 1995).

9. The pastor him/herself may not be giving what he or she knows should be given.
10. Preaching about money may not fit smoothly into the preaching schedule; that is, other faith issues are viewed as more important.
11. Sermons about money create feelings of guilt.
12. Some persons feel they are already giving all they can and are struggling to pay their own bills.
13. The commitment of some persons is shallow and does not include their money.
14. Some persons think, "All they want is my money."
15. Some persons do not like to have their preconceived ideas challenged and their excuses for not giving adequately to the church destroyed.

Yet, even as these fears and anxieties move through the minds of pastor and people, consciously and subconsciously, *a second level of fear* — deeper and largely unrecognized and unsuspected — lurks underneath. What is that deeper level of fear related to? It relates to the reality that money has power. And because money has power, the temptation to worship in its great temples and to bow before its idols is powerful and alluring.

In an insightful article,[12] Ken Gallinger described the church of his childhood as a place where "money was never talked about in the worship service. It was, however, annually fought about at the congregational meeting."[13] He went on to depict money as "dirty, yet desirable. Powerful, therefore both enabling and corrupting. Dangerous, therefore intriguing. Of infinite value, therefore an idol to be feared and a gift to be shared. Bad enough to be worth lusting after, important enough to be treated with care."[14]

There you have it in a nutshell. Money has power and an ability to

12. Ken Gallinger, "Belling the Money-Cat," in *Mandate: Special Edition on Work, Money and Meaning* (Etobicoke, Ontario: The United Church of Canada Division of Communication, 1995), pp. 8-10.
13. Gallinger, "Belling the Money-Cat," p. 9.
14. Gallinger, "Belling the Money-Cat," p. 9.

allure that has us lusting after it. Money has the power to create and the power to destroy. Its power is ambiguous. Money can enable and help us to do ministry and carry out missions in the name of Jesus Christ. Money can also be an entrapment and a snare. We ignore something so powerful at our spiritual peril!

Is it precisely because money is so powerful and so alluring that we are afraid to deal with it in the context of church — especially within worship? Could the fear be that the things of God may be corrupted by the power of money? Perhaps, at root, the fear is that God isn't really God. To put it bluntly, is the love of God (both God's love for us and our love for God) more powerful than our love of money, or is it not?

At its deepest level, the problem is *a crisis of faith.* Is the God of our biblical faith more powerful than the forces of evil unleashed in the world around us? If God is not that powerful, then God cannot be trusted when speaking of love and passion for the world. And the fear may continue. Our fear may also be that God doesn't really know what's going on in the world, or, alternatively, that God does not know how to cope with what's going on.

An Illness in the Church

If the prevailing mind-set is that God cannot be trusted, the church is not well. In a powerful article[15] Murray Joseph Haar wrote about what he identified as the sickness within the church. The illness, which he characterized as rampant, is that Jesus is presented in most Christian churches on Sunday mornings as a product to be marketed. He wrote:

> Many clergy increasingly treat their parishioners as religious consumers with varied spiritual needs, and American churches are busy meeting people's needs, giving people choices, and, what is most ominous, selling a "Jesus" that plays to individualistic and consumeristic "needs."

15. Murray Joseph Haar, "Self-Serving Redemptionism: A Jewish-Christian Lament," *Theology Today* 52, no. 1 (April 1995): 108-12.

The Jesus of American Christian churches has become a product to be marketed and made palatable to the masses, a bargain for wise shoppers to latch onto for religious security. Sermons rarely call Christians to a discipleship of self-sacrifice or to a radical reassessment of the way Americans live their lives. Indeed, many sermons have become "sit-com" homilies. On the surface, all seems well in such sermons. They seem to deal with the problems of "the text," contain many humorous stories, and appear willing to engage the difficult questions of faith. But they really do not. There is no need to worry. Like any television sit-com, all problems are resolved within twenty minutes. Having reassured the flock that all the dilemmas of the text and of life itself are going to work out just fine, the minister sends the people on their way with their personal Jesus, one who is always with them and who is committed exclusively to their individual spiritual happiness and welfare. The Jesus of the "sit-com" sermon makes promises, not necessarily biblical in origin, to meet all their needs. This Jesus gives you "peace in your heart," "a strong self-image," "empowerment," "health, wealth and happiness," "relief from pain and suffering," and, most important, "personal salvation."[16]

This illness — self-serving redemptionism, as Haar named it — is rampant because it works and is marketable. Have mainline denominations in North America fallen into this trap? The answer seems to be yes. Congregations of mainline denominations seem to have the worst of both worlds. Their behavior fits many of the patterns of consumeristic marketing, but the process does not yield a product that is successful in its marketing efforts and strategies. This apparent dilemma is resolved in Haar's words: "This smiling Jesus has become boring! The weekly friendly reassuring pastor who proclaims the loving overly gracious Jesus no longer excites. The Jesus of the hymns is too syrupy. Sermons seem to lack something. Spiritual consumers, who love novelty, are bored."[17]

In *The Mainline Church's Funding Crisis,*[18] the illness of the

16. Haar, "Self-Serving Redemptionism," p. 109.
17. Haar, "Self-Serving Redemptionism," pp. 110-11.
18. Vallet and Zech, *The Mainline Church's Funding Crisis.*

church in North America was described as that of a church trapped in modernity. But the allures and the false promises of modernity are fast fading. Ideas and positions that once seemed to be fixed and immutable are changing before our eyes at a breathtaking pace.

Stephen Toulmin reminded us that the *reversal* of the process of modernity moves from:

> written to oral,
> universal to particular,
> general to local, and
> timeless to timely.[19]

This reversal plays to the strengths of congregational life and experience, which is primarily oral, particular, local, and timely. This advantage may enable congregations to make the transition to a postmodern age more easily than denominations do. The congregation, perhaps more than ever, is the key arena for meaningful change in the church.

The Swinging Pendulum of Stewardship

Understandings of the meaning of stewardship within the church swing like a pendulum from one extreme to another. One extreme holds that Christian stewardship has to do only with money — especially money that individuals give to support a religious institution. The other extreme states that Christian stewardship is holistic and comprehensive and, as such, encompasses all of life. Each extreme of the pendulum's swing has some elements of truth. At the same time, there is danger in holding either of the two extremes as an absolute.

Those who hold that stewardship has to do only with money may find themselves taking a position that money itself — its absence or its presence, how much or how little — is the key to understanding

---

19. Stephen Toulmin, *Cosmopolis: The Hidden Agenda of Modernity* (Chicago: University of Chicago Press, 1990), pp. 186-92.

stewardship. Fund-raising becomes the *sine qua non* of stewardship. Having more money, this position holds, is good for the religious institution, but not good for the individual. In such a philosophy, it becomes the job of the religious institution to devise programs that will appeal to individuals to give their money to the religious institution. Only in this way, it is said, can the institution carry out its programs of good works. And, it is sometimes taught, when an individual gives money to the institution, it is good for the individual as well, because money is evil and would otherwise corrupt the individual.

Others do not teach that stewardship has to do only with money. Instead they take an opposite position: stewardship is inclusive of all of life. While this position can be valid theologically and philosophically, it can be interpreted so broadly that it has no practical focus that will make a vital and practical difference in the lives of individuals.[20] Such words of theology, which are "correct" but make no difference in the lives of people, are like "a noisy gong or a clanging cymbal" (1 Cor. 13:1).

How can these two positions be set in perspective? A look at some biblical texts will be helpful at this point. Nowhere does the Bible teach that money per se is evil. It is clearly taught, however, that the *love* of money is a problem:

> For the love of money is a root of all kinds of evil, and in their eagerness to be rich some have wandered away from the faith and pierced themselves with many pains. (1 Tim. 6:10)

> Keep your lives free from the love of money, and be content with what you have; for he has said, "I will never leave you or forsake you." (Heb. 13:5)

In the Sermon on the Mount, Jesus taught:

> Do not store up for yourselves treasures on earth, where moth and rust consume and where thieves break in and steal; but store

---

20. One aspiring writer once submitted to Ronald E. Vallet a manuscript for an article on stewardship that maintained that stewardship is comprehensive and is about everything *except* money.

up for yourselves treasures in heaven, where neither moth nor rust consumes and where thieves do not break in and steal. For where your treasure is, there your heart will be also. (Matt. 6:19-21)

Though money in and of itself is not evil, the *love* of money can lead individuals away from the Christian faith. Further, Jesus said that where your treasure is, there your heart will be also. Since one's heart — one's desires — follows one's treasure, it is important to consider where that treasure is placed. Christians are called to be stewards of the gospel of Jesus Christ and of all of God's creation.[21] That is where God calls the Christian to place his/her treasure. Two key verses state this clearly:

> Think of us in this way, as servants of Christ and stewards of God's mysteries. (1 Cor. 4:1)

> Like good stewards of the manifold grace of God, serve one another with whatever gift each of you has received. (1 Pet. 4:10)

If Jesus was correct in stating that "where your treasure is, there your heart will be also," does it follow that giving to the church is more vital to donors than it is to the institution? Does the heart — especially as symbolized by energy, time, and talent — follow the giving of money? These are not simple questions with simple answers. The concept of household will help us in our search for meaningful answers.

We have already noted that the Greek word for stewardship used in the New Testament is *oikonomia,* the management of the household. In this book, we are focusing on the household that is the Christian congregation. Some of the related questions include:

> What are the characteristics of the congregation as a household? What are the rules of the household?

21. For a fuller perspective on stewardship viewed as holistic and comprehensive, see Ronald E. Vallet, *Stepping Stones of the Steward: A Faith Journey Through Jesus' Parables,* 2d ed. (Grand Rapids, Mich.: Wm. B. Eerdmans Publishing Co.; Manlius, N.Y.: REV/Rose Publishing, 1994).

What are the instruments of Christian stewardship?
How are economic decisions made by the congregation?
In what ways do resources given to the church benefit the
  donor?

While we will look at the full range of the life and work of the
congregation, a sharp focus will remain on money. As we shall see,
and though we don't like to admit it, attitudes about money affect
all aspects of the life of the Christian and the church.

Before turning to the dilemma of a church caught in modernity
and beset by amnesia, we will look at some of the concepts and
practices of church giving in North America in the past and present.
A knowledge of the past can inform us so that *mistakes* of the past
are not repeated and *positive* aspects of the past are not lost.

CHAPTER THREE

Past and Prevailing Concepts and Practices of Church Giving in North America

Language and vocabulary are important in relationship to acts of giving and sharing.

Robert Wood Lynn

Very few church leaders and members in North America are familiar with the language and methodologies of church giving in North America before their lifetimes. Except for a general sense that things may not be going as well now as they once did, we tend to assume that things now are much as they were in times past. Before I discuss currently prevailing teachings and practices that relate to church giving, it will be instructive to look at some past concepts and practices.

Some English Roots of North American Church Giving

In an important book, William Brackney[1] provided some intriguing and little-known information about English roots of North American church giving. Many of the practices in England had a subsequent impact on the church in North America.

Puritans

When news of the discovery of native peoples in the Puritan areas of New England reached England, Puritan divines immediately accepted the responsibility for the conversion of the Indians as a God-given task. This discovery of a new mission field provided English Puritans with an opportunity to appeal for money to "promote the gospel." In 1651 Parliament was persuaded to incorporate what became the New England Company. This not only gave a legal foundation to Indian charity but also provided a compelling ecclesiastical reason to give to the mission in New England.

John Eliot (1604-1690), the leader of the Puritan effort among the Indians, thought that the best reason for giving was in response for what God had done in prospering the community of faith:

> Come forth, ye Masters of Money, part with your Gold to promote the Gospel; Let the gift of God in temporal things make way for the Indians' receipt of spirituals . . . if you give anything into banke, Christ will keep account thereof and reward it. . . . And as far as the Gospel is mediately advanced by your money, be sure you will be remembered.[2]

1. William H. Brackney, *Christian Voluntarism: Theology and Praxis* (Grand Rapids, Mich.: Wm. B. Eerdmans Publishing Co.; Manlius, N.Y.: REV/Rose Publishing, 1997). It is the third volume in the Faith's Horizons series.

2. J.D., a Minister of the Gospel, *The Glorious Progress of the Gospel Amongst the Indians in New England* (London: Edward Winslow, 1649), p. 27, as cited by Brackney.

The evangelization of Indian peoples fit neatly into the Puritan concept of Christian responsibility as it emphasized God's providence in placing the Indians under the influence of the English; it emphasized the translation of the Scriptures; and it challenged the zeal of Protestants against the advances of the Jesuits.[3] It also promised donors that Christ would keep an account and reward those who gave to the cause.

Tithing in Seventeenth-Century England

Luther P. Powell, in an intriguing chapter, "Stewardship in the History of the Christian Church,"[4] provided fascinating details of the tithing system in England in the seventeenth century. Powell described a book titled *The Parsons Counsellor*, by Simon Degge, which was a guide to ministers in the Church of England regarding all matters with which they might be confronted. The last half of the book deals with the laws of tithes and tithing. Farmers, for example, were confronted with a multiple number of rules and conditions concerning their tithes. Those who received wages and salaries were also covered by the system. The entire system was built on civil laws, ecclesiastical canons, and custom. Once the premises and presuppositions on which the tithing system was built were challenged and were called into question, the system began to collapse. Hostilities against the tithing system grew, and farmers jeered the parsons and stoned auctioneers and bailiffs who were sent to collect the tithe.

Rebellious farmers added the protest of an old harvest song:

We've cheated the Parson;
We'll cheat him again.
For why should a blockhead
Have one in ten

3. William Kellaway, *The New England Company 1649-1776* (London: Longmans, Green & Co., 1961), p. 21, as cited by Brackney.

4. Luther P. Powell, "Stewardship in the History of the Christian Church," in *Stewardship in Contemporary Theology*, ed. T. K. Thompson (New York: Association Press, 1960), pp. 76-131.

For prating so long like a book learned sot,
Till pudding and dumpling burn to pot?[5]

Another song, sung to the tune of The Old Hundredth, also voiced the bitter protest:

God save us from these raiding priests,
Who seize our crops and steal our beasts,
Who pray, "Give us our daily bread,"
And take it from our mouths instead.[6]

Some clergy protested by giving up their livings rather than collect the tithe by legal means. Some of the dissenters were fined and imprisoned for not paying tithes; others were martyred for holding that doctrines of compulsory tithing were contrary to the law of God.[7] Tithing in North American church history will be discussed later in this chapter. This pattern of understanding and acceptance (or nonacceptance) of tithing in England affected how the concept of tithing was received and practiced by churches in North America. Legalistic interpretations of tithing in England tended to lead to rejection of the concept by many North American Christians.

Church Giving in Colonial America and in the Nineteenth Century

English beliefs, customs, and practices had other effects on church giving in North America as well. One result was that, in the American colonies and on the frontier, two opposing philosophies of support for the church were used: voluntary and compulsory. Separatists,

5. "Revolt of British Farmers Against the Tithe," *The Literary Digest,* 23 Sept. 1933, pp. 116-17, as cited by Powell.
6. "Revolt of British Farmers," pp. 116-17.
7. "Prosecutions of Quakers, and the Original of Tythes," *The Gentlemen's Magazine,* March 1737, pp. 154-56; "Some Considerations Touching the Payment of Tythes," *The Gentlemen's Magazine,* March 1737, pp. 131-34, as cited by Powell.

who came from England to America by way of the Netherlands, introduced the philosophy of voluntary support. The Puritans came to the New World with similar convictions. In later years, however, many New England churches turned to public taxation as their method of support. Congregational churches and then early Presbyterian churches followed the pattern of tax support. In the area that was to become New York, planters agreed to be taxed to support the Dutch church in return for the privilege of farming in the area. In the Virginias and Carolinas, taxes were collected for the Anglican Church.

Not surprisingly, the system of compulsory support destroyed much of the willingness to give. "[E]ven where voluntary support was practiced, the giving generally was reluctant. In those denominations which held to voluntary giving, such as the Baptist and Methodist, the people frequently expressed by word and action that the ministers were expected to do the suffering for the cause of Christ."[8]

As the nineteenth century proceeded, a number of methods for support were tried: church glebes (areas of cultivated land), pew sales or rentals, subscription lists, lotteries, and voluntary offerings. All except voluntary offerings had at least one factor that led to partial or complete defeat in accomplishing their purpose.

> Toward the latter part of the second half of the nineteenth century the church was faced with a financial crisis. On the one hand, the limitations of former revenue-producing methods were being felt. Compulsory taxation had been removed in all states soon after the turn of the nineteenth century, pew rents were not equal to the growing financial needs, and the stewardship movement of 1800-1860 . . . had been interrupted so completely by the Civil War that it had lost its effectiveness. On the other hand, the United States had begun a rapid industrial expansion, and the trend was away from a system of barter exchange to cash exchange. Although ministers still were being supported partly in kind, the churches needed money in order to operate in a cash economy.

8. Powell, "Stewardship in the History of the Christian Church," p. 112.

Also, the Christian Church already had launched a world-wide missionary program which demanded more than a "missionary barrel" of old clothes; it demanded cash. Thus, these social, economic, and ecclesiastical factors confronted the church with a financial crisis.[9]

The church responded to this economic crisis in a variety of ways: variations of the lottery; merchandising schemes; soliciting beyond the community; revenue-producing property in both rural and urban settings; church bonds; endowment insurance; and every-member canvas.[10]

Prior to 1850 the few attempts to institute tithing in the American church were generally met with hostility. But, beginning as early as 1885, tithing began to play an important role in the stewardship movement. Four factors led to a growing interest in tithing: (1) the missionary awakening of the eighteenth century; (2) a reaction against liberal theology and higher criticism; (3) a growing dissatisfaction with many of the methods of church support then being practiced; and (4) the layman's movement inspired and led by Thomas Kane, a Presbyterian elder. As early as 1876, Kane began to circulate pamphlets on the subject at his own expense. Millions of copies were distributed.[11]

Generally, the predominant motive was the material reward that was promised; testimonials abounded that tithing brought material blessings. However, in the post–World War II period, more emphasis began to be given to biblical references on tithing, without taking a legalistic or literal approach. The motive expressed in more recent years has been that of a faithful response to the grace of God as revealed in Jesus Christ. Tithing as a rule of the household of God will be discussed in chapter five.

9. Powell, "Stewardship in the History of the Christian Church," pp. 114-15.

10. For a detailed discussion of these items, see Powell, "Stewardship in the History of the Christian Church," pp. 115-25.

11. Powell, "Stewardship in the History of the Christian Church," pp. 120-21.

The Language of Giving in North America

Despite the aphorism "Sticks and stones may break my bones, but names will never hurt me," the names we give to persons, things, and actions, and the language we use do matter. In an important work, Robert Wuthnow[12] noted the importance of the language and vocabulary used by persons in such actions as compassion, evangelism, motivation, and therapy. For example, he used these words to talk about acts of compassion:

> When I talk about "acts of compassion," then, I do not mean a particular set of values, taken simply at face value, such as a visit to the hospital or an afternoon of volunteering at a center for abused women. I mean the cultural framework as well: the languages we use to make sense of such behaviors, the cultural understandings that transform them from physical motions into human action. The discourse in which such behavior is inscribed is no less a part of the act than is the behavior itself. The possibility of compassion depends as much on having an appropriate discourse to interpret it as it does on having a free afternoon to do it. To ask whether compassion is possible, therefore, is to ask about the languages on which its very conceivability depends.[13]

Language and vocabulary in relationship to acts of giving and sharing are no exception. It is important to be able to name the act of giving.

Robert Lynn has made important contributions to a discussion of the language of giving. Much of the following material on the language of giving, as well as a later section on methodologies of giving, was gleaned from his presentations and writings.[14]

---

12. Robert Wuthnow, *Acts of Compassion: Caring for Others and Helping Ourselves* (Princeton, N.J.: Princeton Univ. Press, 1991).

13. Wuthnow, *Acts of Compassion*, p. 45.

14. The material from Robert Wood Lynn is taken from three sources: presentations at the 1991 Winter Event of the Ecumenical Center for Stewardship Studies; a presentation at the 1994 North American Conference on Christian Philanthropy titled "Christian Ideas of Money"; and material found in *Why Give? Stewardship,* a series of articles published on diskette in 1996.

"Charity"

Language that had included the use of the word *alms* for much of the church's history began to change centuries ago. For a time, the word *charity* had been used. In the mid-nineteenth century, the church was casting about for a name for the act of giving by Protestants to their churches. The word *charity* was considered stale and worn out by then. (It is interesting to note an exception, however, when United States President Abraham Lincoln used "charity" in his second inaugural address on March 4, 1865: "With malice toward none; with charity for all.")

As already noted, tithing under legal compulsion had been tried in England and had met fierce and determined opposition. Nevertheless, in North America, some church leaders began to use the word *tithing* and sought to establish the giving of 10 percent of one's income as the norm. In the late nineteenth century and early twentieth century, some Methodists in Canada tried to make tithing a requirement for church membership. In a number of denominations and congregations, struggles and battles took place around the subject of tithing and whether it was the biblical and godly way to raise money for the church. One of the critics of tithing during that period was Alexander Campbell, the leader of the movement that later became known as the Disciples of Christ and is now incorporated into the Christian Church (Disciples of Christ). Campbell reminded his followers that tithing belongs to the old world and represented a tax paid to the state to support the clergy. Because of this, the tithe had often been hated in the Old World. He also argued that the New Testament contains no clear teaching or command about tithing. The word *tithing* continued to be used but never became the generally accepted language to describe church giving.

"Benevolence" and "Beneficence"

Two words used prominently in the nineteenth century as successors to the word *charity* were *benevolence* and its companion *beneficence*. The word *benevolence* had been developed in the seventeenth and eighteenth centuries in the writings of moral philosophers in Great Britain and elsewhere. One of the interpreters of benevolence in North America was Jonathan Edwards, a prominent Congregational minister of the eighteenth century. He defined benevolence in a way that is quite different from how we use the word today. For him, benevolence signified the sense of *joy and exaltation* that people feel when a neighbor is to enjoy a "good." These two words — *benevolence* and *beneficence* — were increasingly used by Protestant churches in the nineteenth century. In fact, the names of some of the church agencies that had responsibility for gathering funds often bore the name of systematic benevolence or systematic beneficence. Even today, the United Methodist Church uses the term "General Benevolences."

Some persons did not consider these words to be appropriate, however, and felt that a new biblical phrase or word was needed — one that would provide a moral constraint against the sin of covetousness. A deep anxiety about money and a spirit of covetousness, with all its attendant perils, developed. For example, in "The Revised Catechism," written in 1871, Mark Twain described the grip of greed. It was a bitter twist on the Westminster Catechism:

> What is the chief end of man? — to get rich.
> In what way? — dishonestly if we can; honestly if we must.
> Who is God, the one and only true?
> Money is God. Gold and Greenbacks and Stock —
> father, son, and ghosts of same, three persons in one;
> these are the true and only God, mighty and supreme.[15]

From the early days of the missionary movement in North America in the early nineteenth century through the televangelists of recent years, one stream of Protestants assumed *an abundant supply of money,* in contrast to others who worried about *the scarcity of money.* Lynn said:

---

15. Mark Twain, "The Revised Catechism," *New York Tribune,* 27 Sept. 1871, quoted in Justin Kaplan, *Mr. Clemens and Mark Twain: A Biography* (New York: Simon and Schuster, 1966), pp. 124-25.

Whereas other Protestants worried about the scarcity of cash, these movement leaders characteristically assumed an abundant supply of money. In that vein, for example, one movement stalwart assured his audiences in the 1820s that "there is capital enough to evangelize the world in a short period of time, and without the retrenchment of a single comfort."

No, the true scarcity lay in the dimension of *time,* not in the realm of money. These folk lived under the pressure of an intense awareness of an eschatological crisis — the crisis of great opportunity. *Now* was the time for giving. God's future was coming. Any invitation to give money to this cause was more than a "once in a lifetime" opportunity. These challenges were, in effect, "once in history" occasions for making a difference in the whole human race.[16]

John R. Mott stood out among this group. Born near the end of the U.S. Civil War, he lived into the 1950s. He was a missionary and ecumenical leader who popularized the watchword of the movement — "the evangelization of the world in this generation." Considered by many to be the most accomplished fund-raiser in the history of North American Protestantism, Mott demonstrated the force of the idea of money. He described money as "stored-up power" and spent his life, in his words, "liberating the money power of the world."

"Stewardship"

Toward the end of the nineteenth century, a word was rediscovered by churches in both Canada and the United States. The word was *stewardship.* This word had two advantages: (1) it was a biblical phrase that was familiar to a Bible-reading public and (2) at the same time the word was fresh and relatively unused.

While the words *stewardship* and *steward* were used occasionally during the nineteenth century in relationship to possessions, Lynn reported that his research indicated that nobody focused on the word

16. Lynn, 1994.

stewardship as the way of naming the Protestant act of giving during that period of time. Yet, almost overnight, it became popular and was used widely by the 1910s.

The influence and contribution of the stewardship idea was viewed as a fundamental contribution of American churchmanship by Bishop Hanns Lilje of Germany:

> The best example is the importance that the idea of Stewardship has gained for the whole of Lutheranism. In this context America has for the first time exerted an important influence on both the theology and the practical church life of the European continent. The Stewardship idea shows that dogmatic definitions are of value only on the condition that they be taken up, confirmed and put into practice through concrete acts of obedience on the part, both of individual Christians and of the churches' congregations. Stewardship rightly understood is equivalent to a program for putting Christ into all aspects of daily life. The need for Christian obedience that the church of the middle ages expressed in the great idea of the imitation of Christ has thus again been made real, but this time by Lutheranism, and in a new, original form, grown out of the Gospel message. These new insights that the Lutheran Church has gained need to be thought out in detail. Our systematic theologians must show us how the theology of justification by faith is completed in the practical sphere by a theology of Stewardship.[17]

Why did such a radical change take place? The word *stewardship* appealed to a rising middle class who thought of themselves as decision makers. The steward, it was said, is expected to exercise discretion on behalf of a master without receiving minute direction. The steward, therefore, was viewed as one high enough in society to be free and responsible.

Another advantage of the word was that it appealed to people throughout the society and not just to church members. For example,

17. T. K. Thompson, ed., *Stewardship in Contemporary Theology* (New York: Association Press, 1960), p. x, quoting Bishop Hanns Lilje in *Lutheran World* (Geneva, Switzerland: The Lutheran World Federation), vol. 1, no. 1, p. 3.

when industrialist Andrew Carnegie realized that the future stretching before him was only to go on making money, he concluded that no idol is more debasing than money. He described the millionaire as "a trustee for the poor, entrusted for a season with a part of the increased *wealth of the community* and the responsibility of administering that wealth for the community." In the 1880s, persons reading parables about stewardship came to the conclusion that the steward was not the owner but the administrator of the wealth that belonged to other persons. This appealed to Carnegie.[18]

In contrast, John D. Rockefeller believed his *wealth belonged to God.* "God gave me my money and I give it to others." This understanding provided another way for people to move toward thinking about trusteeship or stewardship.

The net effect was that stewardship was in the air. It was an idea whose time had come. The word fit very well for Protestant fund-raisers whose job it was to raise money and articulate the relation between faith and money.

Josiah Strong, at the turn of the century, wrote a book titled *Our Country: Its Possible Future and Its Present Crisis,* and was the first to present a whole and complete understanding of stewardship. Though largely unknown now, *Our Country* sold more copies in the United States than any book since *Uncle Tom's Cabin.* He was the first advocate of stewardship. He wrote, "Christian stewardship is the perfect protection against the perils of wealth."[19]

A Baptist minister, Russell Conwell, began to preach one of the most famous sermons ever proclaimed in the United States: "Acres of Diamonds." The thesis of the sermon was: "It is your duty to get rich. God wants you to get rich." That sermon was preached 6,512 times during Conwell's lifetime.

The message of stewardship was also very attractive to a new generation of church bureaucrats in what came to be known as early-twentieth-century systematic benevolence. Today we tend to take

18. This information about Carnegie is taken from "An Alternative Perspective" in *Why Give?* Lynn, 1996, p. 292.

19. See "Vision and Money" in *Why Give?* Lynn, 1996, p. 272, and Lynn, 1991.

church bureaucrats for granted. In the early twentieth century, church bureaucracies were just coming into being.

In 1905 the American Board of Commissioners for Foreign Missions of the American Congregational Church announced the arrival of an unexpected gift: one hundred thousand dollars from John D. Rockefeller. Both the size of the gift and the identity of the donor made the gift a matter of headline news. Rockefeller, one of the world's wealthiest persons, was at the center of a controversy about the issue of the power of American "plutocrats." Almost immediately, criticism flared to new levels. The commissioners at first defended the receipt by stating that it was unsolicited. When it became known that they had spent three years pursuing the gift, their defense crumbled.

Foremost among the critics was Washington Gladden, pastor of the First Congregational Church of Columbus, Ohio. He had been writing about issues of faith and money for twenty years. Ten years before he had written about "tainted money" and the ethical problems of accepting money from plunderers. He used the phrase again to attack the American Board for soliciting and accepting the gift from Rockefeller. His questions and writings were *a call for integrity on the part of persons and institutions that solicit and receive gifts.* Gladden wrote in 1905:

> Certain elementary moral principles appear to be repudiated in the explicit statement of the prudential committee: "Our responsibility begins with the receipt of a gift." The contention is that, no matter what may be the character of the giver, his gifts should be welcomed with thanks. It can hardly be possible that the committee means to stand on this rule. At any rate, it is very important that a clear statement be made respecting the principles which should govern the receipt of gifts from doubtful sources. Our benevolent societies cannot knowingly accept gifts which are the proceeds of lawlessness, nor must they knowingly be the partners of those who are winning gains by methods which, though not yet punished by the law, are yet notoriously and indubitably extortionate and dishonourable. In the complexities of modern commerce it is often possible to take advantage of the necessities of men or of their weakness, and extort from them their property

without incurring the penalty of any law. But property thus acquired is held by no better moral title than the booty of the highwayman, and the principle which forbids complicity in unjust gains applies to this no less rigorously.[20]

Specifically, Gladden was referring to Standard Oil Company and the connection of Rockefeller to Standard Oil. His words make clear his opinion of the Standard Oil Company of that time:

> Not only from these books, and from the authorities to which they refer, but from a great variety of other sources open to the people of the United States, may be drawn abundant materials for a judgment respecting the Standard Oil Company and its methods. It is thus a matter of common knowledge that the Standard Oil Company has been frequently convicted, sometimes out of its own mouth, of transgressions of the laws of the land. A fearless judge of the United States District Court denounced their system of rebates as "gross, illegal and inexcusable," and said of it: "The discrimination complained of in this case is so wanton and oppressive that it could hardly have been accepted by an honest man having a due regard for the rights of others."[21]

The church, Gladden was saying, should not accept "tainted money" from plunderers. His response was based in his convictions about the sacramental nature of money. As such, money is not neutral but carries the spirit of its owner. Accordingly, it is either "consecrated" or "tainted." Money, then, is a test of the church's integrity.

Lynn noted:

> This dispute in 1905 foreshadowed a series of similar arguments throughout the rest of the twentieth century. The phrase — "tainted money" — played a role in fights over investments in liquor stocks, South Africa in the 1970s and 1980s and of course

20. Washington Gladden, *The New Idolatry and Other Discussions* (New York: McClure, Phillips & Co., 1905), as cited by Lynn, "Money, Tainted and Consecrated," in *Why Give?* 1996, pp. 323-24.

21. Gladden, *The New Idolatry,* as cited by Lynn, 1996, pp. 328-29.

tobacco stocks. In all likelihood this now famous phrase will be with us for decades to come.

Yet despite the notoriety of that single phrase, there has never been a serious and sustained debate about the Christian idea of money that lies behind the allusion to "tainted money."[22]

Lynn questioned whether or not such a neat line can be drawn between "tainted" and "consecrated" money and whether that distinction presupposed a presumptuous arrogance about our ability to separate the ethical "goats" from the "sheep." Nevertheless, Lynn indicated, Gladden offered an important corrective for his time and for ours.

> For the most part, nineteenth-century Protestants were tempted to repress any questions about the integrity of the giver. Their primary concerns were elsewhere. They felt an unrelenting pressure to raise the money necessary to keep up with the competition and to support their own ambitious plans for expansion. And so the task of convincing enough church folk to give in a generous and systematic fashion became all important. It was understandable, therefore, that they tended to focus on the gift itself — its size and its regularity — and to bury any sustained worries about the history of the giver. Whether welcomed or not, Gladden's dogged insistence on the question "Who is the giver?" was the right question at the right time.[23]

Most denominations had an office that was often named the Committee for Systematic Benevolence. In the 1910s a new generation took over these agencies and provided extraordinary leadership. Some of the best of these leaders were returned missionaries.

In the previous chapter I referred to Harvey Calkins, a returned Methodist missionary, who wrote a book in 1914 titled *A Man and His Money*.[24] He argued that we have two choices: we can talk about the Christian as a trustee who administers a trust under legal sanc-

22. Lynn, 1994.
23. Lynn, 1994.
24. Harvey Reeves Calkins, *A Man and His Money* (New York, Cincinnati: The Methodist Book Concern, 1914).

tions and restraints and who is under specific instructions from which he may not depart, or we can talk about the Christian as a steward who knows nothing about legal requirements. The steward's ambition is to know his master's mind and then, unbidden, fulfill the master's program. Calkins chose the second of these two options.

Calkins's model seems to have been Joseph as steward for Pharaoh.[25] The book had two themes that still form the basis for an ongoing argument within the stewardship movement: holistic stewardship, which he called stewardship of all of life, and the stewardship of possessions. He chose to concentrate on the steward-ship of possessions, because, as he said, people will try to use talk about the stewardship of all of life to avoid the hardest problem, which is the stewardship of possessions. John Wesley had written: "Earn all you can; save all you can; and give all you can." Calkins updated it to read:

> He will earn *all he can*.
> He will save *all he can*.
> He will *administer all*.[26]

Very soon, leaders in every denomination in Canada and the United States were repeating what Calkins had said. As they did, a remarkable thing happened: as stewardship was introduced in the 1910s, the giving record of the denominations began to ascend rapidly. This was especially true of the American churches, which were un-troubled by World War I until 1917. Canada was deeply involved in the war three years earlier and thus had a different experience.

The giving rate in the United States went up as new programs — the every-member canvas, the pledge, weekly contributions — were introduced. All of these bore the name of "stewardship." By 1918, leaders of the church stewardship offices in the United States were at the top of the status ladder. The spirit was, "We can do anything."

In that spirit of invincibility, stewardship leaders launched what was to be a humbling lesson: an American debacle called the Inter-

25. See chapter one for a different perspective about Joseph as a steward.
26. Calkins, *A Man and His Money,* p. 288.

church World Movement.[27] By way of contrast, the Canadian church leaders never flirted with hubris in the same way American church leaders did.

Lynn said that one American critic, Walter Rauschenbusch, warned the stewardship enthusiasts of what lay ahead. Rauschenbusch originally had been an enthusiast for stewardship, but then began to develop some reservations. *Stewardship does not solve the problem of individualism,* he said. Who is to make the final decision about administering the Lord's money? This is the question of accountability.[28]

The second problem that Rauschenbusch noted was the power of sin when it comes to money. Stewardship advocates, he said, underestimate this power. *The proclamation of stewardship was a new ethical idea and would not protect against the sin of covetousness.* Rauschenbusch reminded church leaders that Francis Xavier once commented that in the confessional booth people confess all sorts of sin, but never covetousness, never greed. The New Testament, he said, put lasciviousness and covetousness on the same level as the two besetting sins of the church. But, he asked, does the church

---

27. Lynn, speaking in 1991 at the Winter Event of the Ecumenical Center for Stewardship Studies, reported that an interchurch committee was formed to raise money for all of the denominations simultaneously. The campaign was to be supported by an interchurch staff who would raise $1.3 billion over a period of five years. When they gathered in January 1920, after a year of preparation, the work involved 140 different boards representing 34 Protestant denominations. The coalition covered between 80 and 90 percent of all American Protestant mission work. By early 1920 the staff had grown to 2,612 and had to be housed in a major building in midtown Manhattan. Plans to create a new skyscraper, to be known as the Interchurch Center, were begun. As it turned out, the campaign was a disaster. The denominations were stuck with the bill for millions of dollars that had been spent in building the staff. They left behind a heritage of debts and disillusions. In the 1910s the stewardship people had been at the top of the status ladder. By the 1920s they were the culprits and considered to be the people who had misled the church in this hapless venture. Calkins, who had written his book *A Man and His Money* in 1914, returned, disillusioned, as a missionary to India. He realized that stewardship education is a process that takes a long time and that it is a disastrous mistake to link stewardship to short-term financial goals.

28. Lynn, 1991.

today do the same? Rauschenbusch noted that though he had heard of exclusions from church fellowship for causes of sexual impurity and though he had made continual inquiry throughout his life, he had heard of only three churches that excluded people because of their covetousness.

Lynn stated that this logic leads to an inescapable conclusion that stewardship is the fruit of conversion upon recognition and repentance of sin. The language of stewardship is powerful, but too often it has been like a cut flower, not rooted in repentance and conversion. The methods used to raise funds for the church have not always — some would say seldom — reflected the understanding of stewardship as rooted in conversion. At their deepest, matters of stewardship concern the core of a person's inner, spiritual life.

Methodologies of Giving

The methods used to raise funds for the church in North America have varied significantly. In the nineteenth century, as benevolent societies were formed by different churches, the chief method of raising funds was through agents appointed by the societies. The agent was often a young man who would travel a circuit for a period of six months to two years, persuading people to provide financial support for the society he represented. The result was great competition among societies and a great deal of pressure on the churches as one agent after another came and went.

According to Lynn, the most responsible and successful fundraisers for mission in the nineteenth century were Protestant women. They were the experts. They gathered money into what they called the Widow's Mite Societies and, later, women's mission groups.

Harry Renfree told the remarkable story of Hannah Maria Norris of Canada, who, in the span of three months and three days, organized thirty-two women's missionary aid societies in the Maritime Provinces:

Another single woman, Hannah Maria Norris, was next to volunteer and with her begins the story of the UBWMU, the United

Baptist Woman's Missionary Union. Minnie DeWolfe had gone to Burma in direct response to a Macedonian call from the women of that land: "Are there no female men who can come to teach us?" and Maria Norris, a teacher at Acadia Seminary, responded to the same call. When it was discovered that the Convention's board did not have the funds to send her, she decided to go to Boston to offer her services to the American Baptists. But when she was on board ship in Halifax harbour ready to sail to Boston, Norris was dramatically persuaded to disembark and reapply to the Foreign Mission Board. This time she was accepted — but on the understanding that she secure financial support by organizing women's missionary aid societies throughout the Maritimes. She accepted the challenge.

After forming the first society in her home church at Canso on June 18, 1870, Maria Norris by phenomenal effort organized a total of thirty-two societies before she sailed for Burma just three months and three days later.[29]

Just as it was difficult to raise money for the missionary societies, so it was also difficult to raise enough money for the support of the church. The most common practice in fund-raising was a *subscription list*. A subscription list was a piece of paper on which a person wrote his or her name and then included the amount of money they were ready to contribute to the cause. One of the experts in using the subscription list was Benjamin Franklin. His astute method was to encourage people to sign up in such a way that the first person who signed at the top was invariably the largest giver. The hope was that people who were to sign the list later would see the size of the first gift and be inspired to a new level of generosity.

Another way of raising money was *pew rental income*. Churches sold or rented pew space. This practice began in colonial New England and elsewhere and continued well into the twentieth cen-

29. Harry A. Renfree, *Heritage and Horizon: The Baptist Story in Canada* (Mississauga, Ont.: Canadian Baptist Federation, 1988), pp. 153-54, as cited by Kenneth R. Morgan in an unpublished letter to Ronald E. Vallet dated January 27, 1997.

tury. Among Methodists the issue became a point of dispute. Benjamin Titus Roberts, in an 1850 article titled "New School Methodism," charged that Methodists had been split into "New School" and "Old School" factions. In the article, he documented how changes introduced by the New School factions departed from Wesleyan teachings and practices. Among the changes he deplored was the selling of pews to the highest bidder to raise money for the benefit of the church. The dispute continued over the next decade. In 1860 Roberts and his followers formed the Free Methodist Church during a convention in Pekin, New York.[30]

The practice of renting pews had some unfortunate consequences, including sharp social distinctions within the congregation. Rich people, by and large, sat in the best seats, usually the four or five rows in the center of the building. Poor people were banished to the balcony or the perimeter of the building. In a church in the nineteenth century that had no central heat, it was easy to understand why those pews were free.

Mark Twain told a story about his experience when going to church. One Sunday, he said, he went to a Presbyterian congregation and took the first available pew that was vacant. During the service, he received a note that said, "You are sitting in our pew for which we pay 50 dollars a year in rent." Twain immediately sent back a note that said, "You are paying too much."

As the causes multiplied, *collections for special causes* multiplied. In some cases, thirty or forty special collections a year were received in some congregations. Other forms of raising money were church suppers, entertainments, and church socials. In Canada, there were sock specials — an occasion where people brought in two socks, both filled with pennies.

Though there were many methods and practices, there was no reliable system to encourage steady habits of disciplined giving. The search was for a system that would move from applying external

---

30. This information about the Methodists was gleaned from Roger Finke and Rodney Stark, *The Churching of America, 1776-1990: Winners and Losers in Our Religious Economy* (New Brunswick, N.J.: Rutgers University Press, 1992), pp. 150-53.

pressure — as in a subscription list — to an inner dialogue with the Bible and one's conscience.

Toward the end of the nineteenth century, one element of such a system fell into place. It was a simple new device called an *envelope*. A person could place money in an envelope and make that the way of giving a weekly contribution. The envelope allowed people to be private in giving their money. One's name and the amount contributed did not appear on a subscription list for everyone to see. Where one sat in church did not automatically reveal the level of one's giving to the church. Giving became a *private affair* between the giver and the treasurer or the financial secretary. The simple device of an envelope got more complicated, however. As the idea of offering envelopes took hold, discussion about the possibility of designating or directing how one's gifts would be used came into play. A debate about whether to use single-pocket envelopes or the two- or three-pocket variety was hotly debated. With the advent of the envelope, the era of confidentiality in giving to the church had begun.

A second simple device — *the every-member canvass* — was adopted around the turn of the twentieth century and took the place of the subscription list. A congregation would send out members to call on other members and present them with the challenge of making an annual pledge to be paid weekly. This device replaced the subscription list and also concentrated the effort within one part of the year. The every-member canvass was not universally popular, however. In poor, urban churches and rural parishes where there was no wage salary, it was difficult for people to anticipate how much money would be available to be pledged for the following year. The every-member canvass is still used, though its peak period was probably in the 1950s.

More Recent Methodologies

A study by a committee of the Commission on Stewardship of the National Council of the Churches of Christ in the U.S.A. in the mid-1980s listed eight categories of generic congregational commit-

ment enlistment plans currently in use, noting that most congregational plans fall under one of the generic categories. The eight generic
categories, together with their strengths and limitations, were described in an article by Robert J. Hempfling:[31]

1. *Every Member Visitation* was described as a plan to make personal contact with all members of the congregation in their
   homes. The plan calls for training teams of two persons to make
   five or six calls to present the congregation's dreams and goals.
   Commitments are given to the callers or presented later during
   a worship service.
2. *Mail Appeal* depends on a series of letters sent to all members
   of the congregation over a period of several weeks. The final
   letter includes a commitment or pledge card to be mailed or
   brought back to the church. The program may include making
   personal calls as a follow up on those who do not respond.
3. *Telephone Appeal* is similar to the every-member visitation, except that the contacts are made by telephone. The callers are
   carefully trained to make effective presentations. Commitments
   are made during the telephone conversation and verified by
   mail.
4. *Personal Delivery* is a plan that has a number of names: Circuit
   Rider, Pony Express, Run for the Roses, ETA Relay, and others.
   The congregation is organized into several trails or chains of
   families. The first family in each chain calls on the second family
   to deliver a packet of materials, including commitment cards.
   The second family then calls on the third family, and the process
   continues until the chain is complete. The signed commitment
   cards are returned to the pouch, or in some cases presented at
   a later worship service.
5. *Loyalty Sunday* concentrates on a twenty-four-hour period
   during which every member of the congregation is expected to
   participate in a worship service and share in a dedication experience where commitments are made. A victory dinner fol-

31. Robert J. Hempfling, "An Enlistment Plan That Fits," *Journal of Stewardship* 39 (1987): 22-29.

lows later in the day. The main thrust of the program is to secure a large attendance on Loyalty Sunday.

6. *Congregational Dinner* is similar to the Loyalty Sunday program, except that the energies of the congregation are focused on the one dinner event. An outstanding presentation is prepared. Commitments are usually presented at a later worship service rather than during the dinner.

7. *Small Group Meetings in Homes* involves recruiting each member to attend a meeting in another member's home. For each meeting, a team of leaders presents a proposed program. Commitments are sometimes made during the meeting, but more often are presented at a later worship service.

8. *Faith-Promise Plan* stresses the relationship to God rather than loyalty to the church and its mission. Members are not asked to submit written commitments or estimates of giving, as in the other plans, but instead are asked to make undisclosed promises of the amount they will give. In some cases, commitment cards are placed in sealed envelopes that are not opened by church officials. A year later, each envelope is returned to the family or individual who turned it in. The family may then open the envelope and compare the amount they had pledged to the amount actually contributed during the preceding year.

In many cases, congregations have developed their own programs by combining elements from more than one of the eight generic categories.

Is the contemporary church in North America doing any better in the area of giving to the church? For decades members of mainline denominations have, on average, given only about 2.5 percent of their income to the church.[32] The use of countless programmatic variations based on one or more of the eight categories described above has failed to change the picture. Though there are exceptions among particular congregations from time to time, the exceptions

32. See Ronald E. Vallet and Charles E. Zech, *The Mainline Church's Funding Crisis: Issues and Possibilities* (Grand Rapids, Mich.: Wm. B. Eerdmans Publishing Co.; Manlius, N.Y.: REV/Rose Publishing, 1995).

are usually short-term in duration. The evidence continues to point to a church caught in modernity: a household of amnesia. We will explore this in more detail in the next chapter.

CHAPTER FOUR

The Church
Caught in Modernity:
A Household of Amnesia

The church — caught in the prevailing assumptions of modernity — lives in a fog of amnesia, having forgotten the promises of God that provide hope and the commands of God that provide a call and direction.

Congregations do not make decisions in a vacuum. Decisions are influenced by *external* factors — the culture of the community, the region, the nation, and the world. This culture contains powerful factors. Congregational decisions are also affected by *internal* factors — those that relate to a congregation's own history, traditions, and practices and the denomination to which it belongs. We look first at internal factors.

Internal Factors at Work in the Church

A myriad of intertwining, interrelated, internal factors are at work in the church in North America in both its denominational and

85

congregational forms.[1] These factors have many facets and point to a church weakened by inner turmoil and uncertainty. The following list of twelve factors is illustrative but not exhaustive:

1. *Denominational Mission Funding Crisis.* Without question, mainline denominations in North America are undergoing a mission funding crisis.[2] Because funding for denominations comes mostly from member congregations, any factor that affects the level of financial resources available to a congregation or how the congregation decides to allocate its financial resources as it makes economic decisions also impacts its denomination.

2. *Allocations from Denominations.* Conversely, those congregations (relatively few in number) that receive financial support from the denomination are directly affected by the amount of denominational funding available for congregations, as well as by the priorities that denominations establish to determine who is to receive such allocations.

3. *Understanding of Mission.* Evidence is accumulating that the understanding of mission by denominational leaders is not consistent with the understanding of mission held by many of its congregations. Denominational leaders need to take an in-depth look at what they understand their mission to be. Unless congregations perceive that the denomination's mission is compatible with theirs and is faithful to their understanding of a biblical vision, financial and other support of the denomination

---

1. Some of the points in this list are adapted from chapter 1 of Ronald E. Vallet and Charles E. Zech, *The Mainline Church's Funding Crisis: Issues and Possibilities* (Grand Rapids, Mich.: Wm. B. Eerdmans Publishing Co.; Manlius, N.Y.: REV/Rose Publishing, 1995).

2. Vallet and Zech in *The Mainline Church's Funding Crisis* documented that the crisis facing mainline denominations is real. Declining membership and declining finances are eating away at their historically solid base. They concluded that a major reason for the crisis is that "for the past three centuries, the church has been deeply enmeshed in the assumptions and presuppositions of modernity. As a result, the church — especially mainline denominations — has found it difficult to avoid the trap of captivity to the reigning culture that has been formed and defined by modernity" (p. 159).

will continue to erode. As loyalty to institutions erodes, congregations and their members are likely to provide a lower level of support for the denomination. It is no longer sufficient for a denomination to say, "This is our program and our budget. Please send in your support." Even those denominations that establish an apportioned amount for each congregation to send to the denomination are discovering that the apportionments do not come as automatically as in the past. *People are increasingly reluctant to support what they may perceive as denominational bureaucracies.*

4. *Changes at the National Level of Denominations.* At the national level, mainline denominations are experiencing restructuring, reduced staff and programming, lower staff morale, program retrenchment, relocations of headquarters, and a loss of vision and clarity about their mission. The distance between congregations and the national level increases in snowballing or spiraling dimensions.

5. *Mid-Level Judicatories.* Regional or mid-level judicatories of mainline denominations in many cases withhold funds completely or pass on to the national level a smaller percentage of the mission funding they receive. This intensifies the budget squeeze at the national level. As a result, responsibility for programming is being shifted from the national level to the regional levels. Regional structures are experiencing their own funding crises.

6. *Comprehensive Nature of Economic Decision Making in the Congregation.* All aspects of congregational life — not just budgets and stewardship programs — affect how much individual members give to the church and how decisions are made by the congregation. For example, the worship experiences of the people and the state of biblical knowledge in the congregation are of great significance in the congregation's economic life and decision-making processes.

7. *Individual Giving.* Congregational income, of course, comes primarily from individuals — men, women, young persons, and children — who attend, participate, and place their money in offering plates and contribute in other ways of their money,

time, and talent. Individuals who are members of mainline denominations continue to make contributions to their congregations. Some give less to their congregation because they also give to parachurch organizations and/or televangelists. In most mainline denominations, as well, there are fewer members to make contributions. This is related, in part, to the relative absence of the baby-boomer generation (born 1946-64) in mainline congregations. As a result, the average age of the members of mainline denominations is rising steadily. Members of the baby-boomer generation who are present in mainline congregations do not give as much from conviction and trust in the institution as they do from being convinced or persuaded. Trust of the institution by boomers is at a lower level than it is in the generation ahead of them.

8. *The State of Biblical Knowledge and Theology.* Many observers have described the currently prevailing state of biblical knowledge in the church in North America as biblical illiteracy. A national poll by the Barna Research Group found that "10 percent of those polled said they thought the name of Noah's wife was Joan of Arc, 16 percent said the New Testament contained a Book of Thomas, and 38 percent said the entire Bible, including the Hebrew Scripture Christians call the Old Testament, was written several decades after Jesus' death."[3] This poll illustrated some of the *symptoms*. But what is the underlying *cause* of the symptoms?

Walter Brueggemann identified the underlying cause as the *amnesia* that afflicts the church.

That amnesia (which on the surface shows up as "illiteracy") causes the church to lack in any serious missional energy. It is only this odd memory, operative at the pre-rational places in our life, that gives energy for social action, generosity in stewardship, freedom for worship, courage in care for outsiders, and passion for God's

3. Reported in "Noah's Wife Burned at the Stake," *The Christian Century,* 1 Feb. 1995, p. 105.

promises. Without memory, there will be little of courage, generosity, freedom, or passion.[4]

In *The Mainline Church's Funding Crisis,* Charles Zech and I
argued that one of the major causes behind the mission funding
crisis of mainline denominations is the short shrift given to matters
biblical and theological in denominational life. On the surface, this
would not seem to be true. Abundant lip service is given to the Bible,
and biblical quotations are sprinkled liberally throughout denominational programs and promotional materials. Far too often, however, denominational programs focus on denominational structures
and the layers of bureaucracy.[5] The temptation to use the Bible as a
"proof text" is powerful and often not resisted. The design and
production of promotional materials are sometimes done by inde-
pendent contractors who have little knowledge of the Bible or the
programs they are asked to promote. In times of financial cutbacks
and staff reductions, the danger, and sometimes the reality, is that a
survival mentality overrides a willingness to take risks as faithful
stewards of the gospel.

As a pastor who had very recently concluded denominational
service, L. E. (Ted) Siverns wrote:

When as a brief but recent part of our national staff I raised the
question about what a denominational office should be doing
these days, the question fell on angry ears. There was no lynching,
but it was obvious it was something like first choice. When I asked
about the purpose of restructuring, the question was received with
a mixture of incomprehension, incredulity, and embarrassment.
When I later suggested that the new structure would cost more

4. Walter Brueggemann, *Biblical Perspectives on Evangelism: Living in a Three-
Storied Universe* (Nashville: Abingdon Press, 1993), p. 90.
5. L. E. (Ted) Siverns wrote of an incident at the time he became executive
director of the Board of Congregational Life of the Presbyterian Church in Canada:
"I met with the executive staff and ruminated on our role which I likened to a
theological faculty where there was a variety of expertise. I was practically hooted
out of the room as I was told that we were not interested in theology and that
theoretical stuff. My experience enabled me to conclude that theology was not
held in high regard."

89

than the old, I met strong denial and was chastised for being uncooperative.[6]

In regard to theological literacy in the church, John Cobb wrote that "theology no longer plays an important role in the church's life. It exists on the periphery, tolerated but not employed in making basic decisions. I am speaking of those churches that once considered themselves 'mainline' and that continue to serve a large segment of middle America."[7] Words such as these should sound a powerful wake-up call to denominational and congregational leaders. Indications are that the call has yet to be heard.

Cobb called for theology to take place within the church, with denominational leaders and pastors functioning as theologians. If the churches should decide that theology is important for them, practical steps could be taken by theological schools to revitalize theology.[8]

"The churches are suffering from theological anorexia," noted Leander E. Keck.[9] He wrote that much of theology has reversed the insight of Anselm that theology is faith seeking understanding. "Insofar as today's theology is propelled and controlled by prior commitments to an agenda for social change, this relation of faith and knowledge is reversed."[10]

The church has reached a point where it needs to be concerned about theology that is faithful to the gospel and not so concerned about style and method. Perhaps the words of Willimon can give us courage to pursue such a course:

6. L. E. (Ted) Siverns, "A Pastor Views Denominational Mission," *Journal of Stewardship* 46 (1994): 42.

7. John B. Cobb, Jr., "Faith Seeking Understanding: The Renewal of Christian Thinking," *The Christian Century,* 29 June 1994, p. 642.

8. Cobb, "Faith Seeking Understanding," p. 644. Cobb offered a number of practical suggestions of collaboration that might take place between denominations and theological schools and noted that the incidental benefits would be enormous.

9. Leander E. Keck, *The Church Confident* (Nashville: Abingdon Press, 1993), p. 46. Chapter 2 (pp. 43-67) is devoted by Keck to the subject of the state of theology in the church.

10. Keck, *The Church Confident,* p. 57.

Modernity told us that our problem with the gospel was that it was trapped in an ancient world of outmoded authority structures (Israel and church), unavailable experiences and incomprehensible concepts. Historical criticism and most of the systematic theology that we learned (with the notable exception of Barth and his heirs) assured us preachers that we had a big problem of *meaning* on our hands in attempting to communicate the gospel, and that therefore our only hope for being heard was to grope for some points of contact in the present lives and understandings of our hearers. Unfortunately, for such homiletics, the gospel proved to be a good deal more intellectually imperialistic than modernity knew.[11]

Willimon, reporting on the work of his colleague Richard Lischer, noted that "historical criticism has taught the mainline church to deal with a biblical text by stepping back from the text. The African-American church, on the other hand, learned that the best way to understand a biblical text is to step into the text."[12] To step into the text is to run the risk that change will take place and structures and familiar patterns come unraveled. Are the leaders of mainline denominations willing to do this?

9. *Belief System.* The belief system has suffered and a crisis of faith has emerged. There is evidence that the single best predictor of church participation is belief. A significant article by Benton Johnson and others offered specifics. Johnson conducted a survey of Presbyterian General Assembly pronouncements on social issues that revealed "an erosion throughout the twentieth century of official commitment to traditional Presbyterian standards of conduct. The erosion proceeded steadily and without instances of reversal, and no new standards requiring equal discipline and sacrifice were adopted in their place."[13] Johnson,

11. William H. Willimon, *The Intrusive Word: Preaching to the Unbaptized* (Grand Rapids, Mich.: Wm. B. Eerdmans Publishing Co., 1994), pp. 41-42.

12. Willimon, *The Intrusive Word,* p. 48.

13. Benton Johnson, Dean R. Hoge, and Donald A. Luidens, "Mainline Churches: The Real Reason for Decline," *First Things: A Monthly Journal of Religion and Public Life,* March 1993, p. 17.

Hoge, and Luidens maintained that the weakening process in the mainline churches continues. The level of participation of the majority of active baby-boomer Presbyterians is *much* lower than that of their parents when they themselves were in their teens.[14] "Given the reluctance of so many baby boomers to talk about religion or to instill their own views in their children, the prospects that their children will make a serious Christian commitment are even dimmer than their own prospects turned out to be."[15]

10. *Gap Between Clergy and Laity.* Evidences of a gap between clergy and laity and a resultant theological quietism are mounting. There are indications of growing unrest among lay members about sermons and how seriously Scripture is taken by pastors. Some clergy, it has been stated, hide or obscure their theological beliefs in order to maintain peace and harmony between themselves and their congregations. It is perceived by some lay persons that Scripture is relegated to a secondary level by their pastor.

11. *Shift in Congregational Focus.* Congregations in Canada and the United States are faced with increased operating costs for building-related items — utilities, insurance, maintenance, and capital improvements. Congregations in the United States have the additional burden of increasing premiums for medical insurance. Ministry in and to the local community is seen as a primary focus of mission for the congregation. Members want to see firsthand the work accomplished by their gifts. This combination of fewer members, increased operating costs, and a focus on local mission results in a lower percentage of the congregation's income being sent to the denomination for mission at the regional, national, and international levels. In addition to all this, some pastors and congregations are withholding, or threatening to withhold, funding to the national level of their denomination as a way of voicing protests about denominational policy. The unified budget system used by many de-

14. Johnson, Hoge, and Luidens, "Mainline Churches," p. 17.
15. Johnson, Hoge, and Luidens, "Mainline Churches," p. 17.

nominations is increasingly viewed as ineffective. More and more, people and congregations want to make decisions and exercise options. More contributions are made with restrictions or strings attached. Persons are less and less willing to fund an old system in which they have lost confidence.

12. *Weaker Loyalty.* Participation in the ecumenical movement and the union or merging of churches has resulted in a fading of denominational distinctions. This has fostered "church shopping" and lessened loyalty to denominations.

These *internal* factors do not exist in a vacuum, however. Most of them are the result of powerful *cultural* factors that have shaped the church in modernity. What are some of these cultural factors?

Cultural Factors That Affect the Church

Cultural forces, when they are allowed to, have great impact on *denominational life and structures.* This in turn creates situations in which institutions take on a life and significance of their own and denominational survival and maintenance drive the agendas of denominational leaders. Personal careers, salaries, and advancement become issues of paramount concern. When the nature of ministry is no longer seen as self-sacrificing, power usually moves from leaders with vision to those with a managerial mind-set. In such a situation, the motivation and the theology of the denomination are agenda-driven and culture-bound.

Congregations, as a result, feel increasingly isolated from bureaucratic structures and lose confidence in denominational leadership. The sense of common vision, purpose, and mission that congregations have traditionally felt with their denomination is eroding. Congregations perceive that the resources provided by the denomination are less likely to meet their needs and situations. Laity, as well as clergy, share these concerns.

When the grass roots perceive denominational theology as agenda-driven and sense an indifference to Scripture, protest cannot be far behind. As already noted, congregations and mid-level judicatories often express their protest by withholding or diverting money from the national level of the denomination. Such protests affect and change the life and decision-making processes within congregations.

An understanding of mission that is based more on cultural considerations and agenda-driven anxiety than on an honest seeking to know and live by the gospel is not enthusiastically supported by the grass roots. It is important to ask, "What is the mission that God has given to the church and how is it affected by the prevailing culture?"

Cultural (external) forces affect and interrelate with the internal life and work of denominations and congregations in North America. The church — caught in the prevailing assumptions of modernity — lives in a fog, having forgotten the promises of God that provide hope and the commands of God that provide a call and direction. There is strong evidence of a cultural captivity of the church in North America. The church may well ask itself, "Can the church be the church God calls it to be if it is bound to and draws its values and agendas from the culture, rather than from biblical principles?"

Kenneth Morgan, drawing from David Bosch, excerpted seven features of the Enlightenment that have undergirded the way in which people have "perceived truth" in the past two and a half centuries:

1. The human mind is seen as the "indubitable point of departure for all knowing."
2. Because rationalism operates on a *subject-object scheme,* the effect is to separate humans "from their environment and enable them to examine the animal and mineral world from the vantage-point of scientific objectivity."
3. Purpose is eliminated from science, that is, science and history have no teleological goal. Direct causality becomes the clue to the understanding of reality.
4. Progress is believed to be inexorable.
5. Scientific knowledge is regarded as factual, value-free, and neutral.
6. All problems are seen as, in principle, solvable.

7. People are emancipated, autonomous individuals.[16]

These features of our culture have had a large, and largely devastating, impact on the church. They are part of the reason the church has often forgotten or forsaken the purpose to which God called it — God's mission.

God's Mission for the Church in a Culture of Technology[17]

The church is confronted by all sorts of cultural diversions and impediments as it seeks to carry out God's mission for the church. A technological, consumeristic society can infect the church with results that are sometimes humorous but that are more often injurious or even deadly.

In 1995 a mainline denomination sponsored, and this author attended, a workshop on "Fund Raising in a Competitive World." The workshop was attended by staff members of the denomination and its institutions who had responsibility for raising funds to support the denomination and institutions they represented. One session on securing and using volunteer leadership was led by a well-known expert on church fund-raising. He said: "Influential, affluent and committed volunteer leadership is an essential ingredient in any fund-raising program because leadership has to have access to major donors." Such thinking is dangerous and destructive. It effectively shuts out low-income, and even middle-income, members of the church from the possibility of full participation in the household of God.

Many consumers in North America are worried about their jobs and deep in credit-card debt. At the same time, the evidence is that

16. Kenneth Morgan in an unpublished paper titled "Stewardship and the Seminary," written for a stewardship course at McMaster Divinity College taught by the author. Morgan cited David J. Bosch, *Transforming Mission* (Maryknoll, N.Y.: Orbis, 1993), pp. 264-67.

17. This section is adapted in part from Vallet and Zech, *The Mainline Church's Funding Crisis*, chapter 5.

those who are rich are "back to being different." John Greenwald reported, "Following a brief, unsatisfying fling with modesty in the early 1990s, they've renewed their lust for luxe and are making upscale stores the brightest spot on the dowdy U.S. retail scene."[18] He went on to specify some of the extraordinary sales figures at luxury stores such as Mont Blanc stores and Tiffany's, while mass merchants such as Caldor and Jamesway went into bankruptcy court and closed hundreds of stores. Stores such as Wal-Mart, Zellers, and Kmart squeeze pricing until their bottom line hurts. Underperforming stores are forced shut. Credit-card delinquencies are at a ten-year high. Amidst all this, the top-end sellers continue to expand.

In a humorous vein, Martin Marty reported on a church secretary who produced a bulletin for a funeral service for a woman named Edna. Using a computer, the secretary prepared the bulletin by updating the bulletin from a prior funeral for a woman named Mary. Using the "search and replace" feature of the word processing program, the secretary gave the command to replace every occurrence of the word "Mary" with the name "Edna." Marty wrote: "Imagine the suppressed giggles when the mourners, dutifully following along in the Apostles' Creed, read that Christ 'was conceived by the Holy Spirit and born of the Virgin Edna.'"[19]

Indeed, technology is often associated with snafus or worse. Julian Dibbell, in an article titled "Everything That Could Go Wrong . . ." discussed some of the ways that technology can go wrong.[20] Drawing on a book titled *Why Things Bite Back: Technology and the Revenge of Unintended Consequences* by Edward Tenner, several examples of the way that "every technological endeavor is riddled with 'solutions' that backfire" were mentioned:

- The South American fire ant, which arrived in the southern U.S. in the 1930s, was targeted for eradication by use of DDT .

18. John Greenwald, "Luxury's Gaudy Times," *Time,* 25 March 1996, p. 48.

19. Martin E. Marty, "Pothole on the Info Highway," *The Christian Century,* 13 April 1994, p. 399.

20. Julian Dibbell, "Everything That Could Go Wrong . . ." *Time,* 20 May 1996, p. 56.

and other superpesticides. After three decades of spraying the infested area with the compounds, the U.S. government discovered that the pesticides had been doing less damage to the invader than to its predators. The chemicals had actually helped to *increase* the population of the fire ants.

- Ten years ago, the personal computer was heralded as the cornerstone of the "paperless" office. Today, most offices are strewn with paper.
- Earlier in the twentieth century, breakthroughs in antibiotics led to predictions that ancient scourges would be eradicated. Now, drug-resistant microbes are increasing and we are running out of antibiotics to fight them.

Corporate marketing is geared to influencing and manipulating consumer opinion in such a way that consumers confuse their real needs in life with their preferences and desires. Products are then designed, produced, and marketed based on consumer confusion. Amnesia has more than one cost.

In North America and other parts of the world, fast food has become an integral part of the diet. In 1994, it was estimated, consumers in the U.S. alone spent $86 billion on fast food — more, for the first time, than they spent at full-service restaurants.[21] McDonalds uses two million pounds of potatoes every day and almost singlehandedly dictates the price of potatoes on the world market. The fast-food industry embodies the symptoms of a culture in which speed and convenience outweigh the values of healthy nutrition and time for the family to gather "at table" in their household.

Disney World and other similar theme parks substitute escapist fiction for reality. Instead of using resources, time, and energy to deal with issues of justice and peace — to live by the logic of the gospel — we as consumers are attracted, seduced, and diverted to fantasies and luxuries that can worsen the plight of most humans on our planet.

Steve Young, a self-made millionaire who is quite active in his

21. "Can Fast Food Be Good Food?" *Consumer Reports,* Aug. 1994, p. 493.

church, used the term "creeping consumption" to describe the behavior he has observed. "It doesn't matter whether you make $100,000 or a million dollars a year, the system is going to cause you to consume 120 percent of it. Social climbing does it to you, TV and advertising do it, your family does, the tax system does. It's ugly. It stinks. So the question is, how do you cap your consumption?"[22] It is ironic that both of the income figures used by Young in his comment are far above the average household income in North America. Persons in poverty can only absorb the advertising and wonder about the world we live in.

A consumeristic philosophy that diverts us from God's mission and leads us to place our trust in consumer technology can be summed up in the words of "A Modern Creed":

I believe in my income and Standard of Living, maker of pleasure on earth:

And in Things-I-Own and Things-I-Want-To-Get, which are conceived by desire for possessions, born of a regular paycheck, suffered under monthly payments, then glorified, cherished and admired. They descend in their value, but on a future day I'll acquire some more, ascending in my status, 'til I sit in quite comfortable retirement, from whence I shall come to enjoy them all without end.

I believe in my home or apartment, my comfortable automobile, my vacation with pay, my insurance for life, the satisfaction of my wants and a bank account ever increasing. Amen.[23]

"A Modern Creed" is consistent with "The Lite Church," summed up in a cartoon billboard that read: "The Lite Church: 24% fewer commitments, home of the 7.5% tithe, 15-minute sermons, 45-minute worship services. We have only 8 commandments — your choice. We use just 3 spiritual laws and have an

22. Robert Wuthnow, quoting Steve Young, in a presentation titled, "Charitable Giving and Church Finance: The Challenge Ahead," at the 1996 North American Conference on Christian Philanthropy.

23. Bruce Gennerson, *The Pulpit* (July-Aug. 1968), as cited by L. E. Siverns in a private communication to this author.

800-year millennium. Everything you've wanted in a church . . . and less."[24]

North American Christians have forgotten that the world in which the church is called to proclaim and to live the gospel is the whole world, whether it is Athens, Georgia; Athens, Ontario; or Athens, Greece. Denominational structures tend to make a sharp distinction between foreign/global/international mission and home/national/homeland mission. These separate structures have often entered into competition with one another and have fostered the notion that God's mission is divided against itself. The point to be remembered is that God's passion is for the whole world.

God's mission for the church is to enable people to answer to and live by the logic of the gospel of Jesus Christ rather than by the logic of the prevailing culture. The implication is that a gospel people must be willing to be countercultural and to take the risks associated with being countercultural. As Willimon wrote: "The ultimate 'proof' for the validity of this gospel is not its alleged universality or applicability, but the church, that counter cultural community. . . . The church is the visible, baptismally derived, very public sign that the news in Jesus Christ is good news indeed, good news for all."[25]

Categories of Liberal and Conservative

In modernity, the church has been uncertain of the mission that God has given to the church. The categories of conservative and liberal that emerged during modernity led to a bifurcation in the mission as understood by the church. It may be a slight oversimplification, though not by much, to say that conservative churches stressed individual salvation and reaching the unsaved for Christ, while liberal churches stressed social systems and structures and the need to bring about systemic change. The tragic result is that these differing perceptions of the mission given to the church by God meant that

24. Concept by Jim Berkley and art by Gerry Mooney in *Leadership* (1983).
25. William Willimon, *Peculiar Speech: Preaching to the Baptized* (Grand Rapids, Mich.: Wm. B. Eerdmans Publishing Co, 1992), p. 94.

only rarely was the whole mission given the attention and resources that were needed. Truncated understandings of the mission became institutionalized within denominations with the result that bureaucratic structures became entrenched in assumptions based in modernity.

Joanne Swenson noted that both the conservative and liberal approaches to theology are limited in the way they present God:

> Both conservative and liberal approaches to theology are hobbled when it comes to presenting a God that is real and comprehensible to the contemporary person. The God of *liberals* is never seen as independent of the apprehension of the believer. Theirs is a privatized God as varied as each believer's sensory calculus. The God of the *conservatives* demands that every advance in knowledge and social justice cohere with pictures gathered between the 12th century B.C.E. and the second century C.E. (or, perhaps, congealed in the 17th or 19th centuries), resulting in a God privatized by the parochial, special pleading for the factual accuracy of every jot and tittle of the Bible. Neither of these will do.[26]

The church's inappropriate use of the categories of "liberal" and "conservative" in modernity has done much to weaken and divide the church.

Evangelism and Church Growth

How does a biblical understanding of God's mission for the church square with current practices of evangelism and church growth? In a book that has attracted considerable attention, Christopher Levan maintained that God is disappointed that the process of institution-

26. Joanne Swenson, "My View: Neither the Liberal Nor the Conservative God Is Adequate," *Bible Review,* Oct. 1989, p. 15. The emphasis is added. (In her article, Swenson observed that B.C.E. and C.E. are the scholarly, religiously neutral designations corresponding to B.C. and A.D. They stand for "Before the Common Era" and "Common Era.")

alization has corrupted the original intent of God's mission.[27] In a section on "The Distortion of Evangelism," Levan wrote that "a myopic preoccupation with church growth has distorted and damaged the Christian idea of evangelism. In most circles, evangelism is equated with recruitment — fostering healthy church membership, enhancing discipleship. In the Madison Avenue hybrid form, Christian evangelism focuses on growth, on making the church a bigger and better enterprise."[28] He continued by noting that the dream is identical for both conservatives and liberals. "Christians wanted an ever-growing, ever-expanding body of Christ. It was intended to be numerically large, giving glory to God, embodying Christ's message. The entire world would be baptized in His name."[29]

Gary Peluso, in writing about Lyle Schaller's vision of the church, stated that for Schaller "faithfulness and growth are closely related if not fully wedded. If a congregation is faithful, it will grow."[30] Schaller, as well as church growth experts and consultants in general, have advocated the homogeneous unit principle (HUP). This principle, which encourages persons who are like one another (financially, racially, ethnically, and otherwise) to worship together, works against the characteristics and rules of the household of God. It is essentially a concession to culture. The next chapter will detail the characteristics and rules of the household of God. Size and growth are not the criteria against which the faithfulness of the household of God is to be measured.

Drawing on Jesus' use of the images of leaven (Matt. 13:33), salt (Matt. 5:13), and mustard seed (Matt. 13:31-32), Levan noted that the images are unimperial and unmajestic. He argued that, in Jesus' parables and sayings, "there is no equation between size and God's favour and not even a hint of providential progress. On the

27. Christopher Levan, *God Hates Religion: How the Gospels Condemn False Religious Practice* (Toronto: The United Church Publishing House, 1995).

28. Levan, *God Hates Religion*, p. 34.

29. Levan, *God Hates Religion*, p. 36.

30. Gary E. Peluso, "What Is Lyle Schaller's Vision of the Church?" *The Christian Century*, 27 Jan. 1993, p. 86.

contrary, according to Jesus, God's imperial rule appears to be a small minority movement. Like yeast in a lump of bread, its role is not to take over or to reproduce itself until its boundaries are equal to those of the society at large, turning everything into yeast. Rather, it is an enlivening agent, a proactive catalyst."[31] By way of contrast, Jesus ridiculed those "who equate largesse with God's blessing and purpose. A glance at the parable of the barns [Luke 12:16]," he continued, "gives adequate testimony to the gospel's suspicion of size as a measure of God's favour."[32] Levan concluded:

> Whether as leaven in the lump, as a grain of mustard, or as salt, the images Jesus employs to describe the coming reign of God are not triumphant or majestic. They are not designed to inspire an ever-growing movement that would take over the hearts and spirits of every being on earth. On the contrary, they seem to call for a committed band of followers whose spirit, compassion, flavour, and zest will inspire the whole — a subverting minority, a band of imaginative followers who turn the world on its head by employing standards of love and justice.
>
> . . . Perhaps for the first time since the church and empire joined together under Constantine and became an "official religion," the disciples of Christ are free to be that small minority movement. Not distressed over its status, but boldly proclaiming the coming reign of God in which everyone has enough and there is a place for all. In the subversive minority church, evangelism means the embodiment of that coming age of God's favour and not the enlargement of church rolls. What a relief.[33]

There is a real sense in which stewardship and evangelism are closely related. Some have described them as two sides of the same coin. And though neither one is *primarily* about numbers, the culture based on modernity tries to convince us otherwise.

31. Levan, *God Hates Religion*, p. 37.
32. Levan, *God Hates Religion*, p. 40.
33. Levan, *God Hates Religion*, p. 43.

Church Buildings

Church buildings are closely related to the issue of the size and status of the church. We have already observed that building-related costs are major factors in congregational budgets. Increasingly, basic decisions about congregational ministry and outreach are controlled and limited by the perceived limitations of financial resources. When push comes to shove, many congregations live by the maxim that "charity begins at home." Jesus said, "Where your treasure is, there will your heart be also." When money goes into buildings and structures, the heart will surely follow. Levan described the misplaced priority in these words:

> Who can doubt the priority of place within institutional religion? Annual budgets, supposedly vehicles for reflecting God's work in the world, weigh heavily in support of maintenance of existing structures. We must ask ourselves if heating a cavernous room for once-weekly use is God's mission, if a mammoth building truly reflects the holiness of the Creator of the universe. Do we believe that God would choose to keep the church doors open instead of selling its assets to feed the hungry and clothe the naked? Every year, many devout Christians struggle to maintain our buildings in the face of desperate unemployment, and yet we proclaim that we are about God's justice.[34]

Church buildings by virtue of their expense, mammoth size, and immovability may be viewed as counterproductive to the fulfillment of God's mission for the church. To become a household of God will require a new vision and point of view.

Portents for the Future of the Church

An overview of a possible future for mainline denominations was presented by Robert Wuthnow in a major study of Presbyterians who went through confirmation classes in the 1960s. Wuthnow noted

34. Levan, *God Hates Religion*, pp. 44-45.

that the major reason the denomination was unable to retain its young people was theological: the church did not teach them a clear, compelling set of religious beliefs.[35]

Wuthnow also reported surveys that indicate that the power of religion to do anything active in curbing greed seems largely to be a thing of the past. In his survey of the U.S. labor force, Wuthnow found that 71 percent agreed with the statement "being greedy is a sin against God." In the same survey, 89 percent agreed with the statement "our society is much too materialistic."

But the same study also showed the following:

- 76 percent said having money gives them a good feeling about themselves.
- 84 percent said they wish they had more money than they do.
- 78 percent said that having a beautiful home, a new car, and other nice things is important to them.
- And religiously active people gave virtually the same responses as people who are not religiously oriented at all.
- 68 percent of the same people agreed that "money is one thing; morals and values are completely separate. . . ."
- Among all church members, only 40 percent claim to have heard a sermon about stewardship in the last year.[36]

As already noted about the mainline denominations in North America, giving by members to the church averages around 2.5 percent of income. Some members give at a higher rate; others give at a lower rate. The figure varies somewhat among the mainline denominations, but the average is 2.5 percent. In fact, this has been the figure for many years, even decades.

If the 2.5 percent of income given were being allocated by congregations in the same way as in the past and if the number of

35. Robert Wuthnow, "The Future of Mainline Protestantism," *The Drew Connection,* Winter 1994, p. 9. The article was a paper delivered at the Frances Youngker Vosburgh Lectures held at Drew University Theological School in October 1993.

36. Wuthnow, "The Future of Mainline Protestantism," p. 10.

households contributing to the congregations were not changing, then we would expect that the financial resources going to denominations, expressed in constant dollars, would not be declining. But the fact is that congregations are sending a smaller percentage of congregational income to denominations and that the number of members (households) in mainline denominations is declining. Details of these changes were given by Vallet and Zech.[37] Shifts in giving are taking place. Many persons regard these as unfavorable shifts.

Perhaps a clue to this low level of giving can be traced to the way the gospel is presented in most Christian churches on Sunday mornings. Members and visitors are treated as religious consumers and are sold a "Jesus" who will meet their needs. We have already noted in chapter two the observation by Murray Joseph Haar that "the Jesus of American Christian churches has become a product to be marketed and made palatable to the masses, a bargain for wise shoppers to latch onto for religious security. Sermons rarely call Christians to a discipleship of self-sacrifice or to a radical reassessment of the way Americans live their lives."[38]

Such sermons, Haar, continued, are "sit-com" homilies.

> On the surface, all seems well in such sermons. They seem to deal with the problems of "the text," contain many humorous stories, and appear willing to engage the difficult problems of faith. But they really do not. There is no need to worry. Like any television sit-com, all problems are resolved within twenty minutes. Having reassured the flock that all the dilemmas of the text and of life itself are going to work out just fine, the minister sends the people on their way.[39]

The dismal possibility is that the culture has so captured the church that its young people and young adults no longer have a realistic opportunity to learn Christian beliefs, but instead absorb the beliefs and values of a consumeristic culture. Yet there can be hope.

37. Vallet and Zech, *The Mainline Church's Funding Crisis*, chapter 1.
38. Murray Joseph Haar, "Self-Serving Redemptionism: A Jewish-Christian Lament," *Theology Today* 52, no. 1 (April 1995): 109.
39. Haar, "Self-Serving Redemptionism," p. 109.

Signs of Hope

At this point, church leaders and members may be tempted to despair and to say, in effect, "What's the use? The die is cast. Nothing we say or do can make a difference." It is my view that change is possible. As already noted in chapter one, there is a biblical and theological rationale for hope that real change can and will take place.

What is needed is the Spirit of God working to bring about a *reversal*. The message needs to be: God is alive and is at work. God *can* change a household of amnesia into a household of God. Persons who know that they are disciples and stewards of the living God and part of the household of God will give abundantly and generously to support God's mission. As a result, the church will not have to beg for money. God's people will do what God has called them to do.

In summary, let it be noted that the current context is a difficult one for congregations and a time in which familiar moorings seem to have washed away. Mainline denominations and their congregations despair. Cuts are made. But there is hope. If the congregation will remember its identity as a household of God there is hope.

We have now reached the heart of the matter. What does it mean to be a household of God? What are the characteristics and rules of a household of God? We turn to these questions in the next chapter.

CHAPTER FIVE

Characteristics and Rules of the Household of God

The obstacle confronting the church is that the reigning assumptions are so ingrained and so powerful that they are scarcely recognized as such, let alone resisted and opposed.

Confronting Reigning Assumptions

In the last chapter, we noted that the church — caught in modernity — has placed its trust in the reigning assumptions of the culture rather than in the living God. Walter Brueggemann expressed the problem as trusting an unreliable script:

> It turns out that the script we have trusted in the Enlightenment (and in the older Euro-American) tradition is an unreliable script, even though we have been massively committed to it. And now, we are wondering, is there a more adequate script out of which we may reimagine our lives? Although few would articulate their coming to worship on such grounds, I believe people are haunted by the question of whether there is a text (and an interpreter) that can say something that will make sense out of our pervasive nonsense. It is my conviction that neither old liberal ideologies nor old conservative certitudes nor critical claims made for the Bible will now do. Our circumstance permits and requires the preacher to do something we have not been permitted or required

to do before. Ours is an awesome opportunity: to see whether this text, with all of our interpretive inclinations, can voice and offer reality in a redescribed way that is credible and evocative of a new humanness, rooted in holiness and practiced in neighbor-liness.[1]

The challenge to the church in North America is to present the biblical text in such a way that persons will respond to a new perception of God's reality. Yet reigning assumptions are so ingrained and so powerful that they are scarcely recognized as such, let alone resisted and opposed. Though the specific assumptions change over time, *the problem of confronting reigning assumptions that are contrary to the logic of the gospel is ongoing. Reigning assumptions are always with us.* The question for the church to ask itself is: with God's help, how can we avoid succumbing to the power and allure of cultural as-sumptions?

William Herzog, in his book on the parables of Jesus as sub-versive speech, reminded us that though Jesus began with incidents taken from daily life, he did not stop there:

> As Freire knew, the danger of beginning with daily life or with dominating institutions was that the peasants had internalized the world of their oppressors and had settled for a reading of the world and its ways offered by their elite rulers. Therefore the codificiation had to jar its hearers out of their almost instinctive acquiescence to the rulers' reading of reality. This need accounts for another characteristic commonly noted in the parables: they not only present ordinary life but contain *extraordinary departures* from it. . . .
>
> Scholars have proposed many reasons why the parables contain these twists and turns. Usually, their reasons revolve around the assumption that *the parables communicate the incongruity between life on earth and life in the reign of God.* This study suggests a different reason for these gaps: the departures trigger the problem-posing

1. Walter Brueggemann, "Preaching as Reimagination," *Theology Today,* Oct. 1995, p. 329. Brueggemann also referred to his article "As the Text 'Makes Sense': Keep the Methods as Lean and Uncomplicated as Possible," *Christian Ministry* 14 (Nov. 1983): 7-10.

questions that begin to explore the scene presented in the parable by holding the scene up as an object for contemplation and analysis.[2]

The church of today may, in some ways, be compared with the ancient peasants of Palestine. Even as the peasants needed to be jarred by Jesus "out of their almost instinctive acquiescence to the rulers' reading of reality," so the church in North America needs to be jolted and awakened to the reality of its acquiescence to its culture. The challenge to the church in North America is to come to an awareness that it is caught in the reigning assumptions of a consumer culture and has forgotten whose household it is. This chapter will explore the characteristics and rules of a household that remembers it is a household of God.

What It Takes to Become a Steward Is the Whole Life of the Congregation

The church is mistaken when it assumes that stewardship is a separate program to fund ministry and mission in the church. Such a limited understanding of stewardship reduces it to fund-raising and barely rises above the survival mentality that is the bane of far too many congregations. Further, such fund-raising understandings and methodologies are scarcely distinguishable from organizations that make no claim to be households of God, bound by the logic of the gospel of Jesus Christ. When a congregation remembers who it is and strives to live as a household of God, it will realize that stewardship is intricately bound up with the basic worship and proclamation and sacramental life of the church. When stewardship is seen as existing outside the church's *diakonia* and *koinonia* and mission, then all the things that are necessary for a person to become a steward

2. William R. Herzog II, *Parables as Subversive Speech: Jesus as Pedagogue of the Oppressed* (Louisville: Westminster/John Knox Press, 1994), p. 261. The emphasis is added. The reference to Freire is to Paulo Freire, whose works Herzog drew from extensively.

are forgotten. As I stated in chapter one, the church is good at developing stewardship programs, but not stewards. *The very heart of what it takes to become a steward is precisely the whole life of the congregation.*[3]

A congregation where stewards can be developed will be a congregation that has a memory. Because it has a memory, it will be generous in sharing with the poor (freed from greed, acquisitiveness, and idolatry) and will live in hope (not despair). In short, it will remember its story; it will know who it is. It will remember that it is a household of God. It will remember that it is a covenanted community and not a volunteer society. *It will have certain characteristics and live by certain rules.*

Characteristics of a Congregation That Is a Household of God

What does it mean for a congregation to be a household of God? What are some of the *characteristics of the congregation?* Three stand out:

Built on the Resurrection of Jesus Christ

The household of Jesus Christ is built on the resurrection of Jesus Christ.[4] In a sermon describing the women who came to the tomb on that Sunday morning, Park Renshaw wrote about the tumult of a new world emerging from the old:

> And so Sunday morning, these women, who were not in on that tumultuous supper, came to the unnamed garden near Cal-

---

3. This insight and some of the suggestions in this section for developing stewards within the whole life of the congregation are adapted from presentations made by M. Douglas Meeks at an Educational Event for Stewardship Leaders in July 1993, held in Bolton, Ontario, and sponsored by the Ecumenical Center for Stewardship Studies.

4. See also the discussion in chapter one regarding the resurrection of Jesus.

110

vary. The Sabbath over, they went shopping for burial spices and arrived, nervous, apprehensive, at the grave. What a shock: it's open, a well-dressed young man is sitting there. He says, "Don't be afraid," and gives them Jesus' forwarding address; and they are so afraid that they don't even go where the young man said to go.

They're paralyzed. Something has gone wrong — or has gone so right they can't take it in. Mark leaves the story there, with the men too afraid to come, and the women leaving terrified. But one thing, they knew: somehow it was clear to them that the world was not the same anymore. It was a new world. They just didn't know what to do with it yet. But they would find out.

In raising Jesus of Nazareth from the dead, God showed us the world according to God. In Jesus Christ the world is now a new world. It is a world where the meek *do* inherit the earth, even when they don't have a deed to it registered in the courthouse. It is a world where the poor in spirit have the only riches, and among the poor the bread is blessed and broken and everyone has enough. It's where everyone knows that *enough is a feast* (in the old world a feast is not enough!). In the new world of the resurrection, those who mourn are more than comforted; they dance before the Lord with their dead — often while they are still grieving. It is a world where the peacemakers know themselves, and everyone else, as children of God, and the merciful know what mercy does: it turns our enemies into sisters and brothers and causes weapons to rust and corrode or be transformed into tools.[5]

The apostle Paul clearly believed that belief in the resurrection of Jesus Christ is foundational to the faith of the church:

Now if Christ is proclaimed as raised from the dead, how can some of you say there is no resurrection of the dead? If there is no resurrection of the dead, then Christ has not been raised; and if Christ has not been raised, then our proclamation has been in vain and your faith has been in vain. (1 Cor. 15:12-14)

5. Park Renshaw, "If It's True It's a Different World; Does That Scare You?" *Journal for Preachers,* Easter 1995, pp. 18-19.

The household of Jesus Christ begins with the dancing and laughter of Easter, or it does not begin at all. The church is a miracle that depends on the resurrection work of God. The church is possible only through God's victory over death in Jesus Christ and God's promise that God will destroy death in all things. The household of Jesus Christ lives between the two realities of the destruction of death in Jesus Christ and the destruction of death in all things. The in-between time — the history in which we live — is what the church calls mission.

Yet far too often the church behaves as though the news of Jesus' resurrection hardly matters, or that it never really happened. The result, either way, is a bland, listless celebration of Easter.

In an intriguing column, Martin Marty wrote about an Atheist Coalition in San Diego that secured a permit to use the site on public land on Mount Soledad where traditionally each year a Christian group had held an Easter morning service. The Atheist Coalition accomplished this feat simply by beating the Christian group in applying for the permit. Perhaps this can be a reminder to the church that celebration of the resurrection of Jesus is a serious matter. Apparently the atheists thought so. Marty observed:

> [The atheists are] not ignoring the shocking news of Jesus' resurrection. In their taunting and opposition they show that they have caught on to this festival's significance.
>
> If Mount Soledad were topped with a cosmic Easter egg, a gigantic stuffed bunny and a field of giant lilies, you would not find any atheists stirring. Much of what happens in many a Christian Easter service is so bland that it is easy to ignore. The Atheist Coalition can help the believing community remember that the resurrection of Christ is offensive and shocking. News of it is worthy of protest. Let's hope the cross, not the cross-claiming element in San Diego, is the scandal, the offense. If so: He is risen. Rejoice.[6]

Michael L. Lindvall told a story that points out in a humorous and effective way the joy and the celebration that are, or should be,

6. Martin Marty, "M.E.M.O: Atheists at the Cross," *The Christian Century,* 10 April 1996, p. 415.

part of the lives of a resurrection people.[7] The story describes a pastor's preparation for preaching an Easter sermon and what happens during the service on Easter. The title of the sermon was "The Lord of the Dance"; the sermon was to be about God's dance of life and was intended to convey that "in the heart of God there is a profound, vibrant, dancing joy, and if there's a dancing joy in our God, so there should be in us." After the sermon was preached, the pastor ended with a prayer "that we, Your people, might be filled with Your joy, that our hearts might dance as David danced before the Ark, that we might dance for the goodness of life." During silent prayer, the pastor asked that God might deepen in him the joy of faith, touch him often with the joy of laughter, and fill him with the spirit of dance. The pastor then described what happened next:

> They say that you should be careful about what you pray for, because you're liable to get it. I hardly dreamed that my prayer would be answered so soon. I said, "Amen," and "let us now receive the offering." I sat down, the four ushers soberly passed the plates while the organist played a somber and tuneless little ditty. When the offering had been collected, she modulated jerkily into the Doxology, and the ushers marched down the aisle, wooden plates in their hands.[8]

The ushers stopped at the foot of the five carpeted steps that led up to the elevated chancel where the communion table sat and on which the offering plates were to be placed. The pastor offered a prayer from the top of the steps and then walked down the steps to take the plates from the ushers:

> All went as usual until I turned, a plate in each hand, to mount the steps to the chancel and place the offering on the communion table. The hem of my robe had come loose and as I took the first step, my toe caught it. But I didn't fall. I should have backed down then and there, but years of liturgical habit kept me aimed onward

7. Michael L. Lindvall, *The Good News from North Haven* (New York: Doubleday, 1991), pp. 69-72.
8. Lindvall, *Good News*, p. 70.

113

and upward. With my next step, I was further inside the garment. By the time I was to the third step, I realized that I was walking up the inside of my black Geneva pulpit robe. I was nearly on my knees; I could have turned around and sat down on the steps, freed my feet, and started over. It would have been a small indignity, but it is what I should have done.

But I decided to stay the course. I straightened up with all my might. My robe gave way and ripped at the bottom button. The force of this sudden freedom sent my arm jerking upward. I managed to hold on to the offering plates, but all their contents flew up and back over my head. Offering envelopes, dollar bills, five-dollar bills, quarters, dimes, and nickels rained down upon the heads of four stunned ushers.

Well, my feet were free, but pride still bound my will. I should have turned around to the congregation, bowed theatrically, and accepted the humorous and humbling grace of the moment. But I marched on up the steps as though nothing had happened, and laid the four empty offering plates on the table. The ushers marched down the aisle through all the offertory debris.[9]

When the pastor turned around and glanced at the larger than usual Easter Sunday congregation, he saw the tops of one hundred twenty heads, bowed deeply in prayer so they would not have to look at him.

After the service he reflected that "faith is a dance with divinity, a mad polka done on the grave, kicking your legs back, and shouting out polka 'whoops' like the fool you are. And maybe we should even throw money in the air. We should certainly laugh at ourselves when we trip."[10] His prayer, "Lord, teach me to dance," had been answered in a way that he had not anticipated.

Tragically, in most congregations in North America, the resurrection of Jesus does not receive major emphasis outside of Easter Sunday. One reason for this, as we have seen, may be a lack of belief. Another may be fear of what it really means if Jesus is alive. These two reasons may, in fact, be intertwined and com-

9. Lindvall, *Good News*, pp. 70-71.
10. Lindvall, *Good News*, p. 72.

bined into a single set of conflicting emotions within an individual Christian.

In regard to the "fear" factor, Ralph Wood referred to Walker Percy's work, *Love in the Ruins,* and his observation that God is dead for most of us because we dread for him to be alive. Wood continued:

> Dr. Thomas More, Percy's protagonist in *Love in the Ruins,* is a man deeply embittered by the paltriness of modern life. Like the psalmist, he sees that his own soul stands in need of radical deliverance. As a lineal descendant of the Renaissance saint for whom he is named, but also as a self-confessed "bad Catholic," More remembers why he did not take his daughter Samantha to Lourdes as she was dying of neuroblastoma. "I was afraid she might be cured," More confesses. "Suppose you ask God for a miracle and God says yes, very well. How do you live the rest of your life?"
>
> For God to have miraculously healed Samantha would have been spiritually too exacting for Dr. More. Such salvation would have robbed him of what he calls his sweet remorse. Once Samantha was dead, More not only grieved; he feasted over her death. It gave him endless excuse for his anger and cynicism, for his drinking and lusting and hating. The psalmist declares that God stands ready to deliver the world from such paltriness with the miracles of his presence, but only if we understand that he matters absolutely.[11]

For the Sake of God's Mission

A second characteristic is that the church exists for the sake of God's mission.[12] It is important for the church to remember that the mission is *God's* mission.

As noted in chapter one, the church sometimes forgets the import of John 3:16, which speaks of God's love of the world — not

---

11. Ralph Wood, "Living by the Word: The God Who Matters," *The Christian Century,* 19 July 1995, p. 707.

12. "God's mission to the world" is discussed further in the next chapter as one of the instruments of Christian stewardship.

God's love for the church. God's love — God's passion — is for the *world*. That is the mission! The church is a subplot in this larger story. The household of God itself is the work of God. The work of the household of God is to carry out God's mission by helping people know and live by the logic of the gospel of Jesus Christ rather than the logic of the prevailing culture. Though the prevailing culture will differ from place to place — from region to region, from country to country, from continent to continent — the heart of the mission is always to present, in words and deeds, God's love and passion for the world.

When the church is a household of amnesia, the emphasis shifts from God's mission to institutional survival, hidden agendas, and personal ambitions. The danger is that church leaders believe, or at least say they believe, that the survival of the institutional church is God's primary mission. Such a survival mentality is both limiting to the fulfillment of God's mission and enervating to those who are involved.

Built Around the Table

A third characteristic of the household of God is that the household is built around and begins at table. The table is where we *remember* who we are and what we are called to do. For the Christian church, this means first and foremost gathering at the eucharistic table — the place where God's people gather in joy and thanksgiving to celebrate the mighty acts of God.

As was noted in the introduction, in the Jewish tradition the Seder question asked by one of the children of the family is: "Why are we doing this?" The Christian church needs to ask itself: Are the church's liturgies odd enough that *our* children ask, "Why are we living this way?" This very question can cause us to remember who and whose we are. Do our gatherings at table lead us to remember with joy the mighty acts of God and to share with God and with one another in thanksgiving?

Chris Levan observed that a meal scene is at the heart of Jesus' ministry. When the Pharisees and others complained about Jesus' eating and drinking with toll collectors and sinners, Jesus replied, "Since when do the healthy need a doctor? It's the sick who do. I have not come to enlist religious folks to change their hearts, but sinners" (Luke 5:31-32, SV).[13] Levan wrote:

> While the meal is not a central part of this story, it could be that Jesus used the fellowship of the table as the central means for conversion. For it is his table practice that precipitates the debate and allow Jesus or the gospel writer or both to make an important point about his messiahship. As you read Scripture, see the common meal as much more than a narrative convention. Whenever the reader encounters a meal scene in the Gospels, one is getting to the heart of Christ's mission.[14]

The act of gathering at a table to eat is a powerful image in Jesus' ministry. The messianic banquet is described in these words in Luke 13:29: "Then people will come from east and west, from north and south, and will eat in the kingdom of God." Levan put the thought into these words, "The coming reign was marked by an open table fellowship . . . where there are no distinctions drawn between pure and impure and the respectable and despised sit side by side."[15]

The question arises: "What might this mean for the church of today?" Levan's words stretch the minds of his readers:

> Imagine what worship would become if it began with a simple meal, one open to all and any. If we cleared away all the furniture in the sanctuary except a single table (not unlike those first church settings), a table at which there is room for everyone. If everyone were invited, rich and poor, prestigious and unknown alike. If at that meal, there were bread, daily bread, just enough. Everyone would have enough. In that company there would be no one more

13. SV refers to *The Complete Gospels: Annotated Scholars Version* (Sonoma, Calif.: Polebridge Press, 1992, 1994).

14. Christopher Levan, *God Hates Religion: How the Gospels Condemn False Religious Practice* (Toronto: United Church Publishing House, 1995), p. 25.

15. Levan, *God Hates Religion*, p. 125.

important than others, no one too lowly or mean to be included. The mark of leadership would be servanthood.

It may sound idealistic, perhaps impractical, but it is precisely this vision that continues to break out of the Christian community. Whenever there are reforms, this primary egalitarian focus re-emerges. This radical community is the antidote to the raging religious fundamentalism that often passes for spiritual zeal in our context.[16]

A remarkable incident recounted by Peter W. Marty describes the incredible power of table ministry. The setting was St. Anthony's Catholic Church in San Francisco, which for years had served meals to people in need. Over the doorway to the dining room hung a sign that read *Caritate Dei*. Marty described what happened one day:

> [A] young mechanic, just released from jail and new to St. Anthony's, entered the door and sat down for a meal. A woman was busy cleaning the adjacent table. "When do we get on our knees and do the chores, lady?" he asked. "You don't," she replied. "Then when's the sermon comin'?" he inquired. "Aren't any," she said. "How 'bout the lecture on life, huh?" "Not here," she said.
>
> The man was suspicious. "Then what's the gimmick?" The woman pointed to the inscription over the door. He squinted at the sign. "What's it mean, lady?" "Out of love for God," she said with a smile, and moved on to another table.[17]

The congregation that has these three characteristics of the household of God will remember what it means for the church to be the economy of God; it will not be a captive to the economy of the household of amnesia, as embodied in a consumer society. The economic assumptions — the market logic — of the Enlightenment can and will be overcome by the logic of the gospel of Jesus Christ.

16. Levan, *God Hates Religion*, p. 127. Use of the table in worship is also discussed in chapter seven of *this* book.

17. Peter W. Marty, "Living by the Word: The Door to Abundant Life," *The Christian Century*, 17 April 1996, p. 427.

Rules of the Household of God

What are the *rules* that a congregation as the household of God is called to live by?[18] To put it another way, what are the *outcomes of the logic of the gospel?* If a congregation follows the logic of the gospel, what will its household rules look like? The claim made about the household rules from the Pentateuch is simple: if the rules are kept, there will be an economy of life and freedom. Unfortunately, much of modern theological tradition has tended to undercut the Torah to make way for the modern market society. In the household, the rules are defined — as are the Ten Commandments — by the words "I love you, accept you, forgive you, and call on you to live a life that is consistent with God's desire for this covenanted community of faith." God's household rules make a better community. The rules and logic of the market economy make the rich richer and the poor poorer.

Rules of the household, even though they are important, may be rejected by many Christians if the rules are presented as laws to be obeyed without question or understanding. Knowing *why* God gave certain commandments is important. Much teaching about laws omits the reasons for the laws. Dennis Prager wrote about his experience in a yeshiva, an Orthodox Jewish day school: "Despite all the encouragement of questioning at yeshiva, one seminal area of Judaism seemed to be off limits to questions — reasons for the laws. Not only were reasons not given, but we were largely taught that looking for reasons bordered on the sacrilegious." Prager says he now believes that every law in the Torah has a rational basis. "The more one understands these laws, the greater one's faith in them."[19]

God gave the "rules" of the household for a reason. As we explore and understand better what those reasons are, we learn that

---

18. M. Douglas Meeks identified the five rules that follow at an Educational Event for Stewardship Leaders in July 1993 at Bolton, Ontario. The details have been developed by the author.

19. "What Dennis Prager Did and Didn't Learn in Yeshiva," *First Things*, Oct. 1995, p. 80.

behind the rules are principles that work for human welfare and blessing, not enslavement — a household of life, not of death.

Despite a common perception to the contrary, the household rules of the Torah lie precisely at the heart of the ministry of Jesus. Too often, the church treats the Torah as legalistic and outmoded — rejected by Jesus. The household rules of the Torah have their parallel in the ministry of Jesus. Memory and hope are the sources of the energy of stewardship in the household of God. The Christian should not assume that the ancient household rules are quaint, dusty rules to be forgotten. They are meant to be rules for today. What are those household rules? Five are lifted up here:

Do Not Charge Interest to the Poor

The first of the rules is *do not charge interest to the poor.* Biblical references for this rule include:

> If any of your kin fall into difficulty and become dependent on you, you shall support them; they shall live with you as though resident aliens. Do not take interest in advance or otherwise make a profit from them, but fear your God; let them live with you. You shall not lend them your money at interest taken in advance, or provide them food at a profit. I am the LORD your God, who brought you out of the land of Egypt, to give you the land of Canaan, to be your God. (Lev. 25:35-38)

> If you lend money to my people, to the poor among you, you shall not deal with them as a creditor; you shall not exact interest from them. (Exod. 22:25)

This rule seems a strange notion to persons enmeshed in the economies of North America, where a debt society is taken for granted. But the debt system will sooner or later put some people into slavery. It is the poor who end up trapped in credit card indebtedness. In the 1960s and 1970s, for example, farmers were told that, in order to make a profit in farming, it was necessary to borrow money to buy more land, more fertilizer, and more equipment. In the 1970s and the 1980s, when the price of land went down, many farmers could not pay their debts and were forced out of business. In the later history of Israel, when interest was allowed, the household rules stated that the creditor could not take as collateral from anyone his or her coat. Jesus reinforced this concept in the prayer that we usually call the Lord's Prayer. Jesus included the words: "And forgive us our debts, as we also have forgiven our debtors" (Matt. 6:12). These words describe the logic of an economy that derives from the gospel.[20]

In a meeting with the author, representatives of several congregations listed some of the programs being done by their own or other congregations that provide substance to the principle of this rule about interest. They mentioned scholarship grants and loans for students, with no interest charged and the students asked to repay the loans as they were able; credit unions run by congregations that helped families (especially poor families) develop a pattern of saving, many for the first time, and secure loans at a nominal rate of interest.

Freddie Mac, a major secondary mortgage lender in the United States, is working with affiliates of Baptist churches to reach potential home buyers who might not qualify for a mortgage without a little help. One of Freddie Mac's partners is the Minority Enterprise Financial Acquisition Corporation, a for-profit company that works with the National Baptist Convention USA and the National Baptist Convention of America. Those who have been helped by the program include people with low to moderate incomes, minorities, and residents of city neighborhoods.

Leave Gleanings

The second household rule is to *leave gleanings*. Scripture references include:

> When you reap the harvest of your land, you shall not reap to the very edges of your field, or gather the gleanings of your harvest;

20. See Appendix Two: "Economic Dimensions of the Lord's Prayer."

you shall leave them for the poor and for the alien: I am the LORD your God. (Lev. 23:22)

The fields were not to be harvested all the way to the edge. Persons who were hungry could then go into a field and pick grain. Gleaning gives the poor access into the household. This tradition continued through the ministry of Jesus (even on the sabbath),[21] the period of the early church theologians, through medieval times, and through the Reformation. But by the seventeenth century, the church began to forget. Amnesia took hold. In the market economy of modernity, milk is dumped, apples thrown into a ravine, and people paid not to grow food! The church, by and large, has trusted these market economy rules rather than the logic of the gospel.

Jesus practiced gleaning. In Matthew 12:1-8, the text states that Jesus gleaned on the sabbath. This text will be looked at in detail in the section on the sabbath later in this chapter.

In recent years, hopeful signs of revival of the ancient practice of gleaning have emerged. A Scripps Howard News Service article described an effort to feed the poor — a gleaning effort — in Florida. Led by Jerry Nichols, program director for the Society of St. Andrew in Palm Beach County, Florida, residents, volunteer pickers, and food banks were teamed up to provide food for the hungry. The non-profit Society of St. Andrew was formed in 1979 by three United Methodist ministers. The goal was simple: to distribute surplus food to those who need it. The society became active in Virginia, Maryland, North Carolina, Texas, and, most recently, Florida. In Palm Beach County the program is called Residential Dooryard Fruit Gleaning. "The term gleaning is used," Nichols said, "because gleaning is a biblical mandate. The farmer leaves behind a portion of his produce for the poor."[22] Both residential and commercial properties participate in the program. The food is distributed to the AIDS network, food banks, and children's homes.

In 1976 the Mennonite Central Committee Canada started the

21. See Matt. 12:1-8.
22. This account was reported in "Florida Man Gleaning Unused Citrus to Feed Hungry," *Syracuse (N.Y.) Herald American,* 14 Jan. 1996, A11.

first Food Bank pilot project as a way to use bountiful Canadian harvests responsibly. In 1983 the pioneer agency was reorganized into the Canadian Foodgrains Bank and has grown to include ten denominations. Over 350,000 metric tonnes of food have been shipped to twenty of the neediest countries in the world. Over the years, Canadian wheat has been the major commodity, but corn, pulses,[23] and cooking oil have also been sent.

In a series of meetings in 1996, representatives from several congregations shared information about programs in their congregations that sought to live out the principle of gleaning. Among the programs described were operating food pantries; organizing food consortiums; providing free sweaters; running clothing closets; securing free toys from manufacturers; and planting, harvesting, and taking food to the poor. The principle of gleaning — helping to give the poor access to food — is an important biblical teaching. Each Christian congregation as a household of God is called to determine the best way for it to practice the principle of gleaning as a rule of the household.

Give the Tithe

The third household rule is *the tithe*.

The tithe has already been mentioned several times in earlier chapters. Unfortunately, in a consumer culture the word "tithe" conjures up images of legalism, compulsion, and fund-raising to support the programs and ministries of the church. Rarely is it viewed as a joyous spiritual exercise that does not primarily have to do with budgets but with celebration.

Among the biblical texts that talk about the tithe is this passage from 2 Chronicles 31:4-10:

> He commanded the people who lived in Jerusalem to give the portion due to the priests and the Levites, so that they might devote themselves to the law of the LORD. As soon as the word

---

23. Pulses are the edible seeds of peas, beans, lentils, and similar plants having pods.

spread, the people of Israel gave in abundance the first fruits of grain, wine, oil, honey, and of all the produce of the field; and they brought in abundantly the tithe of everything. The people of Israel and Judah who lived in the cities of Judah also brought in the tithe of cattle and sheep, and the tithe of the dedicated things that had been consecrated to the LORD their God, and laid them in heaps. In the third month they began to pile up the heaps, and finished them in the seventh month. When Hezekiah and the officials came and saw the heaps, they blessed the LORD and his people Israel. Hezekiah questioned the priests and the Levites about the heaps. The chief priest Azariah, who was of the house of Zadok, answered him, "Since they began to bring the contributions into the house of the LORD, we have had enough to eat and have plenty to spare; for the LORD has blessed his people, so that we have this great supply left over."

In an earlier work, I described my first memory of hearing the word "tithing" at age nine:

My first memory of hearing about stewardship in the church, though I doubt that it was labeled stewardship, was hearing the pastor and my Sunday School teacher stress the importance of tithing. By the time I was ten years old, I had heard the word "tithing" scores of times. Whenever God gave me any income, I was taught, I was expected to calculate what 10% of that income was and to give it to the church. This was an absolute requirement. God expected it and I must do it. While I was told that the tithes of the people enabled the church to carry out its ministry and send missionaries to foreign lands, the stress was placed on the specific obligation of each person to give 10% of his or her income. I remember the preacher once saying that, even if the money I gave were burned and never used, it was still my obligation to give it to the church. Tithing was a requirement! When I got my 50 cents allowance each Saturday, I faithfully placed a nickel in the offering plate on Sunday.[24]

24. Ronald E. Vallet, *Stepping Stones of the Steward: A Faith Journey Through Jesus' Parables,* 2d ed. (Grand Rapids, Mich.: Wm. B. Eerdmans Publishing Co.; Manlius, N.Y.: REV/Rose Publishing, 1994), p. 1.

Of course, my understanding changed and expanded over the years. The tithe has many interpretations and is mentioned in many places in Scripture. Sometimes it is said that the tithe is to be used for one's own celebration. Sometimes the tithe is to be given to the priest either for a religious celebration or because the priest is to be paid. But *the primary reason for the tithe in the Torah is to give to the poor.* Unfortunately, for the most part, the church in North America, when it talks about the tithe at all, presents the tithe as a means to support the church and its ministries. Fortunately a few congregations are remembering the first tithe and using it to minister to the poor in their neighborhoods. This follows the biblical mandate of concern for and hospitality to the stranger, the disenfranchised, the captive, and the oppressed. Habitat for Humanity, known around the world for providing homes for the poor, tithes contributions that it receives for each house in order to provide seed money for the next house.

The tithe, for the Christian, is not a bad thing, but it is not near the standard of giving for the household of Jesus Christ. The standard of giving for the household of Jesus Christ is given by the widow in the temple. When the widow put in two copper coins, she gave her livelihood, her living, her life. She did not give it in the expectation of losing her life. She gave it in the expectation of finding her life and gaining her life. The market economy finds it hard to accept the claim of Jesus that if you save your life you will lose it and if you give your life you will find it. If the church really wanted to follow the tithe, a congregation would say that the first 10 percent of the total income of its members should go to the poor. Then questions should be asked about the church building and salaries.[25]

---

25. Many national governments have programs that provide some help to the poor. Canadians, for example, have a long history of social programs, including Medicare, public housing, day-care subsidies, pensions, and family allowances. Vincent Alfano, then director of stewardship services for the United Church of Canada, noted that, over the past decade, he had heard many church people claim that a portion of their tithe for the poor is paid out in the form of higher taxes. These same people also claim their support of these government programs. It is important to remember that, in times of government budget cuts in Canada and the United States, these social programs are being reduced.

Provide Hospitality

Practicing *hospitality* is the fourth household rule. Hebrews 13:2 states: "Do not neglect to show hospitality to strangers, for by doing that some have entertained angels without knowing it."

Henri Nouwen described hospitality as "the virtue which allows us to break through the narrowness of our own fears and to open our houses to the stranger, with the intuition that salvation comes to us in the form of a tired traveler." He continued:

> Hospitality makes anxious disciples into powerful witnesses, makes suspicious owners into generous givers, and makes closed-minded sectarians into interested recipients of new ideas and insights.
>
> But it has become very difficult for us today to fully understand the implications of hospitality. Like the Semitic nomads, we live in a desert with many lonely travelers who are looking for a moment of peace, for a fresh drink and for a sign of encouragement so that they can continue their mysterious search for freedom.
>
> What does hospitality as a healing power require? It requires first of all that the host feel at home in his own house, and secondly that he create a free and fearless place for the unexpected visitor.[26]

Hospitality is open house to the stranger. The household of Jesus Christ is a household in which the stranger must be present in order for there to be dancing and joy. Hospitality is to create a home for the stranger. That is a main task of stewardship. Congregations need to ask themselves: "Does our church look like a home?" If it does, home to whom? This is not simply a matter of the building's physical appearance. What would make it feel like home to the stranger?

The story of Martha and Mary of Bethany, told in Luke 10:38-42, is typically interpreted so as to pit one sister against the other. Martha is chided by Jesus because of her unneeded acts of hospitality, while Mary is praised for her preference to listen to the teaching of

---

26. Henri J. M. Nouwen, *The Wounded Healer: Ministry in Contemporary Society* (Garden City, N.Y.: Doubleday & Company, Inc., 1972), p. 91.

Jesus. In a household, the kind of work that Martha was doing —
cleaning rooms, washing clothes, preparing meals — may seem unimportant, until suddenly it is not being done. Then everyone in the
house is acutely aware of what is missing. Martha's was the gift and
the practice of hospitality. Margaret Guenther wrote that Martha
should be thanked:

> We need to honor Martha and thank her for the order and
> comfort she brings to our lives. Most of the time I would rather
> be Mary. I prefer study to housekeeping. Presence at the liturgy
> brings me closer to God than mopping the kitchen floor. Time in
> prayer feels richer than time spent in committee meetings.
>
> On the other hand, maybe I am still a Martha. Maybe I want
> to go on being Martha, as long as I can reserve the right to
> occasionally and affectionately complain: "Lord, do you not care
> that my sisters and brothers have left me to do all the work by
> myself? Tell them to help me."[27]

As he quoted from Isaiah 61 when he went to his home synagogue to preach his first sermon, Jesus' words described a place of
hospitality for the stranger:

> The Spirit of the Lord is upon me,
> because he has anointed me to bring good news to the poor.
> He has sent me to proclaim release to the captives
> and recovery of sight to the blind,
> to let the oppressed go free,
> to proclaim the year of the Lord's favor. (Luke 4:18-19)

Isaiah 58 includes a beautiful promise of hospitality realized:

> Is not this the fast that I choose:
> to loose the bonds of injustice,
> to undo the thongs of the yoke,
> to let the oppressed go free,
> and to break every yoke?

27. Margaret Guenther, "Living by the Word: Honoring Martha," *The Christian Century,* 5 July 1995, p. 675.

Is it not to share your bread with the hungry,
and bring the homeless poor into your house;
when you see the naked, to cover them,
and not to hide yourself from your own kin?
Then your light shall break forth like the dawn,
and your healing shall spring up quickly;
your vindicator shall go before you,
the glory of the LORD shall be your rear guard.
Then you shall call, and the LORD will answer;
you shall cry for help, and he will say, Here I am. (Isa. 58:6-9)

Hospitality, at its best, is for members of the household and for the stranger.

Observe the Sabbath

The fifth and perhaps the most important household rule is observing the *sabbath*. The sabbath principle is embedded in the Ten Commandments.

In Exodus 20:8-11 the commandment is tied explicitly to the creation and God's rest on the seventh day:

Remember the sabbath day, and keep it holy. Six days you shall labor and do all your work. But the seventh day is a sabbath to the LORD your God; you shall not do any work — you, your son or your daughter, your male or female slave, your livestock, or the alien resident in your towns. For in six days the LORD made heaven and earth, the sea, and all that is in them, but rested the seventh day; therefore the LORD blessed the sabbath day and consecrated it.

The commandment, as found in Deuteronomy 5:12-15, focuses on justice and obedience:

Observe the sabbath day and keep it holy, as the LORD your God commanded you. Six days you shall labor and do all your work. But the seventh day is a sabbath to the LORD your God; you shall not do any work — you, or your son or your daughter, or your

128

male or female slave, or your ox or your donkey, or any of your livestock, or the resident alien in your towns, so that your male and female slave may rest as well as you. Remember that you were a slave in the land of Egypt, and the LORD your God brought you out from there with a mighty hand and an outstretched arm; therefore the LORD your God commanded you to keep the sabbath day.

Another text about the sabbath is found in Leviticus 23:3: "Six days shall work be done; but the seventh day is a sabbath of complete rest, a holy convocation; you shall do no work: it is a sabbath to the LORD throughout your settlements."

Sabbath as a day to be longed for and desired is described in the novel *Sotah*. Dina, an orthodox Jewish woman, has experienced extreme trauma and change in her life. She is suddenly and unexpectedly taken from Israel to New York City. Her longing for the sabbath is almost palpable:

> She went through the next day like a robot. The ache in her heart, so long numbed by the anesthetic of shocking change, now sent unbearable tremors through her whole being. The only idea that kept her from collapsing with grief and despair was one thought: The Sabbath was coming. Only one more day to the magic, healing balm of its peace and rest. Only one. Then she would have the time she needed to make some sense of all the contradictions, to meditate, to pray for understanding and forgiveness.
>
> She got up two hours early Friday morning, wanting to get all the chores done as soon as possible. She polished and scrubbed and dusted. She made breakfast and prepared the children's sandwiches for lunch.
>
> The day passed. The pale morning light waxed into the white-gold heat of midday, then began the gentle, subtle wane into dusk. She waited for the familiar soft glow of serenity to begin. Yet there was no change. The TV blared. The telephone rang and was answered. The kitchen appliances kept up their ordinary voices of rumbling activity. And outside in the street, cars and buses crisscrossed the restless face of the city.
>
> With a growing dull pain of recognition, Dina felt her heart

129

would finally break: here, in this house that had all the riches a human being could ever dream of, in this great city of overwhelming wealth and abundance, there would never be either peace or rest. The Sabbath would never stray through its heavily carved and polished mahogany doors, never weave its magic healing grace around its great streets and roads and thoroughfares. They were condemned to an eternity of weekdays, each one the same as the next, and she along with them.[28]

Clearly for Dina the need for sabbath transcended simple obedience to a commandment. The need for rest and the clash of two cultures that she experiences were marked and painful for her.

Some scholars have viewed the differing emphases in the Exodus and Deuteronomic texts as offering two distinct reasons for the same law. Though Exodus focuses on divine creation and "holy" rest and Deuteronomy on justice and obedience, the two are not inconsistent or incompatible. The principle of rest and cessation from work is in harmony with the principle of economic justice for workers. Working conditions that are just will include adequate time and opportunity for rest from that work.

A very significant New Testament text about the sabbath is found in Matthew 12:1-14:

> At that time Jesus went through the grainfields on the sabbath; his disciples were hungry, and they began to pluck heads of grain and to eat. When the Pharisees saw it, they said to him, "Look, your disciples are doing what is not lawful to do on the sabbath." He said to them, "Have you not read what David did when he and his companions were hungry? He entered the house of God and ate the bread of the Presence, which it was not lawful for him or his companions to eat, but only for the priests. Or have you not read in the law that on the sabbath the priests in the temple break the sabbath and yet are guiltless? I tell you, something greater than the temple is here. But if you had known what this means, 'I desire mercy and not sacrifice,' you would not have condemned the guiltless. For the Son of Man is lord of the sabbath."

28. Naomi Ragen, *Sotah* (New York: Crown Publishers, 1992), pp. 356-57.

He left that place and entered their synagogue; a man was there with a withered hand, and they asked him, "Is it lawful to cure on the sabbath?" so that they might accuse him. He said to them, "Suppose one of you has only one sheep and it falls into a pit on the sabbath; will you not lay hold of it and lift it out? How much more valuable is a human being than a sheep! So it is lawful to do good on the sabbath." Then he said to the man, "Stretch out your hand." He stretched it out, and it was restored, as sound as the other. But the Pharisees went out and conspired against him, how to destroy him.

This text is often mistakenly interpreted as an attempt to resolve a conflict between Jewish legalism and Jesus' freedom from the Law. To understand the text, it is important to look at the meaning of the sabbath in first-century Jewish life. M. Eugene Boring noted the great significance to observant Jews:

> The sabbath not only was commanded by God as part of the Decalogue, the fundamental covenant Law (Exod. 20:8-11; Deut. 5:12-15, in both cases expressed as the most elaborate of the Ten Commandments), but also was observed and blessed by God at the beginning of creation (Gen. 2:2-3). The sabbath had served for centuries as the distinctive mark of the people of God that separated them from Gentiles and presented a constant testimony to their faith in the one God. Sabbath keeping was not superficial or casual; in times of duress, faithful Israelites would die rather than break God's law by profaning the sabbath. To observant Jews, the sabbath was a joy, not a burden. The sabbath was a festive day of rest from labor, a day of eating and drinking on which it was forbidden to fast. From the beginning (Deut. 5:14-15) an element of social justice had been expressed in the law, for servants and slaves received a much-needed rest of which they could not be deprived, and the poor and hungry joined in the eating and drinking.
>
> Since the sabbath was central in Jewish life, its proper observance was important. In view of the ambiguity of the Scripture itself as to what constituted work, a body of tradition, having the force of religious law, had developed to guide the proper celebration of the sabbath. . . . Humane considerations were paramount.

Jewish tradition had already decided that "commandments that affect relations between human beings" take precedence over "commandments between God and human beings." Thus to set aside strict observance of the sabbath for human need was in Judaism not understood as setting aside superficial ritual in favor of human good, for ritual laws were considered important, a way of honoring God. Nonetheless, God wills that human good take precedence over laws that concern God's honor, so setting aside the strict observance of the sabbath for human good was a way of honoring God. This point was already made in Judaism; its exact application was disputed, however. Some rabbis taught that an animal that fell into a pit on the sabbath could be helped out; others (including the Essenes) specifically rejected this. Some Jews considered healing on the sabbath to be permitted; others only if life was endangered. The latter qualification was often understood very broadly; hunger might be considered life threatening.[29]

The stories about gleaning in the field and curing a man with a withered hand on the sabbath are not about rejection of the law. They were part of a debate within Judaism. It is clear that in first-century Jewish life, the sabbath had to do with economic justice, work, and rest.

The Christian church shifted the relevance of sabbath observance to a question of what can be done on Sundays. Historically, the question of working on Sundays did not become an issue until after the time of Constantine in the fourth century, when biblical sabbath legislation was applied to the Christian celebration. Boring noted that this was not done without hermeneutical violence. Boring continued:

> The Christian institution of the Lord's Day (Sunday), celebrating the resurrection of Jesus and traditionally concentrating on worship as the gathered Christian community, is a different kind of institution from the Jewish sabbath (Saturday), which is devoted to rest from labor and festive eating and drinking. The common

29. M. Eugene Boring, "The Gospel of Matthew," in *The New Interpreter's Bible*, vol. 8 (Nashville: Abingdon Press, 1995), p. 277.

ground between this sabbath text and Christian practice is not the issue of what is legal to do on the day of rest. Instead, we ponder where in our own situation is mercy more than sacrifice. Where is God's Law to be applied, not negated, in such a way that love is at its center?[30]

Did the church lose its way on this issue? Did the trivialization of the sabbath principle into a series of rules and blue laws obscure the core values of the principle and cause people to feel that observance of the rules and laws was trivial and bothersome? And did the subsequent rejection of those rules and blue laws by the North American culture, with support from most of the church, lead to a current situation in which the sabbath principle, if it is remembered at all by the church, is recalled as a quaint relic that has outlived its time and usefulness? The answers to all of these questions seem to be yes. The church now usually teaches that Jesus did away with the sabbath.

In the Torah there are many reasons for the sabbath. One obviously is that God rested on the seventh day. People need rest as well. But the sabbath most basically is about *justice*. During the twenty-four hours of the sabbath, the three things that most often serve as instruments of mutual exploitation come to an end: work, the rules of property, and consumption. Not only did Jesus not reject the sabbath, the sabbath was actually at the heart of Jesus' ministry. What he did was to intensify it — to bring the sabbath out of a twenty-four-hour period into the everyday. When there is no sabbath, as is generally true in North American culture, we create an economy that has no power to humanize and no power to limit greed, no power to limit possessiveness, no power to limit consumption.

On the night of December 11, 1995, a boiler at Malden Mills in Methuen, Massachusetts, exploded and set off a fire that injured twenty-seven people and destroyed three of the factory's century-old buildings. At first the economic implications seemed as devastating as the fire itself. The mill employed 2,400 people in an economically depressed area. Most of these workers assumed that their jobs were

---

30. Boring, "The Gospel of Matthew," p. 279.

gone. Aaron Feuerstein had kept the factory, started by his grandfather ninety years before, open and operating in Methuen when many textile manufacturers in New England had fled to the southern United States and to other countries. After the fire, several companies who bought from Malden Mills sent checks, as did many local citizens. Most significantly, three days later on December 14 when more than a thousand employees gathered in the high school gym, Feuerstein, who had already given out $275 Christmas bonuses and pledged to rebuild, walked to the podium and made this announcement:

> For the next 30 days — and it might be more — all our employees will be paid their full salaries. But over and above the money, the most important thing Malden Mills can do for our workers is to get you back to work. By January 2, we will restart operations, and within 90 days we will be fully operational.[31]

Needless to say, the scene was one of hugging and cheering. It is worth noting that Feuerstein reads the Talmud almost every night. While this story does not directly involve the sabbath, it does illustrate the sabbath principle of economic justice and concern for workers.

Richard Lowery described the power of a vision informed by the sabbath concept:

> Sabbath offers a compelling vision of hope at the beginning of what may not be a "Christian Century," but must be a century of lavish generosity for the sake of human survival. Perhaps in such a world, the love of God will rule and genuine pluralism will be possible. The dark glass will be less cloudy and the holy vision of the exiled poet will shine through with stunning color and detail: "all who keep sabbath without profaning it and who hold my covenant firm, I will bring them to my holy mountain, make them joyful in my house of prayer. Indeed, my house will be called a house of prayer for all peoples" (Isa. 56:6-7).[32]

---

31. "The Glow from a Fire," *Time*, 8 Jan. 1996, p. 49.

32. Richard H. Lowery, "From Covenant to Sabbath," *Journal of Stewardship* 46 (1994): 31.

Probably there can be no Christian stewardship without regaining the sabbath.

Five Rules: One Concern

The concept that binds the five rules of the household of God is concern for the poor, the oppressed, the vulnerable, and the stranger. Each in turn expresses concern that reaches beyond the members of the household: do not charge interest to the poor; leave gleanings (for the poor and the stranger); give the tithe (for the poor); provide hospitality (to the poor and the stranger); and observe the sabbath (with economic justice for the poor, the oppressed, and the vulnerable).

The congregation that seeks to base its life on the characteristics and rules of the household of God will discover new insights and vantage points about what it means to be a household of God. It will be a congregation that cares deeply about the poor, the oppressed, and the stranger. It will be willing to take risks that the world will consider foolish. Yet, merely saying that it wants to be a household of God does not mean that a congregation will become a household of God. The process is not easy or automatic. The bothersome question of "how?" is always waiting to be considered and answered.

In the next chapter, we will look at the life and work of the congregation as a household of God and, specifically, at instruments of Christian stewardship that can help a congregation move from a state of amnesia to become a household of God.

CHAPTER SIX

Life and Work of the Congregation as a Household of God

Preach the gospel always; if necessary, use words.

Francis of Assisi

The Elusive Goal

The reader may think that the household characteristics and rules detailed in the last chapter sound good on paper but wonder how a congregation can move away from being a household of amnesia to become a household of God. What programs exist — or need to be developed — to move toward this desirable but seemingly elusive goal? Is it merely a castle of clouds in the sky that will evaporate in the light and heat of the blazing sun of "reality"? The obstacles and difficulties are real and should not be minimized. With the leading and power of God, however, it is possible to overcome them.

Where can a congregation begin? Most congregations initially look beyond themselves for help, solutions, and resources. Denominational offices, parachurch organizations, for-profit companies, and consultants (some or all of these) may be considered as possible sources for a sense of direction and help in moving from "here" to

136

"there." Some of these may provide resources and materials that give a burst of improvement and bring hope to a congregation. Alas, in most cases the progress turns out to be short-term and illusory. Perhaps the reason is that *the solutions offered are usually based on the same presuppositions of modernity that led the church to become a household of amnesia in the first place.*

Instead, the congregation should seek solutions and methodologies that are built on assumptions rooted in the concept of the congregation as a household of God, bound to outcomes based on the logic of the gospel rather than on the logic of a consumer society whose allegiance is not to God. These solutions and methodologies can be characterized as instruments of Christian stewardship.

An Instrument of Amnesia

Before looking at instruments of Christian stewardship for the congregation, it will be helpful to look at one of the chief instruments used in and by the household of amnesia. I refer specifically to television and the impact that it has had on North American culture. *TV Guide,* the magazine that has grown along with the television industry, reported some startling data from the American experience:

- Half of all U.S. children ages 6 to 17 have a TV in their room.
- The average American child will have watched 100,000 acts of dramatized violence on television by the end of sixth grade, and seen 20,000 murders enacted before turning 18.
- Prior to kindergarten, the average child will see 5,000 hours of television.
- A favorite children's video is watched an average of 13 times.
- Each day, the average American child spends 4 hours watching TV, 10 hours sleeping, 6 hours in school, and 4 hours on other activities (eating, visiting, playing sports, doing chores, homework).
- Children may have watched up to 22,000 hours of TV by the time they graduate from high school.

- 20% of kids who watch more than 5 hours a day are obese.
- The average American child sees 20,000 commercials each year.
- 70% of TV viewers say they tune in for escape; only 1 in 10 look to television for intellectual stimulation.
- 60% of Americans regularly watch TV while eating dinner.[1]

These statistics tell a story of family households engrossed in a medium that can lead to a form of amnesia. This is not to say that the medium of electronic telecommunication is inherently bad. Essentially, the system known as television is a way of conveying a stream of electrons that creates images and sound. What matters is what images and sounds people choose to listen to and watch. It is not encouraging, however, to note that 70 percent of television viewers say they look to television for escape. Escape can easily become a way to forget life's harsh realities — a search for the numbing effects of amnesia. It is almost a way of saying that death (escape) is preferred to life (harsh reality).

The gospel of Jesus Christ, of course, is the story of life triumphing over death. The gospel declares that *new life* is available in Jesus Christ. To proclaim this reality and to be part of a household of God (of life) instead of a household of amnesia (of death) requires countercultural acts. It is to belong not to the culture into which we happened to be born, but to the household into which God calls us. Ellen T. Charry wrote: "[Christians] are directed by God, whose call to live a holy life dedicated to the rescue of others is laid bare in the life, death and resurrection of Jesus Christ."[2]

What instruments does the church have available to create and sustain a household of God? Are they as powerful and effective as the instruments that create a household of amnesia? I believe that instruments to create and sustain a household of God exist and *can* be more powerful and effective than any of the instruments that lead to a household of amnesia.

1. "Digital-Age Data," *TV Guide,* 26 Oct.–1 Nov. 1996, p. 68.
2. Ellen T. Charry, "Sacraments for the Christian Life," *The Christian Century,* 15 Nov. 1995, p. 1076.

Instruments of Christian Stewardship

What *instruments* are available to the church to create and develop a household of God? The instruments of Christian stewardship do not originate in new, sophisticated stewardship programs from ecumenical centers or denominational headquarters. The true instruments of Christian stewardship have been available to the church for centuries. The problem with ministry today is that we have almost systematically forgotten these instruments or have so limited them that they have no power to shape a new household. The instruments of Christian stewardship we will explore are:

1. Word/the news of God; the gospel *(kerygma);*
2. Water/baptism;
3. Table and bread/the Eucharist;
4. Towel/stole *(diakonia);*
5. Community/congregation *(koinonia);*
6. God's mission to the world/outreach/apostolic mission (God's love/passion *[agape]* for the world).[3]

At first glance, these instruments seem staid and outdated. After all, it may be reasoned, if they could provide a solution, the church would not be in the kind of trouble it is. Perhaps the reality is that the church has tended to overlook or neglect these instruments. An in-depth look at each one is in order.

The Word/The Gospel

The first instrument is "the word" or "gospel." But what is meant by these words? To answer this question, let us first look at some biblical texts:

The word *gospel* appears seventy times in sixty-three verses in

3. M. Douglas Meeks presented this list of six instruments of Christian stewardship at an Educational Event for Stewardship Leaders in Bolton, Ontario, in July 1993.

CONGREGATIONS AT THE CROSSROADS

the New Testament — a significant number of times. The text of Mark 8:34–9:1, a statement of Jesus about what it means to follow him, gives a clear indication of the high importance of the gospel. Verse 35 reads: "For those who want to save their life will lose it, and those who lose their life for my sake, and for the sake of the gospel, will save it."

What is the gospel that followers of Jesus should be willing to lose their lives for it? The word *gospel* itself (Greek, *euangélion;* Latin, *evangelium*) is most often understood as good news, specifically the good news of salvation through Jesus Christ. Strangely, it would seem, the primary cause of death and persecution for followers of Jesus was their proclamation of the gospel — the good news about Jesus Christ. Why would people get angry enough to kill because they were told good news? The answer is that what is good news for the outcasts, the poor, and the oppressed can *seem to be* bad news for the oppressors. Reversals can move in two directions.

Not only did proclamation of the gospel lead to persecution and death, other biblical texts, for example, the parable of the sower, make clear that some may lose their faith because concern for wealth and other earthly things takes a position prior to the gospel. Some persons fear God's divine reversals.

Pheme Perkins wrote that "the disciples have participated in Jesus' ministry of preaching and healing. . . . Now they discover that they must also participate in the ministry of suffering. Anyone who attempts to call the world to account before the gospel must be ready to sacrifice self-interest. The gospel was not formulated for the convenience of those who would preach it to others."[4]

Other texts also speak to "word" or "gospel":

Galatians 1:6-7: "I am astonished that you are so quickly deserting the one who called you in the grace of Christ and are turning to a different gospel — not that there is another gospel, but there are some who are confusing you and want to pervert the gospel of Christ."

4. Pheme Perkins, "The Gospel of Mark," in *The New Interpreter's Bible,* vol. 8 (Nashville: Abingdon Press, 1995), p. 628.

140

The term *word* is used to refer both to the gospel and to God:

John 1:1-2: "In the beginning was the Word, and the Word was with God, and the Word was God. He was in the beginning with God."

Matthew 4:4: "But he answered, 'It is written, "One does not live by bread alone, but by every word that comes from the mouth of God."'"

Colossians 3:16-17: "Let the word of Christ dwell in you richly; teach and admonish one another in all wisdom; and with gratitude in your hearts sing psalms, hymns, and spiritual songs to God. And whatever you do, in word or deed, do everything in the name of the Lord Jesus, giving thanks to God the Father through him."

The Church, gathered and formed by the word of God, is called to proclaim the gospel of Jesus Christ. An essential way in which the gospel is proclaimed is testimony. For the making of stewards, testimony is absolutely necessary. This means much more than a preacher in a pulpit. It also means individual Christians who are willing and able to tell the truth about what Jesus has done in their lives. This testimony has validity and power only when it is firsthand testimony. To be credible, the spoken testimony must have a life consistent with the testimony standing behind it. Finally, as in a courtroom, Christians must be able and willing to withstand rigorous cross-examination — to have hard questions about their testimony pressed upon them.[5]

5. The word *testimony* is used here in the sense of a statement made in court as a witness under oath or affirmation. It is a sharing of one's story or faith journey at the deepest level. Such use, for example, is in harmony with Martin Luther's position when he said, "Here I stand; I can do no other." Giving testimony implies a willingness to speak as a witness, even at risk to oneself. This stands in sharp contrast to the way the word *testimony* is sometimes used by individuals to describe emotionally satisfying experiences with God. The giving of testimony is more than saying, "I feel good because. . . ."

141

William Willimon wrote about the danger of allowing a gap between us and the gospel. Often, he observed, we are concerned about a communication gap between speaker and listener or between writer and reader. There is another gap — one that ought to concern us even more — and that is the space between us and the gospel. "Contemporary homiletical thought has focused upon style, rhetoric, or method when theology ought to be our concern. Our problem as preachers is not that we must render strange biblical stories intelligible to modern people but rather that these strange biblical stories render a strange God." He observed that when the preacher tries to answer the "so what" question about those strange biblical stories, the answers are too often "limited by my present horizons, by conventional ideas of what can and cannot be."[6] When such a gap exists, the credibility and power of testimony is diluted — even destroyed.

Willimon argued that people are captured by stories that are not the gospel:

> People live in the grip of stories which are not the gospel, stories which cannot generate the life for which they deeply yearn. Therefore I agree with Walter Brueggemann when he says that "evangelism means inviting people into those stories [the gospel] as the definitional story of our life, and thereby authorizing people to give up, abandon, and renounce other stories that have shaped their lives in false or distorting ways."[7]

Disciples of Jesus are not sent out as conquering heroes into the consumer society of modernity to become burdened with things and goods. When Jesus sent his disciples out (see Luke 10:1-20), they were told that they were sent out like lambs into the midst of wolves, without purse, bag, or sandals. They were to travel light, so as to keep their mobility and not be impeded on their journey.

6. William H. Willimon, "Easter Preaching as Peculiar Speech," *Journal for Preachers,* Easter 1994, p. 3.

7. Willimon, "Easter Preaching," p. 7. Willimon's reference to Brueggemann is found in Walter Brueggemann, *Biblical Perspectives on Evangelism: Living in a Three-Storied Universe* (Nashville: Abingdon Press, 1993), p. 10.

Further, faithful preaching of the gospel is not to be based on consumer polls to determine what the people want. James M. Wall described a preaching event in the life of John Wesley that makes this point forcefully:

> When John Wesley preached standing on a tombstone because he was barred from the local Anglican church — and was too short to be seen otherwise — he delivered a demanding message which no survey would have identified as high on the neighborhood's list of priorities. Wesley was certainly in rebellion against the mainstream tradition of his day, (though the Methodist movement that emerged from his rebellion eventually became a part of the American religious mainstream). But Wesley didn't give his followers what they wanted; he gave them what he felt commanded to preach.[8]

In North America, the "word" that competes with the gospel is the lure of the benefits of modernity. That testimony is easier to hear, and to make, than testimony about the logic of the gospel. The gospel is a powerful instrument and, at the same time, one that can be dangerous to handle. Probably that is why use of this powerful instrument is talked about more than it is practiced.

Baptism/Water

The second instrument of Christian stewardship is baptism/water. The word *baptism* and its variations occur numerous times in the New Testament.[9] Pertinent scriptural passages include two verses that are clear that the act of baptism is an identification with Jesus Christ, especially in his death and his resurrection:

Romans 6:4: "Therefore we have been buried with him by

---

8. James M. Wall, "Viewing the Megachurch: Between a Gush and a Smirk," *The Christian Century,* 22 March 1995, p. 315.

9. *Baptism* occurs 21 times in 21 verses in the New Testament; *baptize* and *baptizes* 10 times in 7 verses; *baptized* 52 times in 46 verses; and *baptizing* 9 times in 9 verses.

baptism into death, so that, just as Christ was raised from the dead by the glory of the Father, so we too might walk in newness of life."

Galatians 3:27: "As many of you as were baptized into Christ have clothed yourselves with Christ."

Other verses refer to different factors:

Acts 2:38 relates baptism to the forgiveness of sins: "Peter said to them, 'Repent, and be baptized every one of you in the name of Jesus Christ so that your sins may be forgiven; and you will receive the gift of the Holy Spirit.'"

1 Corinthians 12:13 connects baptism to the unity of the body of Christ: "For in the one Spirit we were all baptized into one body — Jews or Greeks, slaves or free — and we were all made to drink of one Spirit."

Matthew 28:19-20 views baptism as part of the command to go and make disciples of all nations: "Go therefore and make disciples of all nations, baptizing them in the name of the Father and of the Son and of the Holy Spirit, and teaching them to obey everything that I have commanded you. And remember, I am with you always, to the end of the age."

Most churches — both those that practice infant baptism and those that baptize believers — see baptism primarily as a rite of entry into the church; some see baptism as giving assurance of salvation. These views diminish the full meaning of baptism. Baptism is not simply a passage of entry into the church. It is the way in which the church exists. As noted earlier, *the church is not a volunteer association; it is a covenanted people created by the reality of baptism.* The congregation is called together fundamentally to make a case in word and deed for Jesus. The shape of life in Jesus is what is meant to be the shape of the whole creation. Baptism is not a one-time experience; it is a full-time job.

144

Baptism as an experience that has ongoing meaning and implications was beautifully described by Charry:

> On the occasion of my baptism, a friend wrote: "Try to remember deliberately once a day that you were and are baptized, that your life is underwritten by God and that in a sense this grandest position in life has already been achieved. You can never go higher than simple baptism. In a sense, this is a release from striving. What was sought for long and hard has not been found, it has found you.[10]

In another article, Charry pointed to the mutual responsibility and interrelationship of those who are baptized:

> Churches need to realize that all baptized Christians are responsible for forming one another in Christ. True, parents and teachers are very important. But every time one participates in the covenant of baptism one renews one's own baptismal covenant and promises (in the words of the Book of Common Prayer) to "do all in [one's] power to support these persons in their life in Christ." This public vow is the proper starting point for the formation of Christians.[11]

The gospel expects, promises transformation. In short, it promises conversion.

> [P]ut away your former way of life, your old self, corrupt and deluded by its lusts, and . . . be renewed in the spirit of your minds, and . . . clothe yourselves with the new self, created according to the likeness of God in true righteousness and holiness. (Eph. 4:22-24)

The image of taking off old clothes to be clothed with a new self and putting away our past is clearly baptismal. Baptism is a beginning *and* an ending.

---

10. Charry, "Sacraments for the Christian Life," p. 1076.

11. Charry, "Raising Christian Children in a Pagan Culture," *The Christian Century,* 16 Feb. 1994, p. 167.

The power of baptism is depicted in Ralph Wood's description of a baptism he witnessed in a minimum-security prison. The prisoner had been convicted of a heinous crime — one for which he was despised by the other prisoners. Following a visit by his wife and daughter in which they told him they forgave him, he had knelt and begged for the mercy of God and his family. He had then requested baptism by the pastor of a nearby rural Baptist church. The description is vivid:

> After a pastoral prayer, the barefoot prisoner stepped into a wooden box that had been lined with a plastic sheet and filled with water. It looked like a large coffin, and rightly so. . . . Pronouncing the Trinitarian formula, the pastor lowered the new Christian down into the liquid grave to be buried with Christ and then raised him up to life eternal. Though the water was cold, the man was not eager to get out. Instead, he stood there weeping for joy. When at last he left the baptismal box, I thought he would hurry away to change into something dry. I was mistaken. "I want to wear these clothes as long as I can," he said. "In fact, I wish I never had to take a shower again." And so we walked to the nearby tables and sat quietly in the Carolina sun, hearing this newly minted Christian explain why his baptismal burial was too good to dry off. "I'm now a free man," he declared. "I'm not impatient to leave prison because this wire can't shackle my soul."[12]

Wood also noted that Martin Luther's confession stated that, even in baptism, the old Adam remains a frightfully good swimmer. When faced with satanic assaults, Luther would grab a slate and chalk these words: "I have been baptized."[13]

Baptism is a powerful and much underrated instrument of Christian stewardship.

12. Ralph C. Wood, "Baptism in a Coffin," *The Christian Century,* 21 Oct. 1992, p. 926.
13. Wood, "Baptism in a Coffin," p. 926.

The Eucharist/Table/Bread

We have already noted that the image of table is central to the gospel of Jesus Christ. The words *table* and *bread* are much used in the New Testament.[14] These biblical passages are particularly pertinent:

> Matthew 6:11 indicates that bread is needed daily, and that the source is God: "Give us this day our daily bread."

> Matthew 26:26 describes Jesus' use of bread at the Last Supper: "While they were eating, Jesus took a loaf of bread, and after blessing it he broke it, gave it to the disciples, and said, 'Take, eat; this is my body.'" The passage in 1 Corinthians 11:23-34 is the best-known account of the Last Supper.

> Luke 22:30 speaks of a messianic feast: "so that you may eat and drink at my table in my kingdom, and you will sit on thrones judging the twelve tribes of Israel."

> Luke 24:30-35 recounts how Jesus was made known in the breaking of bread at the home of two followers in Emmaus:

> > When he was at the table with them, he took bread, blessed and broke it, and gave it to them. Then their eyes were opened, and they recognized him; and he vanished from their sight. They said to each other, "Were not our hearts burning within us while he was talking to us on the road, while he was opening the scriptures to us?" That same hour they got up and returned to Jerusalem; and they found the eleven and their companions gathered together. They were saying, "The Lord has risen indeed, and he has appeared to Simon!" Then they told what had happened on the road, and how he had been made known to them in the breaking of the bread.

14. *Bread* occurs 80 times in 74 verses in the New Testament; *table* 26 times in 24 verses.

Acts 2:42-46 describes the sharing that took place around the table in the early church:

> They devoted themselves to the apostles' teaching and fellowship, to the breaking of bread and the prayers. Awe came upon everyone, because many wonders and signs were being done by the apostles. All who believed were together and had all things in common; they would sell their possessions and goods and distribute the proceeds to all, as any had need. Day by day, as they spent much time together in the temple, they broke bread at home and ate their food with glad and generous hearts.

Luke 22:27 speaks to the issue of who is greater at the table: "For who is greater, the one who is at the table or the one who serves? Is it not the one at the table? But I am among you as one who serves."

In a presentation made at a session of the North American Conference on Christian Philanthropy, Catherine Gunsalus González and Justo L. González talked about the third miracle of the manna. They described the surprising gift of bread that Israel received in the wilderness and that the disciples received at the Last Supper. In each case, the gift of bread "shows forth the presence and redemptive work of God in the midst of the people of God."[15] They pointed out that sharing is inherent in the distribution of bread, but it is more than that as well:

> [T]he God of the Bible is the God of the manna, the God who provides food for the people in the desert, and who also redistributes it when the people foolishly produce an unjust distribution. The God of the Bible is the God to whom Christians must pray for the right amount, for daily bread, for that which is neither too much nor too little. Because this is the God whom the

15. Catherine Gunsalus González and Justo L. González in a presentation titled "Managing the Manna" at the North American Conference on Christian Philanthropy in April 1996 in Toronto.

Corinthians claim to worship, their community must be one which seeks to repeat the miracle of the manna, to distribute and share its resources in imitation of what God did for the people of Israel in the desert, so that the abundance of some may supply the want of others, and there be equality, as it is written, "He who gathered much had nothing over, and he who gathered little had no lack."

All around us, God provides the manna — the bountiful resources of the earth. We are commanded to gather it in thanksgiving and praise, as the children of Israel did. And we are also commanded to share it in equality and justice, as faithful followers of the God who in the desert not only provided the manna, but also saw to its distribution.[16]

Having described two events of bread — the manna in the wilderness and the Last Supper — they closed their presentation by saying: "When the Holy Spirit is fully leading the congregation, the church itself is the third miracle of the manna. What a witness to the world that would be."[17]

At table, everybody eats. Much of the ministry of Jesus took place at table. In the early church, when people gathered for dinner, they ate and celebrated. They stayed at the table until the problems of the community, the household, were solved.

As Meeks reminded us, stewards are created at the household's table, at the Eucharist. It is more than an event that takes a few minutes within the worship service. It is an event that gives shape to the whole of life. The sacraments are dangerous. If they are practiced with faithfulness and intentionality, they will change lives. The Eucharist is crucial in the development of stewards because it models sharing.

The Towel/The Stole

The towel, or stole, is the fourth instrument of Christian stewardship. Again, we look at a related biblical text:

16. González and González.
17. González and González.

John 13:4-5 describes the scene at the Last Supper when Jesus "got up from the table, took off his outer robe, and tied a towel around himself. Then he poured water into a basin and began to wash the disciples' feet and to wipe them with the towel that was tied around him."

Just as Christ came into the world not to be served but to serve, so the church, called to carry out God's mission, seeks to serve. Dietrich Bonhoeffer called for a servant church: "The Church is the Church only when it exists for others."[18] Harvey Cox wrote that "the church's task in the secular city is to be the *diakonos*[19] of the city, the servant who bends himself to struggle for its wholeness and health."[20] Paul in Philippians 2:7 wrote of Jesus emptying himself and "taking the form of a servant."

As servant, the church is conscious of its own needs and the needs of the world. The role of servant may well enable the church to overcome its pride, egoism, and callousness. That was the model that Jesus lifted up his inaugural address sermon of Luke 4. Jesus made it clear that "he who is greatest among you shall be your servant" (Matt. 23:11).

The towel, symbolized by the stole worn by many pastors, is a symbol of service. People do not become stewards unless they are working together. Matthew 25 and the seven traditional *diakonic* acts — feeding the hungry, clothing the naked (including housing and shelter), visiting the sick, visiting the prisoner, burying the dead, practicing hospitality, and giving a cup of cold water — are good starting points. It is service done for others without expectation of reward or benefit. It is service done for those who may be undeserving or even unappreciative. It is service that may be unpleasant and even dangerous. It is not done for glory. The one who is a disciple is willing to take risks, even to endanger his or her own life in the process.

18. Dietrich Bonhoeffer, *Letters and Papers from Prison,* rev. ed. (New York: Macmillan, 1967), p. 211.

19. A Greek word meaning "a servant, a deacon."

20. Harvey Cox, *The Secular City* (New York: The MacMillan Co., 1965), p. 134.

As I mentioned in a footnote in chapter one, I once heard of a church that had the custom of presenting a stole to new members of the congregation. During their preparation, each person chose a field of service in the life and ministry of the congregation. Each new member then became a member of an "Abrahamic group" and participated in the type of ministry that he or she had selected. The stole was and continued to be a symbol of commitment to that service.

The symbol in the ministry of Jesus was the foot washing at the Last Supper. Without service *(diakonia)*, we can never get to mission. It is the way to prepare for mission.

The Community/Congregation/Koinonia

The fifth instrument of Christian stewardship is the congregation itself, sometimes referred to as the community or fellowship (Greek, *koinonia*). A number of scriptural passages are relevant:

> Acts 6:2 speaks of the disciples as a community: "And the twelve called together the whole community of the disciples and said, 'It is not right that we should neglect the word of God in order to wait on tables.'"

> The benediction to the community, as described in Ephesians 6:23, is a call for peace, love, and faith, with God as the source: "Peace be to the whole community, and love with faith, from God the Father and the Lord Jesus Christ."

> The church is to go on the offensive, knowing that the gates of hell themselves will not be able to withstand its attack (Matt. 16:18): "And I tell you, you are Peter, and on this rock I will build my church, and the gates of Hades will not prevail against it."

> God provides appointed leaders with the needed gifts to lead the church (1 Cor. 12:28): "And God has appointed in the

church first apostles, second prophets, third teachers; then deeds of power, then gifts of healing, forms of assistance, forms of leadership, various kinds of tongues."

In 1 Timothy 3:15, the church is explicitly identified as the household of God: "if I am delayed, you may know how one ought to behave in the household of God, which is the church of the living God, the pillar and bulwark of the truth."

The church, at its best, has the character of a community. This image is supported by biblical images that speak of the body of Christ (Romans 12 and 1 Corinthians 12). The church is viewed as analogous to a human body with dependence and interdependence of all the parts.

The community is called to walk justly, learning what justice is through love. A new community is formed as the character and rules of the household are remembered and the instruments of Christian stewardship are used.

God's Mission to the World

Finally, we come to the sixth instrument of Christian stewardship: God's mission to the world.[21] Strangely, as much as the church talks about mission, the word itself is seldom used in the New Testament in the sense that the church is accustomed to using it. The text most often quoted in the context of mission to the world is Matthew 28:19-20, where Jesus said:

Go therefore and make disciples of all nations, baptizing them in the name of the Father and of the Son and of the Holy Spirit, and teaching them to obey everything that I have commanded you. And remember, I am with you always, to the end of the age.

21. "God's mission to the world" is also discussed in the previous chapter as a characteristic of the household of God: the church exists for the sake of God's mission.

Yet, as noted in chapter one, this text, usually referred to as the Great Commission, does not use the word "mission" or "commission." The only New Testament text that uses the word "mission" as the church commonly uses it is Acts 12:25: "Then after completing their mission Barnabas and Saul returned to Jerusalem and brought with them John, whose other name was Mark."

It is ironic that the church uses several key biblical words so sparingly and elevates other words that are either not used in the Bible or appear infrequently. Part of the truncation that commonly takes place in the life of the church is when members jump so immediately to mission that they, in effect, bypass the first five instruments. The first five instruments have two factors in common: all five relate strongly to the worship experience of the congregation and they all deal with issues of justice. This "jumping to the end" encourages Christians to skip the work of discipleship in their own lives and to feel good about providing financial support for the mission programs of the denomination. Sometimes, denominations, in their eagerness to raise mission dollars, encourage this mind-set.

The church in North America has almost forgotten the first five of these six instruments; they have been so diminished and under-used that their power to shape a new household is lost. Only when pastor and people work together with the guidance of the Holy Spirit to explore how *all* these instruments can be used effectively to create a new household will the congregation truly become a household of Jesus Christ where new stewards are created. As the instruments are used, the congregation can learn and practice the household rules of the gospel instead of the market society created by modernity. The difference between the economy of gift (the gospel) and the economy of commodity (modernity) is to *remember that God held nothing back.* All that God has given to us is a pure gift of grace.

Where Are the Instruments Used?

In the life of a congregation that is striving to be the household of God, the worship experience is the setting where the six instruments of Christian stewardship can be used most effectively. In worship the invisible reality of God becomes real. Each of the six instruments can and should play a vital role in the worship life of a congregation. In worship the characteristics of the household of God can be developed and made manifest; the rules of the household can be learned and followed; and the instruments that God has given the church utilized. The life of the congregation, especially in its manifestation in worship, will reflect and embody concern for the poor, the oppressed, the vulnerable, and the stranger.

As pastor and people think tangibly and concretely about how to create a new household, the critical importance of small groups in the congregation should not be overlooked. Some congregations have had a good experience with the use of covenant discipleship groups: *covenant* as the reality of baptismal promises made and given and *discipleship* as the means of freedom — the means by which, in obedience to Jesus Christ, the Christian becomes free.

Ultimately, of course, freedom comes because of God's victory over death and sin and evil in the resurrection of Jesus Christ. The resurrection creates a resurrection household with the household rules of the gospel. Then the household can stand against the power of death. The church can echo the words of 1 Corinthians 15:

> When this perishable body puts on imperishability, and this mortal body puts on immortality, then the saying that is written will be fulfilled:
>
> "Death has been swallowed up in victory."
> "Where, O death, is your victory? Where, O death, is your sting?"
> The sting of death is sin, and the power of sin is the law.
> But thanks be to God,
> who gives us the victory through our Lord Jesus Christ.
> (1 Cor. 15:54-57)

Most people gather in worship and participate in the life of the congregation with the odd expectation that they will be subverted — that God will undermine their illusions and unfounded assumptions and bring them to a new reality: new life in Jesus Christ. The church owes them no less.

In the next chapter, we will look at the strategic importance of worship for the congregation that is seeking to become a household of God.

CHAPTER SEVEN

Worship in the Household of God

The church desperately needs to engage in worship that is authentic and an end in itself.

For a congregation that seriously wants to leave a state of amnesia and become a household of God, worship is a critical focal point. In chapters five and six, we commented on characteristics and rules of the Christian congregation as a household of God and instruments of Christian stewardship that the congregation can use to move toward this goal. The question we now consider is how these factors can be brought together and integrated successfully in worship.

The Purpose of Worship

Renewal and transformation of the church will not and cannot come without reform of the worship experience in congregations. Worship will not be a focal point to transform the life of a congregation unless and until the congregation first understands the intent and purpose of worship.

Leander E. Keck described a cartoon in which a man was carrying a sandwich board on which is printed: "Repent!" Near the bottom, in small print, was the sentence: "If you have already re-

pented please disregard this notice."[1] Keck noted that some persons
think that repentance has already taken place through the reform of
worship within mainline denominations. Such persons point to use
of the lectionary, the preacher moving away from the pulpit onto the
floor with the congregation, the wearing of color-coded vestments,
the use of experimental worship, and the practice of embracing one
another and engaging in conversation under the rubric of "passing
the peace." Such change has taken place, but, in the words of Keck,
"in many cases it has amounted to little more than a substitution of
the trivial for the ossified!"[2] What is needed in worship transcends
such issues as use of the lectionary, where the preacher stands, the
colors and types of vestments, experimentation in worship, and
rubrics such as "passing the peace." This is not to say that these
matters are not worthy of discussion and decision, but they hold a
lower level of priority than do other questions to which we shall
turn our attention.

William Willimon wrote: "Because worship is an act of the church
and because the church is before all else a community at worship
before God in Christ, worship precedes theological reflection and
subordinates it. . . . The church's worship is nothing other than the
church's faith in motion, both in its most sublime and on its most
practical levels."[3] While it is true that the word *liturgy* is rooted in Greek
words meaning "the work of the people," it is nonetheless also true that
the pastor carries a crucial role in planning and leading the worship
experience. How seriously this responsibility is taken by the pastor will
affect not only the worship experience itself but the total life of the
congregation. In the next chapter, we will look at the roles of the pastor
and the laity in the congregation. Willimon defined worship as "learning to pay attention," by which he meant that it is not easy to pay more
attention to God and less to myself.[4]

1. Leander E. Keck, *The Church Confident* (Nashville: Abingdon Press, 1993),
p. 25.
2. Keck, *The Church Confident*.
3. William H. Willimon, *Peculiar Speech: Preaching to the Baptized* (Grand
Rapids, Mich.: Wm. B. Eerdmans Publishing Co., 1992), p. 4.
4. William H. Willimon, *The Intrusive Word: Preaching to the Unbaptized*
(Grand Rapids, Mich.: Wm. B. Eerdmans Publishing Co., 1994), p. 43.

Worship, at its best, is an act of praise to God that the one worshiping exists, that the community of faith exists, and that the world exists. Such praise acknowledges that the reason for one's existence lies beyond our individual existence in the generosity of God. Such praise makes us aware that our very existence, the existence of the community of faith, and the existence of the world itself do not depend on us, but on God. The church, as a community of faith, "as an alternative community in the world is not a 'voluntary association,' an accident of human preference. The church as a wedge of newness, as a foretaste of what is coming, as a home for the odd ones, is the work of God's originary mercy. For all its distortedness, the church peculiarly hosts God's power for life."[5]

When worship is seen as praise of God for its own sake, and not for some other purpose, it is subversive. Walter Brueggemann used the story of the shepherds at the birth of Jesus to illustrate a situation where the act of praise became their chief end in life. They "returned, glorifying and praising God for all they had heard and seen" (Luke 2:20). "What they had seen and heard was nothing less than the emergence of a new reality in the midst of their need and deprivation. The shepherds are among the first witnesses, who, when they see Jesus, grasp in an inchoate way that the old world had been invaded, occupied, and transformed."[6]

Worship that is trivialized and secularized cannot transform a congregation. The church desperately needs to engage in worship that is authentic and an end in itself. Though it sounds strange to our modern ears, worship is not for ourselves; it is for praise of the living God. To praise the Creator God with joy acknowledges that we did not make ourselves, but that we "are contingent on the One who cannot and must not be reduced to the guarantor of our cultures."[7]

Denominational calendars give a great deal of space to promote

5. Walter Brueggemann, *Texts Under Negotiation: The Bible and Postmodern Imagination* (Minneapolis: Fortress Press, 1993), p. 36.
6. Walter Brueggemann, *Biblical Perspectives on Evangelism: Living in a Three-Storied Universe* (Nashville: Abingdon Press, 1993), p. 34.
7. Keck, *The Church Confident*, p. 30.

denominational programs on the Sundays listed in the calendar and relatively little space to lift up events and celebrations that are an intrinsic part of the Christian faith. The calendar of one denomination, for example, listed thirty-two denominational programs or emphases in ten months. Only the summer months of July and August escaped such listings. Too often such promotional listings are aimed more at furthering the cause of the institutional church than they are at helping to create and strengthen the church as the household of God. If the listings related to Advent, Christmas, Lent, Easter, and Pentecost were eliminated, little other than denominational promotion would remain. To the extent that congregations follow such a calendar, the worship service is altered significantly. In the words of Keck, "what remains of the worship portion of the hour is related to the real, vital worship of God as junk food is related to a banquet."[8]

Much of the worship experience in North American Christian congregations is joyless and trivial. The praise of God cannot be joyless. If joy is absent, the praise of God is not authentic. Why is worship so often without joy? Keck wrote:

> Perhaps we are more impressed by the problems of the world than by the power of God. Perhaps we have become so secular that we indeed think that now everything depends on us; that surely ought to make us depressed. Perhaps we have simply gotten bored with a boring God whom we substituted for the God of the Bible. We sometimes sing the Doxology as if it were a dirge. Even the Eucharist, despite the words of the Great Thanksgiving, is rarely the thankful, joyous foretaste of the Great Banquet with the One who triumphed over Death, but mostly a mournful occasion for introspection. A joyless Christianity is as clear a sign that something is amiss as a dirty church.[9]

When the church proclaims the gospel faithfully and makes it clear that the church is not captive to the culture, strange things happen. The church voices and begins to live a counterworld that

8. Keck, *The Church Confident,* p. 38.
9. Keck, *The Church Confident,* p. 41.

159

grows out of the text. This in turn acts against the world that has for so long been dominant. The reigning assumptions and presuppositions of modernity are called into question and challenged.

Authentic worship, which includes faithful preaching, will face obstacles and meet resistance. But when the church has a vision of the world as God wants it to be and takes risks in faithful response, obstacles and resistance can be overcome. We turn first to the critical role of preaching.

Odd Preaching and Practices

There was a time in the tradition of many churches, though certainly not all, when the sermon was seen as the central event of the worship experience. When the pastor mounted the pulpit to preach, every eye was turned on him (in the situations I am describing the preacher was nearly always a man). If the pastor had a reputation as an excellent preacher, a hush would descend on the audience.[10] Small babies whose presence and noises might disturb the proceedings were safely tucked away in the nursery. Younger children, who were present earlier in the service for "children's time," had departed to go to a Sunday-school class or to participate in "junior church." *This* was the moment for the adults to listen to the preacher proclaim the word of God — the climax of the service. All of the preliminaries were got out of the way before this moment arrived.

In this model of preaching, the preacher uses powers of persuasion to present a truth so convincingly that the ideas set forth take hold in the minds of the listeners. Much depends on the preacher's voice and oratorical skills, as well as "his" personality. The personal charisma of the preacher is paramount.

Lucy A. Rose proposed conversational preaching as a different model of preaching, which has as its purpose:

10. The words *audience* and *auditorium* were often used, indicating that the key purpose of the worship service was to hear the preacher. Acoustics were very important, the visual less so.

exploring together the mystery of the Word for the lives of the worshippers, as well as the life of the congregation, the larger church, and the world. The preacher and the congregation gather symbolically at a round table where there is no head and no foot, where labels like clergy and laity blur, and where believing or wanting to believe is all that matters. . . . Although one person may do all the speaking during the time set aside for the sermon, it is the priesthood of believers, the entire community of faith, that is responsible for exploring the Word and deciding its meanings, its claims, its direction pointings. Conversational preaching aims to gather the community of faith . . . around the Word.[11]

She continued: "The 'why' of conversational preaching is to gather the community of faith around the Word where the central conversations of the church are refocused and fostered." But, she added, this "why" demands a new "what":

In the postmodern world no "truth" is objective, absolute, ontological, or archetypal. The only way I can speak of "truth" is eschatologically. There will come a Day when we will understand, but until that Day we live by faith and hope, not by sure knowledge, clear facts, or unambiguous truth.[12]

She described the content of preaching not as sliding into relativism but as

a proposal offered to the community of faith for their additions, corrections, or counterproposals. The sermon's content is a tentative interpretation of scripture that acknowledges, as best it can, its limitations and biases. . . . The preacher searches for meaning that makes life livable and, by the secret workings of the Spirit, grace-filled. This meaning is then submitted to the community of faith via the sermon for their answering meanings.[13]

---

11. Lucy A. Rose, "Conversational Preaching: A Proposal," *Journal for Preachers,* Advent 1995, p. 27.

12. Rose, "Conversational Preaching," p. 28.

13. Rose, "Conversational Preaching," p. 28.

Certainly, the conversational preaching that Rose described is helpful. *The danger might be that a slide into relativism could occur and that the content of the preaching might be based more on the content of the developing conversation than on the scriptural text.* Recognition of this danger serves as a firm reminder that the conversation must be based in the "Word," even as it is enlivened and enriched by the ongoing conversation.

On an ABC News Special, "In the Name of God," Peter Jennings interviewed the founder of the Vineyard Christian Fellowships, John Wimber.[14] Wimber said that the first time he went to church he expected dramatic things to happen. After attending three Sundays, he was frustrated. Following the service, he talked to an official-looking man and asked him, "When do they do it?"

"Do what?" the man replied.

"The stuff," Wimber answered.

"What stuff?"

"The stuff in the Bible."

"What do you mean?"

"You know, multiplying loaves and fish, feeding the hungry, healing the sick, giving sight to the blind. That stuff."

"Oh," the man replied apologetically, "we don't do that. We *believe* in it, and we *pray* about it. But we don't *do* it."

The life of the congregation and its members must back up the preaching from the pulpit and be consistent with that preaching.

Saunders and Campbell, in expounding on Acts 2 and 3, stressed the reverse movement *from practice to preaching,* noting that it is equally important to the movement *from preaching to practice.* For example, in Acts 3, it was *after* Peter healed the lame man and the man walked around praising God so that people gathered and asked what was happening that Peter began to preach to tell what had happened to the man.

14. The report of this interview is based on a description by Stanley P. Saunders and Charles L. Campbell, " 'What Does This Mean?' 'What Shall We Do?' Pentecost, Practices, and Preaching," *Journal for Preachers,* Pentecost 1996, p. 3.

The proclamation of the good news of Jesus Christ *follows* the odd life of the Christian community and describes the source and nature of that life for all who wonder, "What does this mean?" Whereas most of us usually think of preaching as stirring up congregations to more faithful discipleship, the texts in Acts remind us that the reverse movement — from practice to preaching — is equally important. Peter's sermons embody a "practice-description" model of proclamation.[15]

The movements from preaching to practice and back again tell us clearly that the gospel, as an instrument of Christian stewardship, is directly and integrally related to the other instruments. We now look at the other instruments, and the related rules of the household, within the context of worship.

Baptism

Baptism, as I have already noted, is usually viewed primarily as a rite of entry into the church. Often the act of baptism is treated as an interlude in or a postlude to the worship service. Sometimes the baptism is even done privately, outside the setting of congregational worship. As a result, the meaning and significance of baptism have a low profile during congregational worship. Even in worship services in which baptism occurs, the sermon may make little or no mention of baptism. In short, baptism is most often treated as a necessary process for a person to become part of the church membership. The congregation is rarely made aware that baptism is the act that binds the members together as a covenanted community and not a volunteer association.

Such a limited view is not enough. Baptism is an identification with the death and resurrection of Jesus Christ. "Baptism," wrote Saunders and Campbell, "is the social practice that marks our transition from the world of sin and death, the realm of fallen creation, to the world of a merciful and reconciling God. The early Christians

15. Saunders and Campbell, "'What Does This Mean?'" p. 4.

practiced baptism in dramatic ways that marked a clear transition from one social space or realm of existence to another."[16]

The issue is *not* whether a church practices infant or believers' baptism, or what the mode of baptism should be. A number of years ago I had the opportunity to observe believers' baptism by immersion among Baptists in Zaire. Nearly a hundred people were baptized in a river by the pastors of nine churches. Several hundred people stood along the bank celebrating with joy and singing hymns of praise. A sermon was preached about baptism and the special meaning of the occasion. It was clear from what was said at the service and what we were told in conversation that preparation for baptism had been thorough, lasting more than a year, and that the members of each congregation had been deeply involved in the process of preparation. It was also clear that for those congregations baptism signified a break with the reigning assumptions of *their* culture and a giving over to newness of life in Christ.

Recently I witnessed a meaningful example of infant baptism at a Presbyterian church in Columbia, South Carolina. During the worship service, with some six hundred members of the congregation present, the pastor baptized an infant girl, Caroline, who had been brought to the front of the sanctuary by her parents. After the baptism had taken place, the pastor walked up and down the aisles, carrying the girl in his arms. As he walked, he explained that this baptism was *an event for the entire congregation* and that she now became part of the congregational household. He paused near the end of each row of pews and gave the people opportunity to see her and even to touch her. As he walked and talked, he reminded the congregation of their household responsibilities to this newest member of the household. It was a "family" event.

How can our baptismal services become more meaningful? The answer is not in simple logistics, such as holding the service outdoors or in some exotic setting. It is not whether the church practices infant or believers' baptism. A key factor is the involvement of the whole congregation — and not just in preparation for the baptismal event and on the day of baptism. The involvement is ongoing — before, during,

16. Saunders and Campbell, "'What Does This Mean?'" p. 6.

and after — because baptism means becoming a member of the household of God. And when anyone comes into a household, *every member* of the household is affected then and in all the days to come.

Whenever a baby is born, a child is adopted, or a marriage brings someone new into a family, the occasion can and should be a time of joy and celebration. At its best, for example, a family anticipating the birth of a child prepares carefully and thoroughly. Perhaps a nursery is redecorated, a crib is obtained or an old one repainted. Plans are made. The household budget is examined and adjustments made. Schedules are rearranged. When a new person comes into a household, change does take place — for that person and for the whole household.

Usually, the "right words" to mark such an occasion of baptism appear in the resources that the church uses. For example, these words, used following the baptism and blessing, appear in *The Book of Common Worship* of the Presbyterian Church in Canada:

> See what love God has given us
> that we should be called the children of God;
> and so we are.
>
> _____, _____, _____
> you are now received by Christ's appointment
> into the holy, catholic church.
> Through baptism, God has made you
> (a) member(s) of the *household of God*
> to share with Christ in the priesthood of all believers.
> Remember your baptism and give thanks.
> Be one with us in the church.[17]

The right words are important, and these are good words. Again, however, more than "the right words" are needed in the household of God.

In Galatians 3:26-28, Paul described baptism as an act that transforms relationships by breaking down barriers of race, national background, social and economic class, and gender:

17. *The Book of Common Worship* (The Presbyterian Church in Canada, 1991), p. 156. The emphasis is added.

[F]or in Christ Jesus you are all children of God through faith. As many of you as were baptized into Christ have clothed yourselves with Christ. There is no longer Jew or Greek, there is no longer slave or free, there is no longer male and female; for all of you are one in Christ Jesus.

Baptized members of a covenanted community — a household of God — have a responsibility for one another and a relationship with one another. Whenever baptism takes place, it is an occasion for joy and an opportunity for each member of that congregation to renew his or her baptismal covenant and to reflect on the promises and the commands of God. Christian formation begins in baptism. As an embodiment of the Christian's identification with the death and resurrection of Christ, baptism is a moment of new creation. This powerful instrument of stewardship deserves to be used as the gift that God meant it to be.

Around the Table

Earlier we looked at the central role of the table in a family household. The table is also central in the household of God. In most North American Protestant churches, except on those Sundays when the Eucharist is celebrated, the table in the sanctuary is not actively used. Often it is adorned with flowers, a cornucopia, candles, a Bible, or offering plates. Seldom is it thought of as a place for food, as the gathering point for the household of God. But at its best, the table is where the household receives daily bread; it is the place where barriers of class, race, gender, and economic status are broken down; it is the place where all are welcome to join the messianic feast. The way we view the table reflects and affects the way we view the world, and vice versa.

Stanley Hauerwas and William Willimon noted the importance of paying attention to the common things we do:

We suspect that much of the difficulty of current church life, and our corresponding theology, is that we have not paid serious attention to how hard it is to understand the common things we

166

do as Christians — such as pray, baptize, eat meals, rejoice at birth, grieve at illness and death, reroof church buildings. Lacking the ability to describe theologically the significance of these activities, we distort what we do by resorting to descriptions and explanations all too readily provided by our culture. Any explanation is to be preferred to no explanation.[18]

Eating is one of the common things we do as members of the human race. What, where, when, how, and with whom we eat are all important and send messages to ourselves and others. In the culture of the first century, the church's mealtime practices were considered peculiar. In the then prevailing culture, persons from different households seldom ate together. Different households usually related to each other in competition, not in fellowship.

A rich householder would often stage a dinner for those whose favor he was seeking to gain. The meal was designed to display one's own wealth and status ostentatiously, and to honor the guest for the sake of anticipated future rewards. An important element at many of these meals was the presence of persons of lesser honor and status, who would be seated at separate tables and served lesser quality food, all as a way of shaming them in order to accentuate the honor of those in the chief seats. All of this was done in dining areas open to the streets, so that passersby could witness and comment upon the affair.[19]

What a contrast to the table of the Lord. The table of God's household is, foremost, the place where the death and resurrection of Jesus are remembered and celebrated with joy and thanksgiving. Far too often, the Eucharist, which literally means "gratitude," is conducted and received as though it were a mournful funeral service. The table of Jesus was joyful. In fact, he was sometimes criticized because of his conduct at the table and because of the persons who had joined him there. At Jesus' table no one was given a special place

18. Stanley Hauerwas and William H. Willimon, "Embarrassed by the Church: Congregations and the Seminary," *The Christian Century*, 5 Feb. 1986, p. 119.

19. Saunders and Campbell, "'What Does This Mean?'" p. 7.

of honor, nor was anyone excluded because he or she was not approved by society. Tax collectors and outcasts were welcome! The same should be true today.

Paul had to warn the Corinthian Christians that their practices at mealtime were reminiscent of their culture, that they were not practicing the Lord's table (1 Cor. 11:7-34). As Saunders and Campbell expressed it:

> Christian mealtime was to be a time of social reintegration and reconciliation, rather than a time of alienation and social violence. In other words, the Lord's Supper was an occasion wherein Christians self-consciously took over an everyday social practice — a practice rooted in fallen imaginations — and transformed it into an embodiment of God's new reality. As a form of social theater, Christian mealtime was a radical, embodied form of proclamation (1 Cor. 11:26), which nurtured the church's oral preaching.[20]

In the church, the table should have a prominent place in the space where worship takes place. If we truly believe that the household begins and is developed "at table," the placement, shape, and size of the table will reflect (or not reflect) the meaning we give to the table. A round table as suggested above by Rose might be considered. Is the congregation as a household of God willing to have a table that cuts across the barriers that divide persons from one another so that the table is open to all? Does the church remember, or has it forgotten?

The same principle applies to dinners and other events that the church holds. Is everyone welcome without regard to race, class, ability to pay, or type of dress? Unfortunately, many church dinners and other functions that bring people together have an admission fee attached. Is the table of the household of God to be accessible only to those who have the money and the appropriate status for admission? Such questions lead to a consideration of the church's views on money and possessions.

---

20. Saunders and Campbell, " 'What Does This Mean?' " p. 7.

The Household's View of Money and Possessions

The Greek word *koinonia* appears twenty times in eighteen verses in the New Testament.[21] Most commonly it is translated as "fellowship." In Acts 2:42, for example, we read, "They devoted themselves to the apostles' teaching and fellowship, to the breaking of bread and the prayers." In *The Interpreter's Bible,* undoubtedly the commentary most commonly used by Protestant clergy in North America in the second half of the twentieth century, both the exegesis by G. H. C. Macgregor and the exposition by Theodore P. Ferris accept the translation of *koinonia* as "fellowship." Macgregor, however, offered some other possibilities as he wrote:

> fellowship (*koinonia*) — first perhaps with the apostles, but also with reference to the wider fellowship of all believers. It is Paul's favorite word to describe the unity of believers with each other and with their Lord. In 1 Cor. 1:9 ("called into the fellowship of his Son") it seems almost to take on the concrete sense of "the body of believers." Its equivalent in Aramaic (*habhura*) seems to have been in common use to describe a group of companions who shared a common life, particularly those who united to celebrate a common Passover meal. Thus there may possibly be a reference here to the table fellowship which becomes more explicit in the breaking of bread. Again, this fellowship found practical expression in experiments in Christian communism (vss. 44-45; for a fuller discussion see on 4:32-37). The original *habhura* of Jesus had shared a common life (cf. John 13:29), and the communism of Jerusalem was simply a continuation of that practice. The word *koinonia* sometimes has the sense almost of "almsgiving" or "relief" (cf. Romans 15:26, "to make some contribution for the poor"). What is in view here is clearly not absolute communism, but a sharing of goods for the benefit of those in need.[22]

21. The word *koinonia* was also discussed in chapters one and six.
22. G. H. C. Macgregor, *The Interpreter's Bible,* vol. 9 (New York and Nashville: Abingdon Press, 1954), p. 50.

In his exposition of Acts 2:42 and the word *fellowship,* Ferris did not call that translation or its usual interpretation into question. He accepted "fellowship" as the translation of *koinonia,* writing that the church "should be the center of a community life in which the lonely find friends, the sinful find understanding and forgiveness, the believers find the support of those who believe the same things."[23]

The word *koinonia* can be translated "fellowship." It can also be translated as "partnership" or "participation," "social intercourse," "communication," "communion," or "distribution." Macgregor's comment about the equivalent Aramaic word, *habhura,* as meaning a group of companions who shared a common life, particularly those who united to share the Passover meal, seems to take the word *koinonia* to a greater depth than North Americans usually associate with its translation as "fellowship." For the contemporary church, the word "fellowship" seems to mean little more than being with people whom you like and get along with, and with whom you share certain beliefs and values. It does not adequately reflect the meaning of *koinonia* in Acts 2:42.

The Acts 2 context of the use of *koinonia* indicates the likelihood that a preferred translation would be a word other than "fellowship." Acts 2:44-45 reads, "All who believed were together and had all things in common; they would sell their possessions and goods and distribute the proceeds to all, as any had need." This practice of the early church of selling possessions and distributing proceeds generally has disturbed the contemporary church. Sometimes the response is simply to ignore the practice, as though it had never existed. Others argue that it was a historical, one-time event that we do not need to take into account today. In general, it is regarded as disturbing or even embarrassing. Actually, it was in keeping with the inauguration of Jesus' ministry, recounted in Luke 4:16-30, when he proclaimed the Jubilee, the acceptable year of the Lord, as reality. The Jubilee concept was revolutionary. On Pentecost, the Spirit-filled Christians put it into practice.

23. Theodore P. Ferris, *The Interpreter's Bible,* vol. 9 (New York and Nashville: Abingdon Press, 1954), p. 52.

Saunders and Campbell observed:

> [I]n contemporary American culture, where people view their possessions in private, individualistic terms and will not even disclose their income or their giving to other church members, the early Christian practice of sharing turns our cultural presuppositions on their head. Were the church today to take seriously this practice, people might have yet another reason to look with amazement at the community of faith and wonder, "What does this mean?" Then again, out of this odd practice, the church's peculiar speech might ring with clarity and vigor.
>
> At a time when preachers often seek to enliven the pulpit through various homiletical techniques — creative metaphors, moving stories, new forms — Luke suggests that power and conviction may return to the pulpit when sermons emerge from peculiar communities of faithful discipleship. Peculiar life and peculiar speech go together. Rather than simply assuming that effective preaching renews the church, we need also to recognize that transformed practices of the church can renew the pulpit.[24]

How and when the offering is received in congregational worship can reveal much about the congregation's attitude about money and its relationship to faith. In some orders of worship, the offering is received prior to the sermon. Any real sense that the offering of the people is a *response* to the word of God is largely lost. Usually, the offering plates are placed on the communion table, although there are congregations where the offering plates are not set down *anywhere* in the sanctuary. Instead, the offering plates are brought forward by the ushers, held there for a brief moment during a prayer of dedication, and then promptly taken to the office, where the financial officers count the money *during* the remaining part of the worship service. The sense that the offerings are gifts to God is greatly diminished. A sense that the offering is first and foremost to and for the budget of the congregation prevails.

Perhaps the greatest tragedy is that the church is forgetting that the offering of the people is to *God* and that *God* then gives the offering to the church to carry out God's mission. To remember that

24. Saunders and Campbell, "'What Does This Mean?'" p. 8.

171

the offering is a response of the people to the love and the goodness of God and is given to *God*, is an act of a people who know they are members of the household of God. This memory is needed in the congregations of North America.

The practices of the church and its preaching about money and possessions will not change unless the viewpoint of the church and its members changes first. The church needs to remember and commit itself to the teachings and core values of Jesus and the early church.

One question to be considered is why North American Christians cling so tenaciously to keeping information about their income and the amount of their giving to the church so secret and confidential. For example, Stanley Hauerwas recounted an occasion when he lectured about business ethics at the business school of Houston Baptist University. Before the lecture he talked at a dinner with the associate dean of the business school. She told him that she was a member of Second Baptist Church of Houston — a church that has between six and seven thousand members and ordinarily grows each Sunday by a hundred or two hundred new members. After the lecture, which was titled "Why Business Ethics Is a Bad Idea," she expressed disappointment to Hauerwas that the lecture was pessimistic if not cynical and suggested that surely there was something they could do to make the business school more ethical. Hauerwas wrote:

> I observed that I certainly felt that there was, but they would have to begin a good deal earlier than business school. I suggested before they let anyone join the Second Baptist Church of Houston, Texas, they ought to have the prospective member turn to the congregation and make public what they earned. "I make $35,000 a year and I want to be a member of Second Baptist Church of Houston, Texas." "I make $185,000 a year and I want to be a member of Second Baptist Church of Houston, Texas." "I make $65,000 a year and I want to be a member of Second Baptist Church of Houston, Texas." She observed that they could not do that. I said, "Why?" and she said "Well, that's private."[25]

25. Stanley M. Hauerwas, "Living on Dishonest Wealth," *Journal for Preachers,* Advent 1996, p. 15.

Financial income and resources are among the many gifts God gives. Does it not follow then that these gifts should be made known and shared with the household in the same way that we share other charismata?

The question remains, why do church members feel so strongly that the amount of their income and how much they give to the church should be considered a matter of such great confidentiality? Is the congregation a household of amnesia or a household of God?

The Role of Children in Worship

The role of children in the life of the congregation, particularly in the worship service, is important to deal with at this point. Traditionally, except during "children's time," children are supposed to sit and behave as miniature adults. When they are not sitting quietly in the worship setting, they are expected to "perform" for the entertainment and amusement of the adults or to participate in a children's time with the pastor. Often the pastor uses this time as an opportunity to send a message to the adults present, knowing that adults tend to listen more intently to the "children's story" than to any other part of the service. Indeed, adults often comment that they "get more out of" the children's story than they do any other part of the service. In most services, shortly after the children's time, the children leave the place of worship to engage in Sunday school or junior church. Babies, if they are present at all, are expected not to cry or make too much noise. In some congregations if the baby cries, the parent is then (quietly) asked to take the baby to the nursery. On more than one occasion I have witnessed the pastor stop in the middle of a sermon and ask that the baby be taken out, once in a way that was even rude to the mother who had come to worship.

Is there a better way? What is the role of children in worship in the household of God? At a conference a number of years ago, John Westerhoff said that children of all ages should be in attendance in worship without overly tight restrictions being placed on them. If they want to color in a coloring book, that is all right. If they want

173

to walk up to the front of the sanctuary and sit down to listen, that is all right. Quiet toys are available for their use. Westerhoff also indicated that the educational program of the church should be tied closely to worship. For example, a worship service on Sunday morning might be preceded by a thirty-minute classroom experience for all age groups in which the focus of the learning is to prepare for the worship experience. The same Scripture to be used in worship would be used in the classrooms. Following worship, each person would return to the classroom to discuss and reflect on what had happened. The entire experience would be integrated in a way that seldom happens in most congregations. The interaction of worship and education would lead to new understandings of the gospel and provide opportunity to discuss and plan life-style changes as individuals and as a congregation.

Regardless of the specifics of design, worship and education should not be separated. David Ng and Virginia Thomas observed:

How did the Hebrew child learn to worship? First, through a relationship with a worshiping parent, a member of a worshiping community; through intentional education built into the rituals of home and community worship; through a multitude of sensory experiences and vivid, thought-provoking symbols and dramas; through a life of ethical actions growing out of worship; through a pattern of sabbath and festivals that recreated the Hebrews' story; and eventually through a form of public, community gathering which made teaching an essential part of the liturgy.[26]

Describing the work of a task force in First Presbyterian Church, Durham, North Carolina, Lori Pistor noted that the "most significant step . . . was rethinking when the children could and should be present in worship." Some of their conclusions were:

- The youngest members of the church were missing the most active, participatory elements of worship: prayers of the people

26. David Ng and Virginia Thomas, *Children in the Worshiping Community* (Atlanta: John Knox Press, 1981), p. 52, as cited by Lori Pistor in "Let the Children Come," *Journal for Preachers,* Pentecost 1996, p. 44.

and the Lord's Prayer, passing the peace, hymns, the offering, the anthem, the doxology, the benediction, and, especially, communion.

- Rather than taking the children out of worship before the sermon as before, the children now continue their time in the classroom and join the congregation in worship during the hymn following the sermon.
- Because the church uses a lectionary-based curriculum for Sunday school, the children have heard the stories/texts that the adults heard during the first part of the worship service.
- The "Time with Children" has continued, but with more variations and enthusiasm.
- At the time of baptism, the children and the rest of the congregation hear the promises together. The children gather eagerly at the front to witness the baptism and are the first to greet the newly baptized members.[27]

Pistor noted that the children now want to come to worship: parents have reported difficulties on those Sundays when their children learned they were not staying for worship after Sunday school! The congregation had made a strong commitment to make worship meaningful for the entire congregation, including children. She concluded: "Children belong with the worshiping congregation because the gospel is for people of all ages."[28] The congregation made great strides toward including children fully in the worship life of the congregation and breaking free from traditional cultural assumptions.

Leslee Alfano, who has served as part of a United Church of Canada task group dealing with children and worship, wrote:

It is not enough that children be present in "adult" worship even if they are present with comfort and welcome. That model is still one of barriers and devaluing in being part of community. The challenge is to discover worship that is accessible to all

27. Pistor, "Let the Children Come," pp. 44-46.
28. Pistor, "Let the Children Come," p. 47.

ages. Children are not simply welcomed to learn how "adults" worship and be socialized or initiated into that. . . . Rather, they are welcomed to the community as those who have something to give and receive in worship. They may offer their leadership and hear a word of God for the living of their lives in school, home and play. Children are honoured for their place in the community through participation in all aspects of worship even as adults and youth. In other words, worship is for all ages and stages.

Thus, worship is neither child oriented nor adult oriented, but seeks to reach out to the needs and gifts of the gathered community. We have yet to articulate, let alone practise, all that such worship might be and become. But the intention is to take steps in that direction.[29]

Only when every member of the household is invited and welcomed to participate can it be fairly said that the whole household is worshiping the living God.

Whither Worship?

If these understandings about worship are taken seriously by a congregation, what will worship look like? The question "whither worship?" can be thought of at two levels. One level is more pragmatic and logistical in nature. The second deals with the intent and purpose of worship.

Looking at logistical questions, a major factor that affects worship in almost all congregations is the place or setting of worship. Too often the worship experience of a congregation is determined in a large measure by its place of worship. The architectural style, size, shape, and furnishings of the space where worship occurs have great influence on the worship life of the congregation. The question to be asked and considered is whether the congregation has seriously wrestled with the elements and style

29. Leslee Alfano, in a letter to the author.

of worship *before* deciding on the space and other logistical matters related to worship.

I began this chapter by stating that worship that is trivialized and secularized cannot transform a congregation. A congregation needs a worship life that is authentic and faithful to the characteristics and rules of the household of God and that uses the instruments that God has provided. Worship is not for the congregation per se; *it is for praise of the living God*.

Leaders of a congregation who desire its worship to be faithful to this purpose will struggle with several questions:

- Who should participate in worship?
- How can our services of worship and liturgies be designed to further the purpose of worship?
- How can we use the instruments of Christian stewardship more faithfully and effectively?
- What should the order of events be?
- Who plans the worship life of the congregation?
- Who provides leadership for worship?
- What is the interaction of pastor and lay members?
- And, above all, is God's mission to the world the primary agenda of worship?

Only *after* these and other questions of intent and purpose are discussed and decided can the congregation turn meaningfully to logistical and pragmatic questions such as:

- What are our space requirements for worship?
- What size and shape should the space be?
- How can the space be made inviting to the stranger, the homeless, and the outcasts of society?
- What furnishings and decorations are needed and appropriate?
- Will the space encourage faithful use of the instruments of Christian stewardship — word, baptism, table, towel, congregation, and God's mission to the world?
- What space should be provided for common meals?
- How can the space encourage participation by everyone present?

- How can the setting encourage the sharing of material goods and possessions for distribution to the poor and dispossessed?
- How do we design the space so as to encourage and enable participatory decision making by everyone in the congregation?

As a congregation struggles with the questions on both levels — the issue of the purpose of worship and pragmatic, logistical questions — it will inevitably bump up against the question of how much money the congregation should invest in buildings.

Christopher Levan observed that much about our buildings and furnishings — fixed pews, baptismal fonts, pulpits, lecterns, communion tables, choir lofts, organs — emanate immovability. All of this works against a church on the move. In a chapter titled "Itinerant or Establishment Church," he wrote:

> The vision of an itinerant community of faith may well mean an adjustment of our church goals and objectives, removing the assumptions of permanence and replacing them with visions of imminence and itinerancy. Perhaps we should design our worship, education, and service to go on the road, living with the people who need healing as those first preachers did. In modern parlance, we would cease being a passive institution and become pro-active. It may be that the time has come to rejuvenate the spiritual pilgrimage, the physical journey that embodies the movement of the soul. Is this not a faithful response to the gospel's story of going out on the road?[30]

Every congregation should struggle with how to be faithful to God's call to be a church on the move and to engage in authentic worship of God.

In the next chapter, we will look at the leadership question: What are the roles of the pastor and the laity in the congregation seeking to be a household of God?

---

30. Christopher Levan, *God Hates Religion: How the Gospels Condemn False Religious Practice* (Toronto: The United Church Publishing House, 1995), p. 57.

CHAPTER EIGHT

Roles of the Pastor and Laity

The work of the pastor is to help people understand the
life-giving logic of the gospel in the totality of their lives.

Pastoral Ministry:
The Dream, the Preparation, and the Reality

Pastors, when asked how they *actually* spend their time, give an answer
quite different than the answer they give when they are asked how they
should spend their time. The answer is often different again if they are
asked how they *wish* they could spend their time. A typical pastor of a
mainline church might describe the dilemma in these words:

> *What I expected ministry to be when I entered seminary bears scant
> resemblance to what it has turned out to be since I left seminary. As a
> matter of fact, what seminary prepared me to do is not what I had
> anticipated, nor is it closely related to what I have ended up doing.
> Before seminary, I had a dream of preparing sermons that would
> transform people. I expected people to be eager to learn about the Bible
> and what it means to be a disciple of Jesus. But it hasn't happened that
> way. On the whole, I'm not sure that seminary prepared me for what
> I have faced in pastoral ministry.*
>
> *The people in my church are not really in agreement about what
> they want me to spend my time doing. Some think I should spend most
> of my time in counseling and calling on the sick and shut-in members.
> In short, they want me to be a chaplain. Others, not as many, want me*

to focus on pulpit ministry and preach sermons "that make them feel good." Others, even fewer in number, want me to make sure that the organization runs smoothly, that money is available to pay all the bills, and that all the elected and appointed positions described in the bylaws are filled. Members say they want the church to grow, but deep down I think they are afraid that new people coming into the church could mean that the new members will take power away from those who have been around forever. I suspect what they really want are new members to give money to support the church budget so they — the older members — won't have to increase their giving to the church.

I obviously can't do all these things and give a high priority to each one. Sometimes, it is very frustrating. What the church wants is a knight in shining armor — a pastor-messiah — who can defeat every enemy and rescue the church from all problems and distress. I feel like I've been put into an impossible situation.

The dream and the reality are far apart.

Pastoral Ministry: Gaps in Understanding

An Associated Press article pointed out the disparity between how members of congregations *imagine* their pastors spending their time each week and how that time is *actually* spent.[1] The *image* held by the members is that the week is spent in study, preparing sermons. The *reality* is different: days are taken over by interruptions, ranging from people calling for service times to vendors selling supplies. Briggs wrote:

A new study in which researchers observed ministers at work for a full week found a third or more of their time was spent on administrative duties. Take away Sunday, and that percentage rises to 50 percent, said the Rev. Gary William Kuhne, an assistant professor of adult education at Pennsylvania State University.[2]

1. David Briggs, "Managerial Duties Cut into Clergy's Sermon Time," Associated Press Article in *Syracuse (N.Y.) Post-Standard*, 4 Nov. 1995, p. C2.
2. Briggs, "Managerial Duties," p. C2.

Kuhne did the study with Joe F. Donaldson, associate professor of higher education at the University of Missouri at Columbia. In the study, they observed five conservative Protestant pastors, ranging in age from 36 to 46, for five days each, or a total of more than 250 hours. Briggs reported: "In observing what ministers actually do in a work week, Kuhne and Donaldson found that nearly half their time was spent in scheduled meetings, a category that included worship services. About a quarter was spent on desk work, half of that involving preparing sermons."[3] Kuhne said, "Overall, it can be said with some certainty that the amount of time spent on administrative tasks is close to 30, 40 percent."[4]

The small size of the sample in the study, the relatively narrow ten-year span in ages, and the fact that all five pastors were described as "conservative," may have skewed the findings. It is quite possible that a similar study done among "liberal" pastors might show the major amount of time spent in counseling and helping members in their interpersonal relationships.

Nevertheless, almost unanimously, pastors, lay leaders, and observers in general agree that how they feel a pastor *should* spend his or her time does not match *reality*. On the other hand, there is not general agreement about what the "should" should be.

Pastoral Ministry: More Than Two Choices?

M. Douglas Meeks noted that most pastors, once they have been in the pastorate for a few years, move toward one of two tasks. These two models, or paradigms, said Meeks, have been a disaster for stewardship, that is, stewardship as it should be for the household of Jesus Christ. The two models are:[5]

3. Briggs, "Managerial Duties," p. C2.
4. Briggs, "Managerial Duties," p. C2.
5. M. Douglas Meeks in presentations made at an Educational Event for Stewardship Leaders in July 1993 at Bolton, Ontario, sponsored by the Ecumenical Center for Stewardship Studies.

1. The external: focusing on the organization. In this model, the pastor's main task is managerial, serving as the chief executive officer (CEO) of the institution. The external model uses principles of organizational development and management as its guide.
2. The internal: focusing on individuals and the inner life. In the internal model, the pastor is a counselor/therapist and psychological principles are the guide.

Meeks said that the ministry of word and sacrament, the ministry of ordination, is a highly specialized ministry: "It is not *the* ministry. *Every* member of the church is called to ministry. The ministry of ordination is highly specialized; people who are given this ministry by the church should spend 90 percent of their time in word and sacrament."[6] Ordination is not for the purpose of establishing a privilege; rather it gives a new responsibility. As we have noted, the stole, often given at the time of ordination, is in actuality a symbol of service — a towel. It is not a symbol of authority! The stole/towel, as a symbol of servanthood, is to enable that person to engage in the work of the household — homemaking.

Many pastors consider that the preparation and delivery of a sermon is the most important part of their ministry. Yet, as important as it is, sermon preparation is a small portion of the work of the gospel — and the pastor. The work of the pastor is to help people understand the life-giving logic of the gospel in the totality of their lives. The totality of life includes relationships in the home, how people make decisions politically, how people make decisions economically, and more. The gospel is meant for the totality of life.

We look next in more detail at the two models for pastoral ministry mentioned above.

6. Meeks observed that he formerly used the figure of 95 percent but lowered it to 90 percent.

External Model

The external model is followed by only a small fraction of the number of pastors who adopt the internal model. Those who follow the external model, and do it well, are viewed as very successful pastors. The external model is more likely to appear in larger-sized congregations in which the pastor's main task is seen as being the chief executive officer of the congregation's organizational structure and life. Because these congregations tend to be larger, pastors who follow the external model have greater visibility in the community and in denominational circles. They are sought out to participate in leadership roles in the community and denomination. Administrative skills are especially sought and valued, both by the congregation and the pastor. Within the congregation, the criteria by which the pastor is evaluated are balanced budgets, boards and committees that function efficiently and effectively, and a staff that knows its job and does it well. The phrase "senior minister" is often used for the title of the pastor. A feeling of hierarchy pervades the organization.

Because the spotlight is so keenly focused on the organization and its chief executive officer, the life and welfare of the organization take on paramount importance. When this happens, the life-giving logic of the gospel is clouded or forgotten inside a household of amnesia.

Internal Model

The use of the internal model is much more widespread in the North American church. In fact, a principal danger in the North American church is that the gospel has become limited to *internal* questions of purpose and meaning in life. That represents a theology that has been given over to the assumptions of modernity — in the arenas of a consumer society, science, politics, and so on — and has kept for itself only the questions related to the meaning and interpretation of life. The gospel is meant to claim the totality of our being and, as such, is a full-time job. For the pastor, it is more than just a sermon to work on, although that is very important. It is helping the congregation understand that the gospel is about the life-giving promises and commands of God that are meant for all of life.

The inner, therapeutic model of pastoral ministry has other dangers as well. In recent years the issue of clergy sexual misconduct has come to the fore in virtually every denomination. One denominational official wrote that in every case of clergy sexual misconduct that he had investigated, the origin and the opportunity for the misconduct arose out of a counseling situation. The danger is twofold:

1. Many pastors participate in counseling situations for which they are not adequately trained or qualified.
2. Insufficient measures are taken to avoid the opportunity for misconduct to arise.

The denominational official wrote that the best advice he could give to pastors who have members who could benefit from counseling is "refer, refer, refer."[7] In the name of therapeutic counseling, the lives of many counselees, as well as their pastors and congregations, have been severely damaged.

How did the church come to a point in which *internal* matters assumed such primacy? A bit of history is enlightening at this point. In the early twentieth century, a handful of reformers began a strategy to introduce psychology into the theological curriculum.[8] Eventually they called themselves the "clinical training movement." Their thought was that the pastor had to have available in his/her pastoral ministry insights from Freud and Jung, whose works were becoming well known. Their strategy was to develop a powerful training movement with high standards of accreditation so they could control the quality of what happened in the training process. They succeeded very well: the clinical training movement has had enormous impact upon not only practical theology but the whole curriculum of theo-

7. Richard E. Rusbuldt, while serving as executive minister of American Baptist Churches of Pennsylvania and Delaware.

8. The historical information in this paragraph is excerpted from a presentation made by Robert Wood Lynn at a Colloquy for Theological Educators in June 1992 in Waterloo, Ontario.

logical education. The movement started with, perhaps, ten or twenty persons who stayed with it over an extended period of time. It took some thirty years to implant the concept on the North American scene. Now virtually every pastor who has finished seminary in the past generation has been affected by this movement.

Most pastors have accepted the internal, therapeutic model of pastoral ministry built on the foundation of the "clinical training movement." Powerful indications that the movement is another symptom of the church's entrapment in modernity and that change may be appropriate are emerging however. In 1993 *Time* featured a cover article titled "Is Freud Dead?"[9] Paul Gray reported on the fierce debate going on in intellectual circles about the validity of Freudian theories and how widespread Freudian theories have become: "Sigmund Freud's rich panoply of metaphors for the mental life has evolved into something closely resembling common knowledge."[10] This "common knowledge," however, is being called into serious question by many scholars. Gray reported that Frank Sulloway, a visiting scholar at M.I.T and a longtime critic of Freud's methods, took a somewhat more apocalyptic view: "Psychoanalysis is built on quicksand. It's like a 10-story hotel sinking into an unsound foundation. And the analysts are in this building. You tell them it's sinking, and they say, 'It's O.K.; we're on the 10th floor.' "[11] Though not willing to declare Freud finished, Gray observed:

> Psychoanalysis and all its offshoots may in the final analysis turn out to be no more reliable than phrenology or mesmerism

9. Two articles were included in the November 29, 1993, issue of *Time:* Paul Gray, "The Assault on Freud," pp. 47-51, and Leon Jaroff, "Lies of the Mind," pp. 52-59. Two years later an article by John Leland titled "The Trouble with Sigmund" appeared in *Newsweek*, 18 Dec. 1995, p. 62. The thrust of the *Newsweek* article was similar to the two articles in *Time*. Leland reported that "Recent research has challenged not only Freud's conclusions, but his ethics as well." He added that Melvin Sabshin, medical director of the American Psychiatric Association, says university psychology departments have moved away from Freud toward more empirical fields, especially biology and pharmacology.

10. Gray, "The Assault on Freud," p. 49.

11. Gray, "The Assault on Freud," p. 51.

or any of the other countless pseudosciences that once offered unsubstantiated answers or false solace. Still, the reassurances provided by Freud that our inner lives are rich with drama and hidden meanings would be missed if it disappeared, leaving nothing in its place.[12]

Gray concluded, "Perhaps Homer and Sophocles and the rest will prove, when all is said and done, better guides to the human condition than Freud."[13] For me, Jesus of Nazareth is a better guide than any of the others.

Despite these evidences that the world of Freudian psychoanalysis may be sinking into quicksand, the world of psychology continues to have a strong hold on the language and mind-sets of ordained ministers. Richard Busch wrote that in his renewal programs with pastors from around the world, a pattern often emerged: "Someone will introduce himself using the language of the Myers-Briggs Type Indicator — as an introvert or extrovert, a feeler or thinker, a sensor or intuitive. Faces light up. Most people understand this shorthand interpretive language, and respond by declaring their own personality type. With this 'Christian horoscope' we begin to tell each other who we are."[14] When participants are directed to tell their stories — to share how they understand God to have been acting in their lives over the years, people respond with excitement. He continued:

> Yet the goal of the assignment — to share how God has been acting in their lives — is not always realized. Traditional Christian language is rarely woven into the narrative. At least 80 percent of the personal stories do not integrate the individual's life with the Christian faith. The vocabulary has a professional, ecclesiastical, or psychological flavor. Because the narratives are powerful, and the connections and associations resonate among the listeners, many fail to notice what is missing.

12. Gray, "The Assault on Freud," p. 51.
13. Gray, "The Assault on Freud," p. 51.
14. Richard A. Busch, "A Strange Silence," *The Christian Century,* 22 March 1995, p. 316.

Christians are "self-interpreting animals." . . . In these renewal programs, competent and articulate leaders of the church are strangely silent about defining themselves in the light of theological and scriptural foundations. It is painful for me to realize that I too share in this silence.[15]

Busch voiced his suspicion that

behind this silence is finally this: the gospel is not the center of our lives, and our spiritual life is disconnected from the things that interest, worry and excite us. We have so many pressing interests, priorities and passions in our lives that we no longer seek first the kingdom. We lack the singleness of heart to be attentive to God. In our desire to be like the people around us, we emphasize the outward *doing* dimensions over the inward *being* dimensions of Christian living.[16]

Are pastors talking about many things yet keeping silent about the life-giving logic of the gospel?

Pastoral Ministry: Theologian in Residence

Is there another model for pastoral ministry? What could be a model for ministry for the pastor? Meeks argued strongly for the role of the pastor as a theologian in residence for the congregation. Because the ministry of ordination is highly specialized, people who are given this ministry by the church should focus on using their time in word and sacrament — preaching the gospel and administering communion and baptism in such a way that they come alive in the congregation. Time in word and sacrament includes more than the worship experiences of the congregation: it includes educational settings, board and committee meetings, conversations, and calls in the homes. Such a holistic, integrated understanding of pastoral ministry will enable the pastor to help

15. Busch, "A Strange Silence," p. 316.
16. Busch, "A Strange Silence," p. 317.

people understand the life-giving logic of the gospel in the totality of their lives.

Lay Ministry Is Not Second-Class Ministry

In most congregations, the ministry of the laity is defined in relatively narrow ways that indicate that lay ministry is not full or "real" ministry, but exists primarily to carry out the secondary tasks in the congregation and to help the pastor do the things that "the pastor doesn't have the time to do." The danger is that lay ministry is not viewed by the pastor or the lay members as full participation in ministry. Lay ministry may be regarded by both the pastor and lay leaders as second-class ministry. It is not!

Lay ministry is usually identified with such tasks as serving as a lay leader in worship, preparing the elements for communion, singing in the choir, greeting and seating people, serving as a con-gregational officer or member of a board or committee, teaching in the Sunday school or youth ministry program, helping maintain the building, preparing budgets, and giving money to support the budget. Sometimes, if the congregation has an outreach program, a few lay leaders participate in ministries to the poor, the hungry, and the homeless. Largely, these in-house and outreach ministries are carried out in a near theological vacuum without an in-depth biblical understanding of *why* they are carried out. An in-depth exploration might even reveal that some of the ministries are inappropriate for a household of God.

Paul, in Ephesians 4:12, wrote that pastors are to help equip members of the church for the work of ministry. The pastor's role is a specialist whose main role is to bring biblical insights and theological reflection to bear on the ministries of that congregation. This does not imply that others in the congregation should not be expected to or are not capable of providing biblical insights and theological reflection. Nonetheless, as one who has received specialized training and is afforded time, the responsibility for the biblical/theological tasks falls mainly to the pastor. The pastor who forfeits this responsibility has abandoned the primary reason for being present as pastor.

A word of caution needs to be noted, however. The pastor's special knowledge and abilities are not to be used in an authoritative style. It is not a matter of the pastor saying, "This is what I have learned and therefore this is the way it is." Rather, it is the pastor saying, "God has given me particular gifts and called me to be your pastor. God has also given each of you gifts to be used in God's mission to the world. Our task together is to determine what are the ways that God wants us to use these gifts from God." Such mutuality will do much to lessen "pastor/people tensions" and help the congregation be faithful to what God has called it to be — a household of God.

Pastor and People in Partnership

The congregation that views the relationship between its members and the pastor as being primarily an employer/employee relationship will find it difficult to become a household of God. Nor does the other extreme work. A congregation that looks to the pastor as a "pastor-messiah" who has all the answers and who carries great authority is not likely to become a faithful household of God.

"Kudzu" is a cartoon feature that offers insights into the life of the church in North America. One of the strips depicted a pastor standing at his pulpit saying, "Brothers and sisters, years ago, the Lord Jesus called me to be your pastor . . . and now I feel like the Lord Jesus is calling me elsewhere." The final box shows the pastor still standing at the pulpit with a somewhat dumbfounded expression on his face. Coming from the direction of the congregation, he hears the words of an old gospel song, "What a Friend We Have in Jesus."[17] This is probably an extreme example of pastor-people relations gone wrong. Nevertheless, it reflects a reality that in many congregations the relationship between the pastor and people is strained and tension-filled.

The need is for a pastor and people who work together in partnership, knowing that the ministry of the church belongs to

17. Marlette, "Kudzu," *The Christian Century,* 15 Nov. 1995, p. 1093.

the *whole* people of God. The role of the pastor is important when it is properly understood. Meeks's suggestion that the pastor's role is primarily that of theologian in residence provides a way for pastor and people to work in partnership and makes it possible for the pastor's specialized knowledge and expertise in biblical studies and theological reflection to be a basic part of the partnership relationship.

In a book that had wide influence on many ministers, Henri Nouwen presented the concept of the minister as a "wounded healer." I believe his concept can be broadened in such a way that the phrase "wounded healer" could apply to pastor and people working in partnership. Nouwen's actual words were:

> If the ministry is meant to hold the promise of this Messiah, then whatever we can learn of His coming will give us a deeper understanding of what is called for in ministry today.
>
> How does our Liberator come? I found an old legend in the Talmud which may suggest to us the beginning of an answer:
>
>> Rabbi Yoshua ben Levi came upon Elijah the prophet while he was standing at the entrance of Rabbi Simeron ben Yohai's cave. . . . He asked Elijah, "When will the Messiah come?" Elijah replied,
>> "Go and ask him yourself."
>> "Where is he?"
>> "Sitting at the gates of the city."
>> "How shall I know him?"
>> "He is sitting among the poor covered with wounds. The others unbind all their wounds at the same time and then bind them up again. But he unbinds one at a time and binds it up again, saying to himself, 'Perhaps I shall be needed: if so I must always be ready so as not to delay for a moment.'" (Taken from the tractate Sanhedrin)

The Messiah, the story tells us, is sitting among the poor, binding his wounds one at a time, waiting for the moment when he will be needed. So it is too with the minister. Since it is his task to make visible the first vestiges of liberation for others, he must bind his own wounds carefully in anticipation of the moment when he will be needed. He is called to be the wounded healer, the one who must look after his own wounds but at the same time be prepared to heal the wounds of others.[18]

What ministry could be done in the name of Jesus Christ if all the members of the household — pastor and people — worked in partnership as "wounded healers." Ministry would be for members of the household but also for those who are "strangers" to the household. Ministries of and by the "wounded healers" would sometimes be done by one or two individuals; other times the entire community would provide ministry.

Envisioning and Planning

How might a congregation envision and plan so as to give flesh and bones to the ideas put forth in this book? Desire by itself is not enough. Specific steps will need to be taken. How can the process begin? If a congregation has within it a pastor and at least a few members who earnestly desire that the congregation move from being a household of amnesia to becoming a household of God, the process can be started.

The following schema *illustrate* a process that could be used to help a congregation move toward becoming a faithful household of Jesus Christ. Undoubtedly, there are many variations to this approach and other approaches that can be used. (Varying understandings about the content of what God's mission is may coexist until the process is well underway.) The end goal or overarching purpose becomes the target toward which all planning is directed. Note that

18. Henri J. M. Nouwen, *The Wounded Healer: Ministry in Contemporary Society* (Garden City, N.Y.: Doubleday & Company, 1972), pp. 84-85. Nouwen wrote this book before inclusive language was widely used. However, he did note in the acknowledgments that many friends had made him aware of his "male-dominated language." He wrote: "I realized how right they are. I hope that the women readers will have patience with my attempt for liberation, and will be able to recognize themselves even in the many 'man's' and 'he's.' I hope to do better next time."

to *create the plan,* the process begins with step one and continues downward to step seven. To *implement the plan,* the direction is reversed. In the schema, dotted arrows indicate the sequence of steps to create a plan; the solid arrows indicate the sequence to implement a plan.

The Planning Process

The starting point of creating a plan is for the congregation to agree that the basic purpose for its existence is to help carry out God's purpose for the world that God loves. God's mission for the world has been discussed at several points in this book, especially in chapters one, four, five, and six. God's mission for the world grows out of God's love — God's passion — for the world. As part of the subplot of God's mission, *God's mission for the church is to enable people to answer to and live by the logic of the gospel of Jesus Christ rather than by the logic of the prevailing culture.*

The pastor and people will need to agree that this process, or one that is comparable, is worth the time and energy that will be required. Steps to launch the process will be needed. *The twelve guidelines, found in the introduction on pages 12-13, can be used as a model to begin.* This book can be a resource to the congregation in the initial and continuing steps of the planning process, as well as in implementing the plan. A congregation that is "between pastors" might agree that they want their next pastor to be willing and able to participate with them in such a process. The congregation that currently has a pastor could begin the process with the mutual agreement of the pastor and key lay leaders.

Conceptually, God's mission for the world is the first step in creating a plan:

Step One in Creating a Plan:

Having agreed on this overarching purpose as a concept, the congregation must agree that the congregation can best accomplish this purpose if it seeks to be a faithful household of God.

Step Two in Creating a Plan:

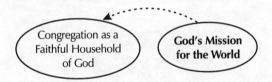

At the heart of the congregation that seeks to be a faithful household of God lie its worship and small group life. The congregation will need to agree that worship and small groups will be used to help the congregation become a faithful household of God.

Step Three in Creating a Plan:

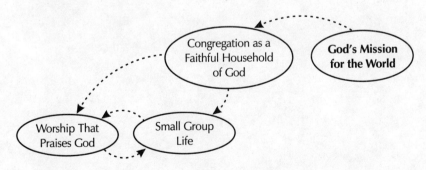

Worship and small group life in the congregation cannot be what God intends unless they grow out of the ministry of the whole people of God of that congregation — pastor and laity working together.

Step Four in Creating a Plan:

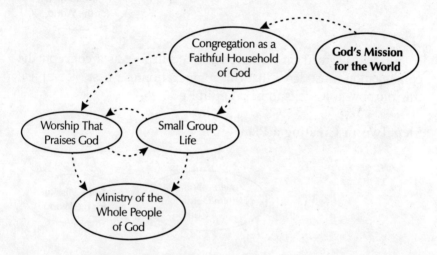

For the ministry of the whole people of God to develop and flourish, the life of the congregation must be bathed in Bible study, theological reflection, and prayer.

Step Five in Creating a Plan:

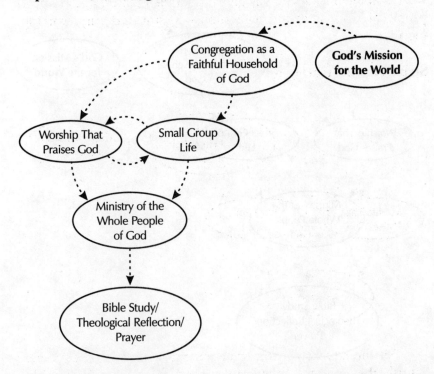

The model of the pastor as a theologian in residence[19] working with the members of the congregation in a mutually-agreed-on partnership defines the key role of the pastor. This model enables pastor and people to be in partnership and to participate meaningfully in Bible study, theological reflection, and prayer that will facilitate faithful worship and small group life.

19. Vincent Alfano suggested the term "teaching elder" as one that would be suitable within the United Church of Canada. Other churches might use different terminology. The key factor is the concept, not the term used.

Step Six in Creating a Plan:

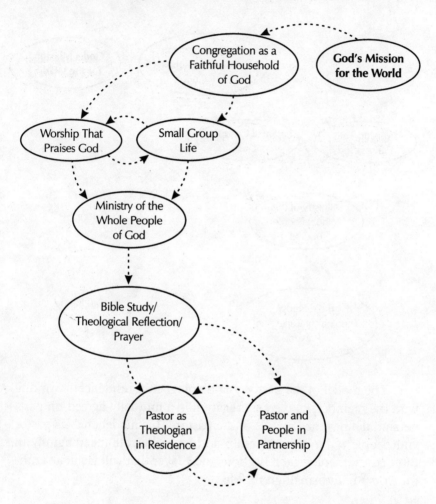

Step seven in the process is to plan the launching of the plan's implementation. In actuality, creating a plan and implementing the plan are closely related, with ongoing evaluation of the implementation phase providing feedback that assists in revising the original plan. The revisions then affect the later stages of the plan's implementation. At its best, the two parts of the process are synergetic.

Step Seven in Creating a Plan:

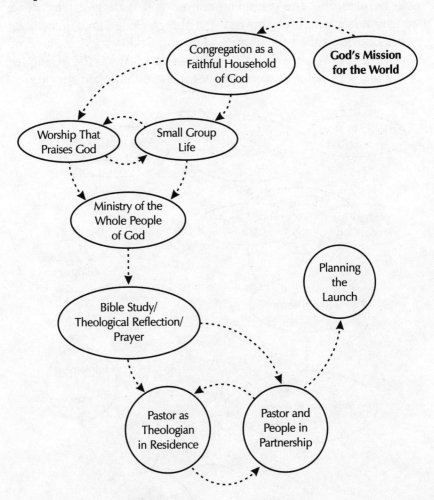

Carrying Out the Plan

Once the congregation has done its planning, it should begin to implement the plan, as indicated by the flow of the solid arrows, beginning with "Implement the Plan." It must be remembered, however, that planning is never finally completed. The plan and its implementation will need to be evaluated on a regular basis and fine-tuned or amended, as indicated by the dotted arrows. Patience and a firm trust in God will be needed. Pitfalls and discouragements will be plentiful. The prevailing culture will issue its siren call to remain a household of amnesia. But the challenge is to remember what God has called the church to be and to do as a household of God. The final scheme shows "Implement the Plan" as the beginning point *and* as a point of reentry after evaluation and adjustments.

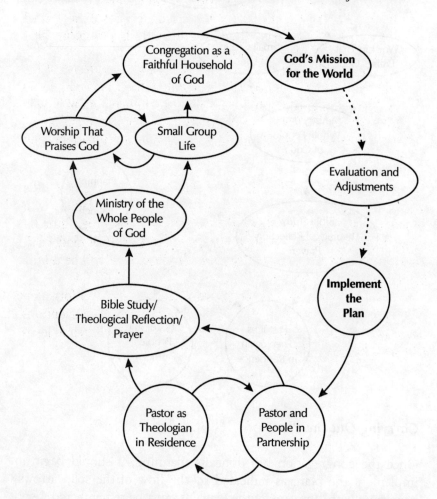

As a young boy, Howard Gordon wrote, he liked to listen to stories told by old Mr. Pollock, who had been a young banker in the coalfields of West Virginia in the late 1890s. Gordon recounted that as Mr. Pollock and his wife got older, Mrs. Pollock developed trouble with her right leg. He continued:

> Mr. Pollock was a true gentleman. After he had opened the door of the car for his wife he would bend down and lift her leg into the car.
>
> One day after Mrs. Pollock had had tea for her now very old friends, Mr. Pollock offered to drive one of them home. He opened the car door for his wife's friend and then, being very polite, bent down and lifted her leg into the car.
>
> The world has a lot of trouble in its right leg. None of the high-powered technology and economic schemes is going to do it. The solution is in clerics who are just a little bit out of it, who embarrass themselves and the world by being gentle and doing the culturally inappropriate things of sacraments, preaching, and worship.[20]

I would go a step farther. More than clerics need to be a little bit out of it. The whole church — made up of congregations with an amazing diversity of pastors and people — needs to be a little bit out of it. Indeed, from the point of view of the culture of modernity, a congregation that is becoming a household of God will be a little bit out of it — or more.

We have come full circle. A congregation that has forgotten who and whose it is and it has become a slave to the conventions of its culture *is* a household of amnesia. God calls the church of Jesus Christ to become a household of God.

20. Howard H. Gordon, Jr., "Protagonist Corner: Lifting the Right Leg," *Journal for Preachers*, Easter 1995, pp. 37-38.

CHAPTER NINE

The Household of God:
A Living Household

Jesus Christ, rejected by the religious leaders of his day, is the cornerstone of the household of God that we call the church. He is both the foundation of this new community and its living presence.

Divine Reversals

The careful reader of this book will have noticed that the word *reversal,* or variations of the word, has appeared frequently. Sometimes, even when the word itself was not used, the implication of the desire for, the fear of, the need for, or the implications of, reversal were apparent.

In the preface I described my 1995 experience of a heart attack that began and then was reversed. Since then, the word *reversal* has taken on an existential dimension for me that it did not have before. I believe that God was the cause of that reversal.

That experience deepened my conviction that God desires to bring, and can bring, reversal to the church in North America, caught as it is in the assumptions and presuppositions of its culture — modernity. If the church is to regain its memory, a reversal is needed. The church, especially in its congregational form, needs to truly become a household of God.

Biblical Examples of Divine Reversals

Biblical examples of divine reversals abound. Many were noted in earlier chapters. A few will be recounted here.

One of the notable reversals found in the Old Testament is in the desert experience of Moses at the burning bush. Not only did it mean a reversal, again, in the life of Moses, it meant a reversal for the Hebrew people. Their conditions of slavery and bondage in Egypt were reversed. Of course, during the forty years in the wilderness before they entered the new, promised land, they sometimes grumbled and longed for "the good old days." The Egyptian king also experienced a divine reversal. From his perspective, it was not a desirable happening. God's reversals can cut both ways: those persons who are lifted up from bad situations rejoice (at least eventually); those persons who are brought low are not happy about their experience (at least initially).

Ezekiel's vision of the valley of dry bones brought hope and the promise of new life to a people in exile in a strange land. God told the people, "I will bring you back to the land of Israel. . . .. I will put my spirit within you, and you shall live." Shattered hopes were restored and Israel did go home. God brought the people back to their land.

The birth, life, and death of Jesus were a series of reversals. Though he was in the form of God, Christ Jesus emptied himself and took the form of a servant, being born in human form. During his ministry he was loved by the common people but feared and despised by the religious elite. On Palm Sunday he was cheered and proclaimed as the Son of David, one who came in the name of the Lord. Five days later he was condemned as a criminal and executed by crucifixion. It appeared that the Jesus movement was over and that his disciples would flee and scatter in fear and despair. Yet, three days later, the greatest reversal of all occurred: the resurrection. Jesus' resurrection is the pivotal event that provides access to the household of life and escape from the household of death. It is the New Testament equivalent to the Exodus event in the Old Testament. It is the supreme stewardship event. And, as we have seen, it is the *first* characteristic of the household of God. The household of God begins here, or it does not begin at all.

Reversal Within Congregations

Many congregations do not seek a reversal in their lives but are content with the status quo. God wants to bring reversal — renewal — to those congregations. The Bible makes clear what the household of God is like: its characteristics and the rules of the household. God has provided ways and means — the instruments — to be used by the congregation. Yet the instruments are poorly used and sometimes not used at all.

Of course, a congregation that considers even the possibility of seeking divine reversal knows that reversal will mean *not doing business as usual* in the congregation. The pastor and leaders of a congregation may dream and fantasize about change — about reversal — but fear can loom large. Especially where money and possessions are concerned, the fears are real and may prove overpowering. As we noted, the fears lie at two levels: (1) The first level is the type of fear that shows up in studies and surveys of pastors and lay members of the church. This level ranges from the practical and logistical to statements that because money is material and therefore unspiritual, it should not be talked about in the church. (2) Yet, even as these fears and anxieties move through the minds of pastor and people, consciously and subconsciously, *a second level of fear* — deeper and largely unrecognized and unsuspected — lurks underneath. This second level of fear relates to the reality that money has power. And because money has power, the temptation to worship in its great temples and to bow before its idols is powerful and alluring. It becomes a crisis of faith: is money, or our love of and desire for money, more powerful than our love of and desire for God? And, as we saw, disciples of Jesus Christ are called to participate in the ministry of suffering. The gospel was not formulated for the convenience of Jesus' disciples, nor for those who preach it to others. Some persons choose to follow the god of mammon, which says that money can alleviate, and even prevent, suffering.

On a more positive note, as we have seen, the reversal of the process of modernity plays to the strength of congregations. The locus of the church that is most apt to be freed from the culture of modernity is the congregation. Faithful use of the instruments that

God has provided can help to reverse the erosion of the belief system that is taking place in so many congregations.

Characteristics of Divine Reversals

Though divine reversals vary widely in their scope and type, they share certain characteristics:

> Divine reversals unsettle the status quo. Because of this, reversals are usually resisted and are hard to come by.
>
> The rate of change of divine reversals is not predictable. Reversals may come quickly or slowly.
>
> Short-term reversals are not enough and are not real. The long term is important. Long-term reversals have far-reaching consequences.

A House of Living Stones

One of the most striking images in the New Testament appears in 1 Peter 2:4-10:

> Come to him, a living stone, though rejected by mortals yet chosen and precious in God's sight, and like living stones, let yourselves be built into a spiritual house, to be a holy priesthood, to offer spiritual sacrifices acceptable to God through Jesus Christ. For it stands in scripture:
>
> "See, I am laying in Zion a stone,
> a cornerstone chosen and precious;
> and whoever believes in him will not be put to shame."
>
> To you then who believe, he is precious; but for those who do not believe,
>
> "The stone that the builders rejected
> has become the very head of the corner,"

and

"A stone that makes them stumble,
and a rock that makes them fall."

They stumble because they disobey the word, as they were destined to do.

But you are a chosen race, a royal priesthood, a holy nation, God's own people, in order that you may proclaim the mighty acts of him who called you out of darkness into his marvelous light.

Once you were not a people,
but now you are God's people;
once you had not received mercy,
but now you have received mercy.

Jesus Christ, rejected by the religious leaders of his day, is the cornerstone of the household of God that we call the church. He is both the foundation of this new community and its living presence. The description of Christ as a living stone is a reminder of his resurrection and of the newness of life he brings to those who build their house on him. He does not build the house alone. He invites others to join with him in building the household of God.

The members of the household are also "living stones" of the household. The emphasis is not on the individual; it is on the whole community that constitutes the household. The house, of course, is not a physical building; it is a spiritual house. Peter Marty painted a beautiful picture of this house formed on Jesus Christ, the cornerstone:

With our modern minds we struggle to think in such beautifully collective terms. Our most wholesome conceptions of the church rarely resemble a unified church anchored by a precious cornerstone. We're more apt to think of ourselves as individual rocks strewn about a building site, awaiting the builder's chisel or the soft mortar or the dreaded toss of rejection. Idolatrous forms of individualism entice us. Old patterns of denominationalism comfort us. A strong sense of community is more a dream than a pursuit in many quarters.

But Peter's perspective, and the understanding of the New Testament world in general, was far more attuned to people becoming part of a corporate body. This emphasis on the collective or communal character of faith is hard to appreciate in an era in which many Christians no longer consider identification with a specific church community to be central to their identity. But the apostolic church understood it differently. God does not make covenants with individuals. Covenants are made with the community of faith. "Once you were not a people, but now you are God's people." The people who were once considered a heap of dry and disparate bones have become a house of living stones.[1]

Lest We Forget

The danger is that the people whom God has called to be a household of God built on Jesus Christ the cornerstone will forget! Seduced by a culture that promises much but delivers pain and estrangement, the people form a household of amnesia in which individuals take precedence over the community of faith. In effect it is "every man for himself," to use an old term expressed in exclusive language.

In a household of amnesia, people forget the higher calling, preferring to remember and to celebrate themselves and their material gains and possessions. Edgar Krentz reminded his readers that when Queen Victoria celebrated her diamond jubilee in 1897, the *London Times* printed Rudyard Kipling's poem "Recessional." Krentz noted that this "scandalized the English because instead of celebrating their empire, the poem called them to repentance. The refrain 'lest we forget — lest we forget' ended each stanza. England too stood under God's judgment and might vanish as a power on the world stage."[2] One stanza reads:

The tumult and the shouting dies;
The captains and the kings depart:
Still stands Thine ancient sacrifice,

1. Peter W. Marty, "A House of Living Stones," *The Christian Century,* 24 April 1996, p. 451.
2. Edgar Krentz, "Justice and Judgment," *The Christian Century,* 6 Nov. 1996, p. 1071.

An humble and a contrite heart.
Lord God of Hosts, be with us yet,
Lest we forget — lest we forget!

The church must not forget who and whose it is and why God called it into existence.

Burning Hearts

At the heart of who and whose we are is the need to remember that we are a resurrection people. The appearance of Jesus to two disciples on the road to Emmaus is a remarkable story. The account in Luke 24:13-35 states that "on that same day" — the day of the resurrection — two persons were going to Emmaus, about seven miles from Jerusalem. One of them was named Cleopas. We do not know the name of the other.

As they traveled, they talked with one another about all the things that had happened. During their journey Jesus came near and went with them, but "their eyes were kept from recognizing him." The subsequent conversation indicates that the two travelers were part of the extended group of Jesus' followers in Jerusalem. Jesus asked what they were talking about. Cleopas answered, apparently surprised by Jesus' question: "Are you the only stranger in Jerusalem who does not know the things that have taken place there in these days?" Jesus asked, "What things?" Their reply recounted the ministry of Jesus, his condemnation and death by crucifixion, and the reports of some women who said they had gone to the tomb and did not find his body there and that angels had told them he was alive.

Jesus responded, "Oh, how foolish you are, and how slow of heart to believe all that the prophets have declared! Was it not necessary that the Messiah should suffer these things and then enter into his glory?" Then, beginning with Moses, he interpreted the things about himself in the *Scriptures*. Earlier, they had not understood. His death had dashed their hopes. Now they began to know that the suffering of Jesus and his entering into his glory were necessary to the fulfillment of Scripture as part of God's plan.

206

As they came near the village of Emmaus, Jesus walked ahead as if he were going on. But they strongly urged him to stay with them because it was almost evening. He did not impose on them to offer *hospitality,* but with their urging he went in to stay with them. Near Eastern custom dictated that a guest turn down an invitation unless it was vigorously repeated. Jesus did not force himself on them, or on others.

The meal scene at Emmaus is a treasure mine of information for those who want to explore it for reflection, preaching, and teaching. At the *table,* Jesus, the guest, became the host. Jesus took *bread,* blessed and broke it, and gave it to them. R. Alan Culpepper wrote: "The four verbs are Jesus' signature, which the disciples (or at least the readers) may remember from the feeding of the five thousand (9:16) and the last supper (22:19)."[3]

The four verbs — took, blessed, broke, and gave — are powerful words. They are words used in the Eucharist. In fact, these four words — and the principles behind them — permeate our Christian faith. God provides us with gifts that we can receive or *take*. We can ask God to *bless* them for our use and for the use of others. Use of the gifts requires that they be *broken* so they can be *given* to others.

At the table Cleopas and his companion finally recognized who Jesus was. In the act of sharing bread, Jesus was made known to them. "Their eyes were opened." Jesus then vanished from their sight. Jesus had opened the Scriptures, opened their eyes, and finally opened their minds. They said to one another, "Were not our hearts burning within us while he was talking to us on the road, while he was opening the scriptures to us?"

That very hour, they returned to Jerusalem and found the eleven and their companions gathered together. Those who had remained in Jerusalem were saying, "The Lord has risen indeed, and he has appeared to Simon!" Then the two from Emmaus told what had happened on the road and how Jesus had been made known to them in the breaking of bread. They proclaimed the *word* — the good news — of their experience.

3. R. Alan Culpepper, "The Gospel of Luke," in *The New Interpreter's Bible,* vol. 9 (Nashville: Abingdon Press, 1995), p. 480.

Notice how many of the words and concepts that we have focused on in this book appear in this story: stranger, Scripture/word, hospitality, table, and bread. And all are in the context of the appearance of the *risen* Christ. The concepts embodied in these words are key parts of the life of the household of God.

Later disciples may not experience the risen Christ in the same way that the travelers to Emmaus did. But it is important to remember that Easter did not end at sunrise on the day of resurrection. For us, as for them, the risen Christ provides a memory that can move us from being a household of amnesia to becoming a household of God — a household of Jesus Christ. Peter Marty summed up the experience of the two travelers to Emmaus in these words:

> Until Jesus reminded the travelers to Emmaus who the Messiah was and what his resurrection meant, they were as desperate as most of us are to make sense of life. Their existence was as phantom as their faith. Their identity was as elusive as people believed the risen Christ to be. Their hope was as uncertain as the future of their nation. Then they remembered. They remembered that they wouldn't have to make up life anymore. Jesus had set them free.[4]

The Household of God as Countercultural

God calls the church to be countercultural — to live by the logic of the gospel and not by the logic of the prevailing culture. What does this mean for the church in a North American context? Unfortunately, during most of North American history, the church has related to its culture so closely that it was hard to tell the two apart. Mainline Christian churches often were so closely tied to the culture that to criticize one was viewed as criticizing the other. Christianity and the state were so closely linked in the minds of many persons that it was routine to speak of the United States and Canada as Christian nations.

4. Peter W. Marty, "Living by the Word: Burning Hearts," *The Christian Century*, 10 April 1996, p. 397.

Non-Christians were tolerated at best, and resisted, discriminated against, and persecuted at worst.

When the religious practices of groups that are not Christian are prohibited, many Christians do not protest. For example, when the U.S. Supreme Court upheld the law prohibiting the use of peyote by the "Native American Church," George Will commended the opinion written by Justice Scalia because it held firm to the common-sense approach of Thomas Jefferson, "patron saint of libertarians."

> A central purpose of America's political arrangements is the subordination of religion to the political order. . . . The founders . . . wished to tame and domesticate religious passions of the sort that convulsed Europe. They aimed to do so not by establishing religion, but by establishing a commercial republic — capitalism. They aimed to submerge people's turbulent energies in self-interested pursuit of material comforts.
>
> Hence religion is to be perfectly free as long as it is perfectly private — mere belief — but it must bend to the political will (law) as regards conduct. . . . Mere belief, said Jefferson, in one god or 20, neither picks one's pockets nor breaks one's legs.
>
> Jefferson's distinction rests on Locke's principle . . . that religion can be useful or can be disruptive, but its truth cannot be established by reason. Hence Americans would not "establish" religion. Rather, by guaranteeing free exercise of religions, they would make religions private and subordinate.[5]

When the church is a household of God, it will not allow itself to be subordinated to, or tamed or seduced by, the political order — especially in the "self-interested pursuit of material comforts." To be able to claim free exercise of religion at the cost of making religion private and subordinate is a price not to be paid. Whenever nation-

---

5. William H. Willimon, "Christian Ethics: When the Personal Is Public Is Cosmic," *Theology Today*, Oct. 1995, pp. 367-68. Willimon cited Stanley M. Hauerwas, *After Christendom?* (Nashville: Abingdon, 1991), pp. 30-31. Willimon noted his indebtedness to Hauerwas for many of these insights on the public/private split, referring particularly to chapter 3 of Hauerwas's book.

alism takes precedence over our faith in the living God, our faith is diminished.

Jesus was not condemned and executed because he saw religion as private and subservient to the ruling authorities. He was seen as a threat. The authorities did not dismiss him as a harmless crank who went about the countryside preaching the "pop psychology" of his time. As Willimon put it, "The world was quite right in seeing Jesus not as a crisis in their self-understanding or a challenge to their existential selves but as a politically disruptive revolutionary who would have to be killed if peace with justice was to be preserved."[6]

God has not called the church in the North America to be "good citizens" above all else. To be convinced that our most pressing task is to make the world of democracy work is to abandon the household of God.[7]

As a household of God, our responsibility is not to try to convince or persuade others that they are wrong and we are right. God calls the church to *be* a household of God and to live a life-style that is consistent with that calling. And, I am convinced, the congregation is the key, strategic arena where this can happen. The congregation that seeks humbly before God to become a household of Jesus Christ, living according to the rules of the household and using the instruments of Christian stewardship that God has provided, will become a shining light within a dreary culture. Willimon wrote:

> Our greatest ethical, political need right now is not for new or better rules. What we're dying of is lack of imagination. We need some great gift that would enable us to imagine our little lives as caught up in something greater than ourselves, as contributing, in their countless personal acts, to something public and cosmic. Our ethics is thus an aspect of our worship, our risky, corporate,

6. Willimon, "Christian Ethics," p. 370.

7. Willimon, "Christian Ethics," pp. 370-71, wrote that Reinhold Niebuhr and other Christian thinkers "convinced American Christians that our most pressing political, ethical task was to help make the world of American democracy work. In jettisoning our language of faith for language that had been approved by the secular order, we became functionally atheistic."

every Sunday attempt to take God a little more seriously and ourselves a little less so. Thus Jesus preaches to us of a kingdom where enemies are forgiven and cheeks are turned, not as a social strategy but as our part in being a sign, a signal, a witness, that God, not nations, rules the world.[8]

When the church truly becomes an alternative, countercultural community, a light to a culture living in the shadows, many will rejoice. Those who are poor and oppressed will welcome an alternative to a culture that tramples the downtrodden. Such a countercultural community will be a household of life, not of death.

Called Out to Stand Up Again

The Greek word most commonly used in the New Testament for "church" is *ekklesia,* which literally means "a calling out." The word appears 116 times in the New Testament. It was used to refer to a popular meeting, especially a religious congregation (both a Jewish synagogue and a Christian community of members on earth or saints in heaven or both). The church then is made up of those who are "called out" by God. But for what purpose?

Jesus said to Peter, "On this rock I will build *[oikodomeo]* my church *[ekklesia],* and the gates of Hades will not prevail against it" (Matt. 16:18). Without getting caught up in the varying interpretations of what "this rock" refers to in this text, note that the Greek word *oikodomeo* translated as "I will build" has as its prefix *oikos,* which as we have already seen means "household." The church that Jesus said he would build has the nature of a household.

The first characteristic of the household of God is that it begins with the resurrection of Jesus. The Greek word translated "resurrection" is *anastasis,* which translated literally means "a standing up again."

Putting together the concepts of these three Greek words, we can say that the church is *a household* of those who are *called out* by

8. Willimon, "Christian Ethics," p. 373.

211

God *to stand up again.* To be such a household means remembering that God is a God of life and helping people live by the logic of the gospel of Jesus Christ rather than by the logic of an amnesiac culture enslaved in the trappings of death.

A New Beginning

In the introduction, I recounted the parable of a crude little lifesaving station whose members, over time, forgot their mission to save persons in peril at sea. When the purpose of the lifesaving station was forgotten, it changed into a social club that placed emphasis on the beauty of its building and its exquisite furnishings. Professionals were hired to do the work of lifesaving. Those rescued were not allowed into the building for fear that their presence would besmirch the ornate facilities. But some persons remembered what their mission was, and there was a new beginning.

What to us appears to be an ending can, through the work of God, become a new beginning. Joseph S. Harvard recounted and commented on a story told by Paul Tillich:

> The story is told about a witness at the Nuremberg War Crime Trials. He had escaped a death camp and the gas chamber. This witness survived by living for a time in an open grave in a Jewish cemetery in Wilna, Poland. While he was there, he saw a young woman give birth to a child in a nearby grave. In her delivery, she was assisted by an eighty-year-old grave digger. When the baby uttered its first cry, the old man prayed, "Great God, has thou finally sent us the Messiah? For who but the Messiah could be born in a grave?" Who indeed? Who but God the Finisher can turn endings into new beginnings?[9]

God waits patiently for congregations whose members will begin the process of remembering that we are called to be God's

---

9. Joseph S. Harvard, "A Witness to the Resurrection: When Finished Isn't Final!" *Journal for Preachers,* Easter 1995, p. 17, citing Paul Tillich, *The Shaking of the Foundations* (New York: Charles Scribner's Sons, 1948), p. 165.

resurrection people — a household of Jesus Christ. In the providence of God, faithful pastors and church leaders will respond to that call of the living God.

A Sermon

"Jesus: An Alternative to Bread, Circuses, and Political Power"

Matthew 4:1-11

Then Jesus was led up by the Spirit into the wilderness to be tempted by the devil. He fasted forty days and forty nights, and afterwards he was famished. The tempter came and said to him, "If you are the Son of God, command these stones to become loaves of bread." But he answered, "It is written,

'One does not live by bread alone, but by every word that comes from the mouth of God.'"

Then the devil took him to the holy city and placed him on the pinnacle of the temple, saying to him, "If you are the Son of God, throw yourself down; for it is written,

'He will command his angels concerning you,' and 'On their hands they will bear you up, so that you will not dash your foot against a stone.'"

Jesus said to him, "Again it is written, 'Do not put the Lord your God to the test.'"

Again, the devil took him to a very high mountain and showed him all the kingdoms of the world and their splendor; and he said to him, "All these I will give you, if you will fall down and worship me." Jesus said to him, "Away with you, Satan! for it is written,

'Worship the Lord your God, and serve only him.'"

Then the devil left him, and suddenly angels came and waited on him. (Matt. 4:1-11)

Introduction

Sometimes, without meaning to, we trivialize Jesus' temptation experience. We tend to think that the experience was recorded simply to remind us that Jesus was without sin and that he set a good example for us. While that is true, it only scratches the surface of the implications of Jesus' temptation experience.

Actually, following his baptism — which was in effect his ordination — Jesus' ministry was defined by the wilderness experience. As M. Eugene Boring wrote:

> Instead of the bread, circus, and political power that "kingdom" had previously meant, represented in Jesus' and Matthew's day by the Roman Empire . . . in the Matthean Jesus we have an alternative vision of what the kingdom of God on earth might be. This is what was at stake in the temptation.[1]

He continued: "to be a 'child of God' . . . means to have a trusting relationship to God that does not ask for miraculous exceptions to the limitations of an authentic human life."[2]

What it boils down to is that the Bible asserts that Jesus is an alternative to bread, circus, and political power. We too often fail to remember what is at stake here: that to be part of the reign of God is not like being under the crushing authority of a Roman Empire. Rather, the reign of God means that we are invited to be part of God's household. Let us turn to the temptation experiences to see what that means.

1. M. Eugene Boring, "The Gospel of Matthew," in *The New Interpreter's Bible*, vol. 8 (Nashville: Abingdon Press, 1995), p. 166.
2. Boring, "The Gospel of Matthew," p. 166.

Stones into Bread

First, note that Jesus' experience in the wilderness is reminiscent of the desert wanderings of Israel. Remember how the Israelites complained to Moses that he had led them out of Egypt and brought them into a wilderness without food.

> The whole congregation of the Israelites complained against Moses and Aaron in the wilderness. The Israelites said to them, "If only we had died by the hand of the LORD in the land of Egypt, when we sat by the fleshpots and ate our fill of bread; for you have brought us out into this wilderness to kill this whole assembly with hunger." (Exod. 16:2-3)

In the first temptation, Satan urged Jesus, who had fasted forty days, to use his power to convert the stones into bread *in order to still his hunger*.

The desert was full of stones. An ancient legend says that when the earth was created, God sent an angel with two bags of rocks to spread around the whole earth. One of the bags broke over Palestine and it got half the world's supply.[3] It wasn't easy for Jesus to see all those stones and to have them remind him of bread when he hadn't eaten for forty days.

Just as Israel in the wilderness had complained and clamored for a change in living conditions, so the temptation before Jesus was to rebel against God and demand a change in the situation *for his own betterment*.

Jesus responded by quoting Deuteronomy 8:3: "It is written, 'One does not live by bread alone, but by every word that comes from the mouth of God.'" Through his answer he refused to use such power, "since it is God's business to perform a miracle when it is needed. It is more important to trust God than to demonstrate the power of the Spirit. Christians have no obligation whatsoever to save the world through their wonderful accomplishments."[4]

---

3. LaRue A. Loughhead, *Sayings and Doings of Jesus: His Parables and Miracles Firsthand* (Valley Forge: Judson Press, 1981), p. 18.

4. Helmut Koester, *Proclamation*, Series A, Lent (Philadelphia: Fortress Press, 1974), pp. 14-15.

Jesus could have succumbed to this temptation. "He could go buzzing around in the air turning the desert into a gourmet bakery or he could keep his feet on the ground and live with the ache in the pit of his stomach, as hungry and tired as anyone would be after a six-week fast. . . . He refused to cross over the line God had drawn."[5]

In this temptation, bread becomes a form of power. Even today, we often use the word *bread* as a synonym for money. Does money have power? It has exactly the amount of power that we give to it. Jesus' reply told us, "That is not all there is."

Acrobatics at the Center Ring at the Circus

For the second temptation, there was a change of scene from the wilderness to the capital city of Jerusalem and the pinnacle of the temple. Satan took the lead. Satan, in effect said, "Well, you said that trust in God is important. Show how much you really trust God by throwing yourself off the pinnacle. Surely a legion of angels will come to your rescue and no harm will come to you." Satan even threw in some Scripture (Ps. 91:11-12) to buttress his argument.

Jesus quoted from Deuteronomy (6:16) to provide the answer: "Again it is written, 'Do not put the Lord your God to the test.'"

> [The one] who asks for a miracle makes experiments with God. If Christians do that, they are not demonstrating their trust in God, but they are frivolously creating situations which do not leave any other choice to God than to perform a miracle.[6]

In the wilderness *Israel* had tested God by insisting that God should miraculously provide water to prove that God had not abandoned them to death. With *Jesus* the temptation was to test God to prove that God would fulfill the promise to protect Jesus from harm. About 329 B.C. in ancient Rome, the empire built a coliseum

5. Barbara Brown Taylor, "Living by the Word: Remaining Human," *The Christian Century,* 7 Feb. 1996, p. 127.
6. Koester, *Proclamation,* p. 15.

— known as the Circus Maximus — where the emperor and the ruling elite gathered for entertainment. It was a large amphitheater used for chariot races, games, and so on. Gladiators — men who fought other men or animals in order to amuse the spectators — often died for the entertainment of the people. When the climactic moment came, it was customary for the people to vote for or against allowing a defeated gladiator to live by displaying a thumbs up or a thumbs down. The final and decisive vote was that of the emperor.

Do we have modern equivalents of the Roman circus? I believe we do. And not only in the form of show business that goes by the name of circus.

Bow Down and Worship

For the third temptation the scene was a high mountaintop. Satan dropped all pretense of piety. In effect he simply said, "Worship me." "What is at stake is the opposition of mutually exclusive claims of power."[7] It was a *political* struggle.

In election years in the United States, we are treated to the sorry spectacle of attack and counterattack among those who wish to be nominated and elected. Those in power, of whichever party, are tempted to use their power not for the welfare of the many but for the welfare of the privileged few and the moneyed interests. The church also can and does succumb to the deadly attraction of the political process. Church leaders become enamored and are seduced by the centers of political power.

Again Jesus quoted from Deuteronomy (6:13) — the great confession of faith of Jews and Christians that there is only one God whom one must worship: "Away with you, Satan! for it is written, 'Worship the Lord your God, and serve only him.'"

Every human being worships someone or something. The ultimate issue of power is, "Whom do you worship?" Worship is terribly important. It goes beyond mere submission; it is a surrender of mind, body, and spirit.

7. Koester, *Proclamation,* p. 15.

Conclusion

All of which brings us back to the heart of the matter and raises the key question: Is there any other way in the human situation to impose order other than by bread, circus, or political power? Is the reign of God accomplished only through the elements of bread, circus, and political power? The answer is no. Jesus is an *alternative* to bread, circus, and political power, but this will have meaning in our lives only if we remember who we are, and who Jesus is.

When we forget — or fail to remember — that to be part of the reign of God is to be part of the household of God, confusion and uncertainty inevitably follow.

Christopher Levan wrote about his Aunt Jane:

> I was reminded of the importance of memory when I got an emergency call about Aunt Jane from the nursing home.
>
> We all have an Aunt Jane. She lives in the senior's complex over town, has that sit-around-the-fire grandmotherly charm, and, as of late, she's losing her mind. Actually, it's not really her mind that is deteriorating, just her memory.
>
> My Aunt Jane is dignity personified. In younger years, she would never set foot outside her door in anything but the latest fashion. Dressed to "the nines" with none of this polyester and pearls, my aunt looked her Paris-collection best at all times.
>
> You can imagine my dismay when her memory loss became serious. There was the time she called the house in a breathless fluster. "I can't remember where I put my teeth." (Jane had replaced the real ones with a set of dentures — a great blow.)
>
> I asked the obvious question: "Where did you put them last?" Talking her through the apartment, she scouted out the bathroom and her night stand by the bed. "They're not in the glass," she said. A search of the kitchen counter was equally fruitless.
>
> In desperation, I asked her to recall what she was doing just before she missed them. "I was eating a sticky bun, but I didn't like it. They make them so sweet these days. I threw the whole thing out."
>
> A light blinks on!
>
> "Say, Aunt Jane," trying to sound nonchalant, "why don't you

look in the kitchen garbage can?" Sure enough, there were her false teeth still stuck to the half eaten Chelsea roll. Still wedged in the dough, they went into the waste basket along with the bun; she hadn't even noticed.

That's sad, but not nearly as tragic as the time she came to the door not remembering what to wear. My knock caught her between bath and clothes closet. She knew she should do something, but had no memory of what exactly was needful. So she opened the door with a towel around her neck and a smile — nothing else.

My heart sank for her lost dignity. How could the loss of memory be so cruel to a woman who wore her self-respect with such poise and class?

When we forget, we do embarrassing, undignified things.

In a mad dash to shore up the cracks in our religious institutions and balance our church budgets, we're a bit like [my] Aunt Jane. Forgetful and naked, stripped of the assurance that grows from a knowledge of our past, we are prone to grasping at easy answers or accepting half measures that promise finality. This would be an error. There are many texts that offer the latest in ecclesiastical management techniques. It seems wise that our understanding of any twenty-first century programs be based on a solid appreciation of history's judgments and questions concerning the merits of church life and the role of stewardship within that.[8]

When the church forgets what it means to be God's household, it is a disaster. Because God's promises for the future were given in the past, if we don't have a memory of them we have no real knowledge of God's promises and, therefore, no hope. We need the miracle of memory.

If we forget that we are God's household, we will be tempted to worship the gods of bread, circus, and political power.

Jesus resisted the temptation to cease being human. By resisting, he stayed with us on our own side of the line. This reminds us that

---

8. Christopher Levan, in the introduction to *Living in the Maybe: A Steward Confronts the Spirit of Fundamentalism* (Grand Rapids, Mich.: Wm. B. Eerdmans Publishing Co.; Manlius, N.Y.: REV/Rose Publishing, 1997).

the primary temptation confronting us is not that we might become bad human beings — the real danger is that we try to become godlike and cease being human. We are called not to curse our humanity but to enter into it as fully as we dare — as Jesus did.

Satan can be beaten. "[T]he secret in keeping the tempter at bay is out: it is in being faithful to one's vocation to be God's child [part of the household of God], clinging tenaciously to the divine calling."[9]

9. Charles B. Cousar, *Texts for Preaching: A Lectionary Commentary Based on the NRSV — Year A* (Louisville: Westminster John Knox, 1995), p. 191.

APPENDIX TWO

A Sermon

"Economic Dimensions of the Lord's Prayer"

Matthew 6:5-13

And whenever you pray, do not be like the hypocrites; for they love to stand and pray in the synagogues and at the street corners, so that they may be seen by others. Truly I tell you, they have received their reward. But whenever you pray, go into your room and shut the door and pray to your Father who is in secret; and your Father who sees in secret will reward you.

When you are praying, do not heap up empty phrases as the Gentiles do; for they think that they will be heard because of their many words. Do not be like them, for your Father knows what you need before you ask him. Pray then in this way:

"Our Father in heaven,
hallowed be your name.
Your kingdom come.
Your will be done,
on earth as it is in heaven.
Give us this day our daily bread.
And forgive us our debts,
as we also have forgiven our debtors.
And do not bring us to the time of trial,
but rescue us from the evil one." (Matt. 6:5-13)

Mostly, the common folk whom Jesus taught were peasants who barely scratched out a living on small farms. They and the daily circumstances of their lives were the context for Jesus' teaching, including the model prayer provided by Jesus.

To the modern ear, Jesus' model prayer is strange; it is exclusively one of petitions. The prayer does not have a simplistic formula of adoration, confession, thanksgiving, petition, and intercession. Rather, it basically requests God to do something. "The disciples are being taught what their real needs are and to whom they need to go for satisfaction. God in turn is being asked to fulfill the promises previously made regarding God's name and reign and regarding the care and protection of God's people."[1]

Structurally and theologically, the Lord's Prayer is at the center of the Sermon on the Mount. "Each petition is primarily eschatological, with an impact on the present that calls for corresponding action."[2] Each petition has a present dimension that is basically economic. While acknowledging that the Lord's Prayer deals with ultimate matters of death, judgment, and resurrection, this sermon will focus on economic implications in the here and now. To pray this prayer is to commit oneself to the fulfillment of God's will in the economic realm in the present and to pray that other persons will also submit themselves to God's reign.

The prayer is addressed to one with whom the disciples are familiar: "Father." Without getting into issues of inclusive language concerning the word *father*, it is clear that the term provides a context of family and intimacy. In prayer, the disciples are taught, they can approach our parent God with confidence. The prayer puts disciples in touch with God's incredible generosity. To pray that the reign of God come and that God's "will be done on earth as it is in heaven" is to pray for a good and joyful thing. It is not a prayer for streets paved with gold; it is a prayer for economic justice. "'Successful prayer' depends not on the methods or strategies of the disciples

1. Charles B. Cousar et al., *Texts for Preaching: A Lectionary Commentary Based on the NRSV, Year C* (Louisville: Westminster John Knox Press, 1994), p. 447.
2. M. Eugene Boring, "The Gospel of Matthew," in *The New Interpreter's Bible*, vol. 8 (Nashville: Abingdon Press, 1995), p. 203.

(what time of day one prays or the posture one assumes), but on a listening Father, to whom the petitioners are constantly referred."[3]

The words of the Lord's Prayer are used in hundreds of thousands of congregations around the world almost every time men, women, and children gather to worship. On some occasions it has profound meaning for those who use the words, as they pray to a God who, they feel, loves and cares for them. Other times the words are used mechanically or automatically, with little thought given to what is said.

David Beebe, a good friend of mine who is a stewardship officer for the United Church of Christ, once shared that he prays the Lord's Prayer every day. Each day he continues to repeat the prayer until it takes on real meaning and comes alive for him in the context of his life on that particular day. Perhaps there is a lesson for all of us in this practice. Even under the best of circumstances, the danger is great that Jesus' words may be "spiritualized" — removed from the context of a world of blood, sweat, and tears — in a way that would have shocked Jesus.

Who were the people who were taught the model prayer by Jesus? They were Palestinians who lived in the land where Jesus lived and ministered; they were not wealthy or affluent, or even middle class. They were mostly peasants — men, women, and children who struggled from dawn to dark and from day to day to make ends meet and to stay ahead of an oppressive regime, symbolized by the dreaded tax collector.

William R. Herzog II gave me some interesting insights into the economic context of the people whom Jesus taught.[4]

Most of the people farmed small plots of land that had been farmed by the same family for generations. Many grew crops of barley and some chick peas, from which a wonderful paste was made. But there was just barely enough to get by.

The landlord was always at the door, demanding more money for the rent. Herod's tax collectors and the Romans were everywhere,

3. Cousar, *Texts for Preaching*, p. 446.
4. William R. Herzog II in Bible studies given in June 1995 at the Biennial Meeting of American Baptist Churches in the U.S.A., in Syracuse, N.Y.

demanding more tribute. The rich, however, didn't pay taxes. Instead they took from the poor. The peasants did what they could to hide their crops and their herds. When they knew the tax collector was coming, they would run some of the sheep and goats up into the hills. They hid what they could, fought for every ounce of barley, and survived.

The words "give us this day our daily bread" were not part of an idle or inconsequential prayer. The words were real and grew out of a life-threatening concern.

Catherine Gunsalus González and Justo L. González interpreted the phrase "give us this day our daily bread" to mean "give us what we need, our daily ration, our just portion." They described this as "the amount that is best for us." "[W]hen we pray the Lord's prayer we are actually asking to be given the right amount, that which is necessary, wholesome and just, and neither less nor more."[5]

Herzog observed that, for the peasants, the sabbath observance at the synagogue was very important. On the sabbath the peasants weren't animals — beasts of burden working the soil to barely scratch out a living. On the sabbath they knew they were God's own people. It was something to celebrate!

The struggle to keep from losing the land was a daily one. The landlord would even try to call in the loan before the agreed-on date. Neighbors often put money into a village fund to prevent the land being lost to the landlord. If a man lost his land, he was out on the street — without a home and without a means of livelihood. After a few years of working hand to mouth and begging, death inevitably followed. It was Herod's contract with Galilee.

In such an economy most persons barely had enough. Sometimes the landlord's steward would throw all of a family's possessions outside, pick through them, take what seemed to have value, and order the family out. The family would be left to pick up what they could carry and leave — many times without a good-bye because they didn't want to put the village in danger. No one dared speak.

5. Catherine Gunsalus González and Justo L. González in a Bible study given at the North American Conference on Christian Philanthropy held in April 1996 in Toronto.

Other times, villagers simply disappeared or were thrown into prison — often *debtor's* prison. The soldiers would show up, grab the villager, and cart him off. No explanation, no trial! Even when the prisons were full, the pattern continued.

That is why Jesus taught us to pray "Forgive us our debts as we forgive our debtors." Not sins or transgressions, whatever they are. The debts were economic debts, with real consequences.

The economic nature of the words "forgive us our debts as we forgive our debtors" was described by Christopher Levan:

> For instance, we could translate the petition about forgiveness in the Lord's prayer as "Forgive us our loans, as we forgive those who have outstanding loans with us." This didn't make a lot of sense to the traditional religious mind, so we have spiritualized the meaning of the Greek original, turning "loans" into "debts," and hence into "trespasses."[6]

When we pray "Forgive us our debts as we forgive our debtors," that prayer is dealing with real daily problems. Jesus was not speaking of some vague abstract notion of "sin." He was describing daily realities of economic life. It has to do with food and shelter.

"Rescue us from the evil one" were words that voiced concrete concern about the "evil empire" in which they were economic prisoners.

The words that Jesus taught them were words of life for people in a society in which the rulers did not care what happened to the average person. It was a society of death in which the economy was stacked against the common people who desperately needed — and longed — to hear words of good news. Jesus' words were practical, good news in an economy of death in which people were commonly dragged away and imprisoned.

Herzog said that we who are Christians in twentieth-century North America think that the big question is whether God will forgive us. Will we accept God's forgiveness and be saved? *The real question is "Can we forgive God?"* Can we forgive God when cancer

6. Christopher Levan, *God Hates Religion: How the Gospels Condemn False Religious Practice* (Toronto: The United Church Publishing House, 1995), p. 13.

takes a loved one? Can we forgive God for loving people whom we consider enemies or unworthy of God's love? Can we forgive God for making people so different and then calling all of us to be disciples of Jesus? Can we forgive God for injustices that take the bread out of the mouths of children? Can we forgive God for making people who think differently and come to different conclusions than we do?

The prayer that God is looking for is not the accumulation of words upon words. It is not the rote recital of a litany that has lost any inner meaning for us. The prayer that God desires is prayer that grows out of pains and struggle and is a search for justice.

The agonizing and experiential nature of prayer is revealed in a story recounted by Christopher Levan:

> During the drought of the 1930s, farmers in western Canada were losing their livestock at alarming rates. Farmyards were literally filled with the carcasses of dying animals. There was not enough water for the people, let alone the cattle. Into this desperate situation came a young and zealous theological student. It was his summer job to visit these farms and offer what pastoral support he could. At one sheep ranch, he bounded up the steps of the house to pay his pastoral visit and, upon encountering the curiously tongue-tied farmer, suggested they go inside for prayer. "Surely God will not ignore the pleas of a righteous man," said the practicing pastor.
>
> The farmer was unmoved for a moment, looking off to a hazy horizon. Then, sensing the untried eagerness of his visitor, he agreed. "I'll come and pray with you, but first come and visit my sheep." So the pair walked out into the pasture by the homestead. There, they found dozens of sheep, bleating for water and dying because there was none to be found. In the midst of the moaning and anguish of his sheep, the farmer turned to the student and said, "Now, pastor, if you can pray better than those sheep, you go right ahead."[7]

Let us hear again Jesus' words about the Lord's Prayer, this time

7. Levan, *God Hates Religion*, pp. 136-37.

as found in the Scholars Version translation. The depth and bite of Jesus' words ring loud and clear.

> And when you pray, don't act like phonies. They love to stand up and pray in houses of worship and on street corners, so they can show off in public. I swear to you, their prayers have been answered! When you pray, go into a room by yourself and shut the door behind you. Then pray to your Father, the hidden one. And your Father, with his eye for the hidden, will applaud you. And when you pray, you should not babble on as the pagans do. They imagine that the length of their prayers will command attention. So don't imitate them. After all, your Father knows what you need before you ask. Instead you should pray like this:
>
> > Our Father in the heavens,
> > your name be revered.
> > Impose your imperial rule,
> > enact your will on earth as you have in heaven.
> > Provide us with the bread we need for the day.
> > Forgive our debts
> > to the extent that we have forgiven those in debt to us.
> > And please don't subject us to test after test,
> > but rescue us from the evil one. (Matt. 6:5-13, SV)[8]
>
> Amen!

8. *The Complete Gospels: Annotated Scholars Version* (Sonoma, Calif.: Polebridge Press, 1992, 1994).

Select Bibliography

Birch, Bruce C. "A New Heart and a New Spirit." In *Stewardship Worship Resource.* Indianapolis: Ecumenical Center for Stewardship Studies, 1992.

Bonhoeffer, Dietrich. *Letters and Papers from Prison.* Rev. ed. New York: Macmillan, 1967.

The Book of Common Worship. The Presbyterian Church in Canada, 1991.

Boring, M. Eugene. "The Gospel of Matthew." In *The New Interpreter's Bible,* vol. 8. Nashville: Abingdon Press, 1995.

Bosch, David J. *Transforming Mission.* Maryknoll, N.Y.: Orbis, 1993.

Brackney, William H. *Christian Voluntarism: Theology and Praxis.* Grand Rapids, Mich.: Wm. B. Eerdmans Publishing Co.; Manlius, N.Y.: REV/Rose Publishing, 1997.

Briggs, David. "Managerial Duties Cut into Clergy's Sermon Time." Associated Press Article in *Syracuse (N.Y.) Post-Standard,* 4 Nov. 1995, p. C2.

Brueggemann, Walter. "As the Text 'Makes Sense': Keep the Methods as Lean and Uncomplicated as Possible." *Christian Ministry* 14 (Nov. 1983): 7-10.

————. *Biblical Perspectives on Evangelism: Living in a Three-Storied Universe.* Nashville: Abingdon Press, 1993.

————. *Texts Under Negotiation: The Bible and Postmodern Imagination.* Minneapolis: Fortress Press, 1993.

————. "The Book of Exodus." In *The New Interpreter's Bible,* vol. 1. Nashville: Abingdon Press, 1994.

————. "Preaching as Reimagination." *Theology Today*, Oct. 1995, p. 329.

Busch, Richard A. "A Strange Silence." *The Christian Century*, 22 March 1995.

Calkins, Harvey Reeves. *A Man and His Money*. New York, Cincinnati: The Methodist Book Concern, 1914.

"Can Fast Food Be Good Food?" *Consumer Reports*, Aug. 1994, p. 493.

Charry, Ellen T. "Raising Christian Children in a Pagan Culture." *The Christian Century*, 16 Feb. 1994, p. 167.

————. "Sacraments for the Christian Life." *The Christian Century*, 15 Nov. 1995, p. 1076.

Cobb, John B., Jr. "Faith Seeking Understanding: The Renewal of Christian Thinking." *The Christian Century*, 29 June 1994, p. 642.

The Complete Gospels: Annotated Scholars Version. Sonoma, Calif.: Polebridge Press, 1992, 1994.

Cousar, Charles B., et al. *Texts for Preaching: A Lectionary Commentary Based on the NRSV, Year C*. Louisville: Westminster John Knox Press, 1994.

Cousar, Charles B. *Texts for Preaching: A Lectionary Commentary Based on the NRSV, Year A*. Louisville: Westminster John Knox Press, 1995.

Cox, Harvey. *The Secular City*. New York: The MacMillan Co., 1965.

Culpepper, R. Alan. "The Gospel of Luke." In *The New Interpreter's Bible*, vol. 9. Nashville: Abingdon Press, 1995.

Dibbell, Julian. "Everything That Could Go Wrong. . . ." *Time*, 20 May 1996, p. 56.

"Digital-Age Data." *TV Guide*, 26 Oct.–1 Nov. 1996, p. 68.

Elliott, John H. *A Home for the Homeless: A Sociological Exegesis of 1 Peter, Its Situation and Strategy*. Philadelphia: Fortress Press, 1981.

"Europeans Seek the Grave's Anonymity." *The Christian Century*, 15 May 1996, p. 541.

Ferris, Theodore P. *The Interpreter's Bible*, vol. 9. New York and Nashville: Abingdon Press, 1954.

Finke, Roger, and Rodney Stark. *The Churching of America, 1776-1990: Winners and Losers in our Religious Economy*. New Brunswick, N.J.: Rutgers University Press, 1992.

"Florida Man Gleaning Unused Citrus to Feed Hungry." *Syracuse (N.Y.) Herald American,* 14 Jan. 1996, A11.

Forrester, Jay W. "Counterintuitive Behavior of Social Systems." In *Toward Global Equilibrium: Collected Papers,* edited by Dennis L. Meadows and Donnella H. Meadows. Cambridge, Mass.: Wright-Allen Press, 1973.

Frost, Robert. "The Death of the Hired Man." In *The Complete Poems of Robert Frost.* New York: Holt, Rinehart and Winston, 1962.

Gallinger, Ken. "Belling the Money-Cat." In *Mandate: Special Edition on Work, Money and Meaning.* Etobicoke, Ontario: The United Church of Canada Division of Communication, 1995.

Gennerson, Bruce. *The Pulpit,* July-August 1968. As cited by L. E. Siverns in a private communication to this author.

Gladden, Washington. *The New Idolatry and Other Discussions.* New York: McClure, Phillips & Co., 1905. Cited by Robert Wood Lynn, "Money, Tainted and Consecrated," in *Why Give? Stewardship,* 1996.

"The Glow from a Fire." *Time,* 8 Jan. 1996, p. 49.

Gordon, Howard H., Jr. "Protagonist Corner: Lifting the Right Leg." *Journal for Preachers,* Easter 1995, pp. 37-38.

Gray, Paul. "The Assault on Freud." *Time,* 29 Nov. 1993, pp. 47-51.

Greenwald, John. "Luxury's Gaudy Times." *Time,* 25 March 1996, p. 48.

Guenther, Margaret. "Living by the Word: Honoring Martha." *The Christian Century,* 5 July 1995, p. 675.

Haar, Murray Joseph. "Self-Serving Redemptionism: A Jewish-Christian Lament." *Theology Today* 52, no. 1 (April 1995).

Harvard, Joseph S. "A Witness to the Resurrection: When Finished Isn't Final!" *Journal for Preachers,* Easter 1995, p. 17.

Hauerwas, Stanley M. *After Christendom?* Nashville: Abingdon, 1991.

————. "Living on Dishonest Wealth." *Journal for Preachers,* Advent 1996, p. 15.

Hauerwas, Stanley, and William H. Willimon. "Embarrassed by the Church: Congregations and the Seminary." *The Christian Century,* 5 Feb. 1986, p. 119.

Hempfling, Robert J. "An Enlistment Plan That Fits." *Journal of Stewardship* 39 (1987): 22-29.

Herzog, William R. II. *Parables as Subversive Speech: Jesus as Pedagogue of the Oppressed.* Louisville: Westminster/John Knox Press, 1994.

Jaroff, Leon. "Lies of the Mind." *Time,* 29 Nov. 1993, pp. 52-59.

J.D., a Minister of the Gospel. *The Glorious Progress of the Gospel Amongst the Indians in New England.* London: Edward Winslow, 1649.

Johnson, Benton, Dean R. Hoge, and Donald A. Luidens. "Mainline Churches: The Real Reason for Decline." *First Things: A Monthly Journal of Religion and Public Life,* March 1993, p. 17.

Keck, Leander E. *The Church Confident.* Nashville: Abingdon Press, 1993.

Kellaway, William. *The New England Company 1649-1776.* London: Longmans, Green & Co., 1961.

Koester, Helmut. *Proclamation,* Series A, Lent. Philadelphia: Fortress Press, 1974.

Krentz, Edgar. "Justice and Judgment." *The Christian Century,* 6 Nov. 1996, p. 1071.

Leland, John. "The Trouble with Sigmund." *Newsweek,* 18 Dec. 1995, p. 62.

Levan, Christopher. *God Hates Religion: How the Gospels Condemn False Religious Practice.* Toronto: The United Church Publishing House, 1995.

————. *Living in the Maybe: A Steward Confronts the Spirit of Fundamentalism.* Grand Rapids, Mich. and Cambridge, U.K.: Wm. B. Eerdmans Publishing Co.; Manlius, N.Y.: REV/Rose Publishing, 1997.

Lindvall, Michael L. *The Good News from North Haven.* New York: Doubleday, 1991.

Loughhead, LaRue A. *Sayings and Doings of Jesus: His Parables and Miracles Firsthand.* Valley Forge: Judson Press, 1981.

Lowery, Richard H. "From Covenant to Sabbath." *Journal of Stewardship* 46 (1994): 31.

Lynn, Robert Wood. Presentations at the 1991 Winter Event of the Ecumenical Center for Stewardship Studies; a presentation titled "Christian Ideas of Money" at the 1994 North American Conference on Christian Philanthropy; and *Why Give? Stewardship,* a series of articles published on diskette in 1996.

Macgregor, G. H. C. *The Interpreter's Bible,* vol. 9. New York and Nashville: Abingdon Press, 1954.

232

Marlette. "Kudzu." *The Christian Century,* 15 Nov. 1995, p. 1093.

Marty, Martin E. "Pothole on the Info Highway." *The Christian Century,* 13 April 1994, p. 399.

———. "M.E.M.O: Atheists at the Cross." *The Christian Century,* 10 April 1996, p. 415.

Marty, Peter W. "Living by the Word: Burning Hearts." *The Christian Century,* 10 April 1996, p. 397.

———. "Living by the Word: The Door to Abundant Life." *The Christian Century,* 17 April 1996, p. 427.

———. "A House of Living Stones." *The Christian Century,* 24 April 1996, p. 451.

Meeks, M. Douglas. *God the Economist: The Doctrine of God and Political Economy.* Minneapolis: Fortress Press, 1989.

Morgan, Kenneth. "Stewardship and the Seminary." Unpublished paper written for a stewardship course at McMaster Divinity College taught by this author.

Nelson, William R. "Reflecting on Paul's 'Great Collection.'" *Journal of Stewardship* 41 (1989): 8-19.

Ng, David and Virginia Thomas. *Children in the Worshiping Community.* Atlanta: John Knox Press, 1981.

"Noah's Wife Burned at the Stake." *The Christian Century,* 1 Feb. 1995, p. 105.

Nouwen, Henri J. M. *The Wounded Healer: Ministry in Contemporary Society.* Garden City, N.Y.: Doubleday & Company, Inc., 1972.

Peluso, Gary E. "What Is Lyle Schaller's Vision of the Church?" *The Christian Century,* 27 Jan. 1993, p. 86.

Perkins, Pheme. "The Gospel of Mark." In *The New Interpreter's Bible,* vol. 8. Nashville: Abingdon Press, 1995.

Pistor, Lori. "Let the Children Come." *Journal for Preachers,* Pentecost 1996.

Powell, Luther P. "Stewardship in the History of the Christian Church." In *Stewardship in Contemporary Theology,* ed. T. K. Thompson. New York: Association Press, 1960.

"Prosecutions of Quakers, and the Original of Tythes." *The Gentlemen's Magazine,* March 1737, pp. 154-56.

Ragen, Naomi. *Sotah.* New York: Crown Publishers, 1992.

Renfree, Harry A. *Heritage and Horizon: The Baptist Story in Canada.*

Mississauga, Ont.: Canadian Baptist Federation, 1988. As cited by Kenneth R. Morgan in an unpublished letter to Ronald E. Vallet dated 27 January 1997.

Renshaw, Park. "If It's True It's a Different World; Does That Scare You?" *Journal for Preachers,* Easter 1995, pp. 18-19.

"Revolt of British Farmers Against the Tithe." *The Literary Digest,* 23 Sept. 1933, pp. 116-17.

Rose, Lucy A. "Conversational Preaching: A Proposal." *Journal for Preachers,* Advent 1995, p. 27.

Saunders, Stanley P., and Charles L. Campbell. "'What Does This Mean?' 'What Shall We Do?' Pentecost, Practices, and Preaching." *Journal for Preachers,* Pentecost 1996.

Saxe, John Godfrey. "The Parable of the Blind Men and the Elephant." In *Concern: Communication,* edited by Jeffrey Schrank. Morristown, N.J.: Silver Burdett Co., 1970.

Siverns, L. E. (Ted). "A Pastor Views Denominational Mission." *Journal of Stewardship* 46 (1994): 42.

"Some Considerations Touching the Payment of Tythes." *The Gentlemen's Magazine,* March 1737, pp. 131-34.

Stark, Rodney. *The Rise of Christianity: A Sociologist Reconsiders History.* Princeton, N.J.: Princeton University Press, 1996.

Sullivan, Robert. "Americans and Their Money." *Worth Magazine,* June 1994. This article was accessed on the Internet at "www.worth.com/articles/Z9406CO1.html."

Swenson, Joanne. "My View: Neither the Liberal Nor the Conservative God Is Adequate." *Bible Review,* October 1989, p. 15.

Taylor, Barbara Brown. "Living by the Word: Remaining Human." *The Christian Century,* 7 Feb. 1996, p. 127.

Thompson, Joy, of Knight-Ridder Newspapers. "'Prosperity Gospel' Doesn't Jibe with Scriptures." *Syracuse (N.Y.) Post-Standard,* 21 Dec. 1996, B2.

Thompson, T. K., ed. *Stewardship in Contemporary Theology.* New York: Association Press, 1960, quoting Bishop Hanns Lilje in *Lutheran World,* Geneva, Switzerland: The Lutheran World Federation, vol. 1, no. 1, p. 3.

Tillich, Paul. *The Shaking of the Foundations.* New York: Charles Scribner's Sons, 1948.

Toulmin, Stephen. *Cosmopolis: The Hidden Agenda of Modernity.* Chicago: University of Chicago Press, 1990.

Twain, Mark. "The Revised Catechism." *New York Tribune,* 27 Sept. 1871, as quoted in Justin Kaplan, *Mr. Clemens and Mark Twain: A Biography.* New York: Simon and Schuster, 1966.

Vallet, Ronald E. *Stepping Stones of the Steward: A Faith Journey Through Jesus' Parables.* 2d ed. Grand Rapids, Mich.: Wm. B. Eerdmans Publishing Co.; Manlius, N.Y.: REV/Rose Publishing, 1994.

Vallet, Ronald E., and Charles E. Zech. *The Mainline Church's Funding Crisis: Issues and Possibilities.* Grand Rapids, Mich.: Wm. B. Eerdmans Publishing Co.; Manlius, N.Y.: REV/Rose Publishing, 1995.

Wall, James M. "Viewing the Megachurch: Between a Gush and a Smirk." *The Christian Century,* 22 March, 1995, p. 315.

Wedel, T. O. "Evangelism — The Mission of the Church to Those Outside Her Life." *The Ecumenical Review,* Oct. 1953.

"What Dennis Prager Did and Didn't Learn in Yeshiva." *First Things,* Oct. 1995, p. 80.

Willimon, William H. *Peculiar Speech: Preaching to the Baptized.* Grand Rapids, Mich.: Wm. B. Eerdmans Publishing Co., 1992.

————. "Easter Preaching as Peculiar Speech." *Journal for Preachers,* Easter 1994, p. 3.

————. *The Intrusive Word: Preaching to the Unbaptized.* Grand Rapids, Mich.: Wm. B. Eerdmans Publishing Co., 1994.

————. "Christian Ethics: When the Personal Is Public Is Cosmic." *Theology Today,* Oct. 1995, pp. 367-68.

Wilson-Kastner, Patricia. *Preaching Stewardship: An Every-Sunday Theme.* New York: The Office of Stewardship, The Episcopal Church, n.d.

Wood, Ralph C. "Baptism in a Coffin." *The Christian Century,* 21 Oct. 1992, p. 926.

————. "Living by the Word: The God Who Matters." *The Christian Century,* 19 July 1995, p. 707.

Wuthnow, Robert. *Acts of Compassion: Caring for Others and Helping Ourselves.* Princeton, N.J.: Princeton Univ. Press, 1991.

————. "The Future of Mainline Protestantism." *The Drew Connection,* Winter 1994, p. 9.

————. *God and Mammon in America.* New York: The Free Press, 1994.

Index of Subjects

236

Index of Subjects

Freud, Sigmund, 185-87
Fund raising, 58
Future, portents for, 103-5

Giving by individuals, 87-88, 104-5;
confidentiality about, 172-73; lan-
guage to describe, 67-70; methodolo-
gies of, 78-84; recent methodologies
of, 81-84
Giving to church, in colonial America,
64-65; in England, 63-64; in
nineteenth century, 65-66
Gladden, Washington, 73-75
Gleanings, as a household rule, 121-23
Gospel. *See* Word
Great collection, the, 42-43
Great Commission, 41-42
Greed, 104

Heart, as used in Hebrew context, 33
Hope, signs of, 106
Hospitality, 207, 208; as a household
rule, 126-28
Household, characteristics and conditions of, 21-23
Household of amnesia, 1, 15, 16, 84,
85, 88-89, 116, 118, 137-38, 205,
208
Household of God, 37, 38, 41, 109-
10, 152, 200; and biblical texts, 16;
characteristics of in a congregation,
19, 28, 110-18; as countercultural,
138, 208-11; guidelines for becoming a, 12-13; Jesus as cornerstone of,
204, 205; lives from promise and
command, 31-32; members of congregations as living stones of, 204-5;
questions about, 1-2; and the reign
of God, 219; and the resurrection,
13-15, 41, 201, 206-8, 212-13;
rules of, 15, 119-35; table central in,
166; as those who are called out to
stand up again, 211-12; worship in.
See Worship, in the household of
God

Household of Jesus Christ. *See* Household of God

Instruments of Christian stewardship,
139-55; use of, 202-3
Interchurch World Movement, 76-77
Interest, do not charge to the poor, as
a household rule, 120-21
Internal factors, in church life, 85-93

Jesus: as an alternative, 219; baptism
of, 37-38, 215; birth of, 36-37;
birth, life, and death of as reversals,
201; death of, 40; miracles of, 39-
40; model prayer of, 38-39, 222-28;
parables of, 38-39, 108-9; resurrection of, 40-41, 201; resurrection of,
a characteristic of the household of
God, 110-15; teachings of, 58-59;
temptations of, 37-38, 214-21
Joseph, 27-28

Kerygma, 139-43
Koinonia, 17-18, 43, 139, 151-52, 169-
70, 170

Laity, in partnership with pastor, 189-91
Lay ministry, 188-89
Liberal, as a category, 99-100
Lord's prayer, 38-39, 222-28
Love, God's, 20, 139

Manna, 15, 148-49
Memory, need for, 17; recovery of, 15-
16; role of, 14-15; urgency of, 4-6
Mission, God's, 17-18, 20, 139, 152-
53, 192; as a characteristic of the
congregation as a household of God,
115-16; and the church, 95-99
Mission, understanding of, 86-87
Modernity, 33-34, 56-57, 84, 122,
137, 153, 202-3; assumptions of,
85, 107-9, 200; reversal of, 57
Money, as bread, 217; and faith, 7, 55;
fears about, 53-55, 202-3; house-

Index of Scripture References